Making
Magnificent
Marriages

To Debbie,

God Bless!

Dr. Jared Pingleton

Jared Pingleton, PsyD

Prov. 21:21

Book Layout ©2013 BookDesignTemplates.com
Cover Design by Joel Pingleton at PopularPixels.com

All scripture quotations, unless otherwise indicated, are taken from the Holy Bible, New International Version®, NIV®. Copyright ©1973, 1978, 1984, 2011 by Biblica, Inc.™ Used by permission of Zondervan. All rights reserved worldwide. www.zondervan.com. The "NIV" and "New International Version" are trademarks registered in the United States Patent and Trademark Office by Biblica, Inc.™"

Scripture quotations from *THE MESSAGE*. Copyright © by Eugene H. Peterson 1993, 1994, 1995, 1996, 2000, 2001, 2002. Used by permission of NavPress Publishing Group.

Scripture quotations taken from the New American Standard Bible®, Copyright © 1960, 1962, 1963, 1968, 1971, 1972, 1973, 1975, 1977, 1995 by The Lockman Foundation. Used by permission. (www.Lockman.org)

Scripture quotations taken from the Amplified® Bible, Copyright © 1954, 1958, 1962, 1964, 1965, 1987 by The Lockman Foundation, Used by permission.

Marriage Improvement Tools
2131 South Eastgate Avenue
Springfield, MO 65809

Quantity sales. Special discounts are available on quantity purchases by corporations, associations, and others. For details, contact the "Special Sales Department" at the address above.

Making Magnificent Marriages/Jared Pingleton. —1st ed.
ISBN-13: 978-0989918909
ISBN-10: 0989918904

Endorsements

Advance praise for *Making Magnificent Marriages:*

"We know from experience and also from hard science, growth comes from focused attention. Quite simply, what is attended to is what grows, and what is not, does not. What I love about this book is that Jared has given us a great guide to focus on the absolutely vital aspects to having a great relationship, or helping one that hurts."

> **Dr. Henry Cloud**, Leadership Consultant, Clinical Psychologist, and Best-Selling Author and Co-Author of over 20 books, including the *Boundaries* series
> Beverly Hills, Calif.

"Marriage is one of God's highest gifts to us. Sadly, couples don't often have the skills necessary to experience this gift. The result is alienation and worse. Jared Pingleton has done an exceptional job of creating a biblically sound and highly practical resource that will help transform marriages. I highly recommend *Making Magnificent Marriages!*"

> **John Townsend, Ph.D.**, Organizational Consultant, Leadership Coach, Clinical Psychologist, and Best-Selling Author and Co-Author of over 25 books, including *Boundaries*
> Newport Beach, Calif.

"I have known Dr. Jared Pingleton for many years and consider him to be a premier marriage counselor. I am delighted he has written *Making Magnificent Marriages*. This outstanding book not only covers every aspect of marriage in an effective and humorous way; it presents strategies for establishing a healthy marriage, doing "preventative maintenance," and repairing damaged relationships. Along with the created tools, *Relationship Health Score 1.0* and his accompanying workbook, *A Marriage Maintenance Manual*, he helps couples in a superior way."

George W. Westlake, Jr., D.Min.
Pastor Emeritus, Sheffield Family Life Center
Kansas City, Mo.

"*Making Magnificent Marriages* is not just another garden variety book on marriage relationships. The practical tools and godly wisdom Jared provides in this excellent resource are gleaned from his many years of ministry to hurting couples. His counsel is solidly biblical, clinically astute, and directly relevant for married couples of all ages. Ideal for both church-wide and small group study, I highly recommend this creative and powerful book to pastors, church leaders, and all those who minister to marriages."

George O. Wood, D.P.Th., J.D. General Superintendent,
The General Council of the Assemblies Of God
Springfield, Mo.

"*Making Magnificent Marriages* is a fun and exciting new resource which will prove valuable for couples, clergy, and counselors alike. Based on his many years of clinical experience, Jared gives fresh and powerful insights into achieving marital intimacy and fulfillment. Biblically sound, solidly practical, and highly relevant, this book will provide realistic help for couples who are struggling or for those who want to make a good marriage better."

> **Greg Smalley, Psy.D.**, Clinical Psychologist and Author of eleven books; Vice-President of Family Ministries, Focus On The Family
> Colorado Springs, Colo.

"*Making Magnificent Marriages* equips couples with the knowledge necessary to build a successful and satisfying marriage. Covering twelve critical areas of marriage, Dr. Jared Pingleton's book is grounded in biblical principles, provides insights from the best research and authors on marriage, and draws on his own personal clinical experiences. Each chapter includes discussion questions and provides a list of recommended resources to lead to deeper application and further study. The humor and amusing examples keep the book lighthearted, while packing a heavy-hitting message. Pingleton has given couples the gift of insight on greatly improving their relationships. I highly recommend this exceptional marriage book."

> **Todd Hudnall, D.Min.**
> Senior Pastor, Radiant Church
> Colorado Springs, Colo.

"I have always been impressed by Jared Pingleton's wealth of psychological, marital, and biblical knowledge and insight. This book puts on display in an enjoyable way his wisdom and years of experience in helping marriages thrive. Couples at any stage of their relationship will be blessed by his writing."

> **Brett K. Sparks, Psy.D.,** Licensed Psychologist, Lead Intensive Marriage Counselor, National Institute of Marriage
> Branson, Mo.

"Healthy marriages may be designed in heaven but they are made here on earth. This fun and innovative new resource will help you do just that. Filled with fresh insights, challenging concepts, and practical exercises, *Making Magnificent Marriages* is a powerful and helpful book. We enthusiastically recommend it!"

> **Claudia and David Arp,** Co-Authors of over 30 books on marriage and family relationships
> Great Falls, Va.

"Marriage has been around for a long time, but it doesn't seem to be getting any easier! This innovative new book provides a powerful set of tools to help us do it better. I have known and respected Jared for many years, so I am not surprised that he expertly blends biblical wisdom and his clinical experience in a very helpful, practical, realistic, and encouraging way. *Making Magnificent Marriages* can bring hope and healing to many relationships."

> **Gary Collins, Ph.D.,** Clinical Psychologist and Author of over 50 books
> Distinguished Professor of Coaching and Leadership, Richmont University, Atlanta, Ga.
> Distinguished Visiting Professor in the School of Psychology and Counseling, Regent University, Virginia Beach, Va.

"Not only has Jared Pingleton written an easy-to-read book that you will simply enjoy reading, but the book is exceptionally useful. It is heavenly minded, yet down to earth. He integrates an on-line assessment system with practical targeted advice. What a great book!"

Everett L. Worthington, Jr., Ph.D., Professor of Psychology, Director of Counseling Psychology Program, Virginia Commonwealth University, Author of over 20 books

Richmond, Va.

Dedication

Solomon, the wisest man who ever lived, asserted that "He who finds a wife finds what is good and receives favor from the Lord" and that "A wife of noble character is her husband's crown..." (Proverbs 18:22, 12:4). Like no other man I know, I have definitely found what is good and have received favor from the Lord! Simply put, I am the most fortunate and blessed guy I know because of you, Linda, my precious and pretty wife.

I deeply resonate with Solomon's renowned rhetorical question: "A capable, intelligent, and virtuous woman—who is he who can find her? She is far more precious than jewels and her value is far above rubies or pearls. The heart of her husband trusts in her confidently and relies on and believes in her securely..." (Proverbs 31:10-11, Amplified). Darling, you were certainly never lost, but I am thoroughly thrilled that I "found" you that wonderful Sunday morning when our eyes first met across that proverbially crowded room! Eureka! What an unforgettable experience—the first of many of the awesome adventures of life with all its tragedies and triumphs that we have been privileged to share together.

Sweetheart, you epitomize these virtues and values of which Solomon speaks. I am honored and humbled to have had the fabulous opportunity to be able to hang around you for over 28 years now. Being married to you has been by far the best and most fulfilling part of my life. Accordingly, as Solomon declares, "...her husband joins in with words of praise: 'Many women have done wonderful things, but you've outclassed them all!'" (Proverbs 31:28-29, The Message).

As my best friend, lover, co-parent, financial partner, and playmate, you know all too well (and unfortunately painfully) my many faults, foibles, and failures as a man and as a husband. But I want you know that in dedicating this book to you, I likewise dedicate myself to trying to purposively and progressively practice what I preach within it! The words herein will hold me accountable towards that end.

Contents

Acknowledgments

What you hold in your hand represents the culmination of a long-held dream. In graduate school over 35 years ago, the Lord gave me several book ideas—which for various reasons have not been able to be realized before now. Foremost, I am grateful to Him for the inspiration and impartation of these ideas and insights about His sacred, sensational human institution of marriage, which He designed for His glory and our growth.

But we humans need other people, too, to help us along the way. I am very thankful to my loving, lovable, and lovely wife, Linda, who has taught me more about the delightful yet daunting dynamics of marriage than anyone anywhere else. Thank you so much for marrying me! (And for still being married to me.) You are the best wife I could ever dream of or ask for.

I also want to thank our four sons and our daughter-in-law for their support, encouragement, and understanding while so much of my time has been consumed with this project. Jordan, Josh and Anna, Joel, and Joseph—I am very proud of you and love you very much. You guys are awesome and a wonderful blessing (most of the time—you must admit you have given us some gray hair over the years!) to your mom and me. A special thanks goes to you, Joel, for your creative genius and expertise in designing the cover for the book through your graphic arts enterprise, Popular Pixels. Great work—it's really cool!

To my friends and colleagues at Marriage Improvement Tools, LLC, Josh Spurlock and Andre Soumiatin, many thanks for your support, encouragement, and assistance in making this project materialize. The innovative and creative efforts you men collaborated on to minister to married couples are ones with which I know the Lord is pleased, and I trust they will prove to be a blessing to many. I so appreciate your hearts and help.

Thanks to my (old!) buddy, Dr. Dan Call, lead pastor at New Life Church in Springfield, MO, and the Wednesday evening married class for volunteering to be "guinea pigs" to test out the material on a live audience. It was fun to share and interact with you all, and your feedback was both instructive and inspiring. This book, workbook, and online assessment are markedly better because of all of you—thanks!

Special gratitude goes to Jon Jones with Springfield BackOffice for his expertise and patience in the layout and formatting of the manuscript. His technical skill and ability translated and transformed the typewritten text into this beautiful book you now hold.

There is no other way to say this: my editor, Patty Roberts, was an absolute God-send. I am extremely appreciative, Patty, for your excellence and expertise with the written word. You are a superb wordsmith, and your skills and facility with the language have resulted in a much better and more easily readable text. It was indeed an honor and a blessing to work with you! You have really helped me write a lot more gooder!

Finally, I want to express my sincere, heartfelt gratitude to the thousands of couples with whom I have had the privilege of serving in my counseling practice over the past 36 years. You have taught me much from the pain and pathos of your personal hurts and heartaches. You have impacted my heart and life mightily, and I am forever indebted. Thank you for having the courage to reach out for help, to reach up to the Lord for strength, to reach down inside for healing, and to reach over to your spouse for growth in your relationship. I hope and pray the readers of this book will do likewise.

Step 1:
Take The Relationship
Health Score 1.0

You care about your marriage. That's why you are reading this book. We care about your marriage too—that's why we created *The Relationship Health Score 1.0* and its companion, ***Making Magnificent Marriages***.

To get the maximum benefit out of reading this book, first take *The Relationship Health Score 1.0* assessment at:

www.RelationshipHealthScore.com

A unique feature of this book is a personalized free assessment of your marriage relationship, which is included with your purchase. This brief, clinically validated inventory is designed for both you and your spouse to take. The assessment, which you'll learn more about in the **Introduction** of this book (please be sure to read) will help you specifically identify and apply the material in the chapters which are most important for your marriage. It will, in effect, equip you to "customize" the book to your marriage in a highly personal and relevant way.

If you have questions about the book or the assessment feel free to email us at: MMM@marriagetools.org or call 888-972-4MIT (4648).

Wishing you a *Magnificent* Marriage,

Jared, Andre, and Josh
The Marriage Improvement Tools team

Introduction

*M*ediocre, mundane, and monotonous marriages are miserable. But no marriage relationship starts off that way. Normally, most couples fall deeply in love and launch into a wonderfully romantic, naïvely blissful, and fairytale-like dream of living happily ever after. In the storybooks, the handsome prince in shining armor valiantly rescues the beautiful fair maiden from her distress and sweeps her off her feet into his strong arms. Then they gallop off into the sunset astride his white steed toward the faraway castle.

Yet somewhere along the way, for most couples, the honeymoon eventually comes to an unceremonious and unfulfilling end. The armor rusts (providing he can still squeeze into it!), the horse comes up lame, the utility bills for the castle are astronomical, and the beautiful maiden? Well, let's just say that time and gravity inevitably exert an unfortunate and unintended effect upon her physical appearance. Needs get neglected, dreams are dashed, hearts become hardened, and thus love seems lost.

But it doesn't have to be like that. Magnificent marriages can be made. However, doing so requires much prayer, planning, patience, and persistence, along with some objective guidance and direction.

Let's back up to the beginning. It could be said that the process of mate selection in our culture is somewhat like the acquisition of a new automobile. A prospective car buyer will typically look at many different models, compare various features, read a few consumer magazines, perhaps kick some tires, and then take a few test drives. Finally, they choose their

5

favorite color and options on their selected model, negotiate the very best bargain possible, and drive it proudly off the show-room floor.

This wonderful new set of wheels provides them with a great deal of fulfillment, fun, and freedom. It is fancy, shiny, smells new, and looks and performs superbly. They proudly show it off to all of their family and friends who agree that it is indeed a valuable acquisition. The vehicle provides pleasure, safety, and reliability. They quickly become acclimated to and familiar with it, learning its specific features and mechanisms, driving it eve-rywhere they go. Since it is brand new, the owners are spared the expense of breakdowns, major repairs, and the hassle and inconvenience of frequently working on it or taking it to the shop.

Then a few years later, while idling at a traffic signal minding their own business, they happen to casually look over at a shiny, brand-new car, which just pulled up alongside them. They are startled yet captivated by the sleek, sporty, aerody-namic lines of this elegant new model, with its luxurious glisten-ing wheels and its freshly waxed, beautiful new coat of paint. Quickly glancing back at their own vehicle, they are surprised at how dull, dingy, and dirty their car has gradually become.

As the other driver confidently revs his or her sophisticated power plant into a deep, throaty roar, the owners notice for the first time that their own car isn't running quite as smoothly as it used to. Then the light turns green and the new car races off, showcasing the impressive horsepower of its finely tuned, well-engineered engine. Now, for the first time, the original car pur-chasers start to become dissatisfied, disappointed, and disillu-sioned with their original dream car. Analogously, in marriage, the glitz and glow of honeymoon happiness typically tends to silently and subtly deteriorate into grumbling and grief after a few years.

Unfortunately, it is all too often the case that at this point many people start entertaining thoughts of trading their original vehicle in on a fresher, fancier, and faster (and generally much more expensive!) model. Or, after years of friction, frustration, and futility, they may simply be tempted to push it off the nearest cliff! Whereas that may seem delightful when it comes to vehicles, it is disastrous when it comes to relationships.

The simple reality is that both vehicles and marriages naturally need ongoing maintenance and upkeep in order to run smoothly and function optimally at their factory-designed levels. Without regular attention and ongoing investment, even the best cars and marriages will inevitably rattle, rust, sputter, and eventually die. The basic difference between a head-turning classic and a dilapidated junk heap boils down to how much and how well its owner invests in and cares for it!

> **The sad but simple fact is that most marriages aren't running very smoothly or efficiently.**

While everyone in our culture is aware of the abominable divorce rate in our society (which God hates; see Malachi 2:16) with about half of all marriages failing legally, many people aren't aware that most of the other half of marriages actually fail functionally. Research shows that *only about 5 to 12% of marriages in the United States of America are described by both spouses as being mutually fulfilling*. And to make these numbers even more sobering, 90% of those 5 to 12% of "mutually fulfilled" married couples have been married 30 years or longer! These statistics are both a tragedy and a travesty to the intimacy and institution of marriage. The sad but simple fact is that most marriages aren't running very smoothly or efficiently.

We must do better! And we can. The problem with the drivers in the above example is that they apparently did not read, or at least did not apply, the information the manufacturer specified in its maintenance manual for that particular vehicle. It takes time, money, and energy to regularly change the oil, re-inflate and rotate the tires, wax the paint, clean the interior, re-place the spark plugs, change the filters, and keep all of the flu-id levels topped off.

In the same way, maintaining a healthy marriage is also a lot of work and requires an ongoing commitment to be observant and intentional about what one's marriage needs and how it is functioning. We all become accustomed to just jumping in the car, turning on the ignition, putting it into gear, and accelerating. No one intends to take either their automobile or their marriage for granted—but most people do. Then, when the marriage fails to operate normally or no longer runs smoothly, they call for a tow truck. Hopefully they take it in to the repair shop (i.e., a qualified and certified relationship "mechanic") instead of the junkyard (i.e., a divorce attorney)!

Seldom will an automobile break down—much less have its wheels fall off—without some warning lights or signals first be-ing activated. Neither will marriages. But unfortunately, over the years in my clinical practice, I have sadly observed that many couples ignore the relationship indicators of things that need attention; maintenance that must be done if they want to keep their marriage operating at peak efficiency. The ugly truth is that flashing warning lights on the dashboard and loud buzz-ers can be distracting and even downright annoying.

Taking the time to pull over to try to attend to the problem could make them late, might cost them something, will certainly be an inconvenience, may possibly be unsafe, and could keep them from meeting their own agenda. So, many couples just keep on driving. They either ignore the warning signals, or they try to make them go away by metaphorically slapping duct tape over the flashing lights or reaching underneath the dash to dis-connect the wires. They would do much better to slow down, pull over, stop, and open up the hood to look inside and see what's wrong.

> **The terrible and tragic truth is that the majority of broken marriages do not suddenly "crash and burn"— typically they gradually rust and break down from negligence and inattention!**

The terrible and tragic truth is that the majority of broken marriages do not suddenly "crash and burn"—typically they gradually rust and break down from negligence and inattention! Such failures can generally be prevented by following specific servicing recommendations (and using appropriate equipment or parts), but our society has failed miserably in educating and equipping couples with the tools they need to make their marriages successful, sustainable, and satisfying.

One extremely important principle I have learned over the years is that with both vehicles and marriages, *prevention is easier than cure!* The sooner a problem is identified and addressed, the easier and cheaper it is to solve.

Let me illustrate this universal wisdom principle another way. I really enjoy landscaping and gardening. Plain common sense tells you that the smaller the weed in your garden is, the easier it is to pull. And if you mulch your garden, not only will there be fewer weeds to begin with, but the plants will flourish with the moisture preservation and root protection provided by the organic covering. Preventative maintenance in your marriage works just like that.

Regularly cleaning and waxing your car will not only prolong the life of the paint, it will prevent the development of rust. Regularly changing the oil will not only prolong the life and increase the performance of the engine, it will prevent the need for an overhaul. Regularly airing up and rotating the tires will not only prolong the tread life of your tires, it will also produce the added benefit of increasing your gas mileage. Lots of cars—and marriages—become prematurely worn out and eventually break down because of a failure to maintain them well.

No one walks back up the aisle from their wedding ceremony flipping a coin to see what the 50-50 odds of staying married will be for them and their new mate. Yet without proper training and instruction, including professional pre-marital counseling, *most couples are not adequately prepared to operate and keep their marital relationships running smoothly for a lifetime.* They can only run on the high octane and new car smell of newlywed bliss for so long. Dissatisfied, disappointed, and disillusioned premarital expectations of one's mate are inevitable. And we all have them.

Advertising focuses on attempting to convince drivers that they must always have the newest and most improved status symbol model with the latest bells, whistles, gizmos, and doodads, so they can keep up with the Jones' new vehicle. In a similar way, rather than investing wisely in their marriage relationship, many individuals start looking around for someone new when the romantic infatuation of their relationship starts to lose its original luster and allure, or when something doesn't work like it used to. It has been said that love at first sight often results in divorce at first slight! In this respect the old adage, "What's good for General Motors is good for the country," may be valid economically but not relationally.

Years ago, my friend, Ron Kelly, in Independence, Missouri provided me with a profound illustration of how beautiful and awesome a classic car can be, as well as how much dedication and hard work the restoration process involves. Ron helped his dad, Bill, completely restore a rusted out, broken down shell of a 1912 Model T Touring car into a magnificent mechanical masterpiece.

As you can see from the "before" photo, this car was in very poor condition and was missing many of its original parts. It was rescued from a chicken coop on a farm outside Manhattan, Kansas. Beginning in 1993, Ron and his dad meticulously restored, reassembled, and repainted every single bolt, nut, rivet, and part on the vehicle. In a true team effort, his mom, June, refurbished the top and the black leather tufted upholstery to its original elegant beauty.

1912 Model T
before restoration

The "after" photo on the next page was taken shortly after the restoration project was completed. On June 28, 1997 the vehicle was used by Ron's daughter and son-in-law, Debbie and Scotty Moon, as their wedding "getaway" car. The car was absolutely pristine. From the gleaming brass headlamps, side lanterns, radiator, horn, and other fixtures, to the hand-rubbed wild cherry steering wheel and floorboards, to the engine, which was almost clean enough to eat off of, this grand 85-year-old touring car was truly magnificent. Debbie and Scotty were ceremoniously chauffeured away from the church in the coolest coach ever!

The timeless spiritual and relational lessons of transformation and redemption were crystal clear to me at that beauti-

1912 Model T
after restoration

ful wedding. First, it was very easy to see the deleterious and destructive effects which negligence, passivity, and inattention had exerted upon this once classic automobile. Second, it was very powerful to see how focused effort, careful planning, determination, and organized teamwork could restore a broken down, rusted out vehicle. The parallels to marriage relationships are obvious: *Our marriage can become either a gross clunker or a gorgeous classic. It all depends upon how well we maintain it!*

Introducing the "Relationship Health Score 1.0"

This unique and exciting book has been created to help you make your marriage become magnificent. Toward that end, it is designed to be both personal and practical. The book directly corresponds with an amazing new individualized and innovative free online marriage relationship assessment tool called the *Relationship Health Score 1.0* (located at: RelationshipHealthScore.com), created by the clinical professionals at Marriage Improvement Tools. Drawing from over 40 years of collective direct clinical experience, and the accumulated insight and wisdom derived from working with real-life couples' marital concerns and conflicts, this inventory was developed to be used by both marital professionals (to help couples with whom they work) and couples just like you.

The *Relationship Health Score 1.0* is a fun, insightful, and helpful instrument which can be used by couples to clearly and accurately assess the current functioning of their marriage systems. This powerful tool equips you with an excellent opportunity to apply the principles and concepts of this book in a real and relevant way, in order to help and heal your marriage. Just as all vehicles have various gauges to measure and give feedback about their operating condition (e.g. a speedometer, tachometer, altimeter, etc.), the *Relationship Health Score 1.0* measures and gives feedback for your relationship.

The *Relationship Health Score 1.0* is a simple, yet technologically sophisticated inventory, which helps you quickly, accurately, and easily evaluate how well your marriage is operating. By utilizing the power and convenience of the Internet, the results are rapidly available in a confidential, user-friendly, electronic format. In just 15 minutes or less, you can go online and answer the questions as they pertain to your own marriage. The clinically validated results will yield an easy-to-interpret, customized, diagnostic printout to gauge how your marriage is currently operating. Then, if you so desire, you can be referred online to a marriage professional in your area who is familiar with this helpful tool and can help you do additional work on your marriage relationship.

The *Relationship Health Score 1.0* explores 12 fundamental aspects of marriage functioning by asking you and your mate to rate each area of your marriage on a 1 to 10 scale. The results yield valuable information about the strengths and weaknesses of your marriage relationship, which you can then utilize to specifically help and heal your marriage.

After addressing specific areas of concern here in the book, you can re-take the inventory in order to accurately measure your growth and progress. Or, on your wedding anniversary or after periods of intentional growth (e.g. marital counseling, retreats, etc.), you can re-assess your relationship—comparing your new Health Score results to your original inventory profiles—to monitor and measure your progress and growth. This type of tune-up can help to keep your marriage running smoothly and satisfactorily. Hopefully, using these customized tools will prevent the need for a complete overhaul, or worse yet, the tragedy of a complete breakdown. Again, prevention is always better than cure!

As you experience challenges or difficulties in certain areas of your marital relationship (e.g., trust, finances, and/or recreational activities), you can focus specifically on the appropriate chapters in the text which address these concerns, study the biblical passages regarding that topic, think about and talk through the discussion questions, and find other resources you can utilize for further growth. Each of the following 12 chapters of *Making Magnificent Marriages* corresponds to and addresses in-depth those topics covered in the *Relationship Health Score 1.0,* while offering valuable guidance and insight on how to troubleshoot, repair, or even overhaul problems in your relationship.

Chapter Descriptions

In addressing the 12 primary areas of marital functioning, the chapter titles and topics for this book, the accompanying workbook *A Marriage Maintenance Manual*, and the *Relationship Health Score 1.0* online inventory are as follows:

Spiritual Synergy. Spiritual synergy means that the spiritual core of your relationship is a source of strength and support for you and not a subject of strife or separation between you. Your beliefs are balanced, your values are validated, and your spiritual activities are aligned. You spend meaningful time in Bible study, devotions, worship, and prayer with each other.

Concrete Commitment. Concrete commitment involves more than just a definite determination to hold on through the rough times; it's about consistently making mature choices that have a positive impact on your relationship. This is the essence of an unconditional covenant—you choose to love the other person no matter what. No marriage is likely to survive, much less thrive, through life's disappointments, drudgeries, and difficulties without a rock solid commitment.

Total Trust. Total trust is the decision to rely unswervingly on the character, consistency, and conduct of your spouse. It is based upon truthfulness, dependability, and integrity. Total trust is the foundation of all healthy relationships, and it results in feelings of safety, security, confidence, and optimism.

Compassionate Caring. Compassionate caring demonstrates that you have a deep, heart-felt concern for how your spouse thinks and feels. What matters to him or her matters to you simply because it is important to them. You lovingly care for the health, emotional well-being, and protection of your spouse, and you are willing to provide for their needs to the best of your ability.

Rigorous Respect. Rigorous respect means you value, honor, and appreciate who the other person is as a unique individual by building up their self-esteem, complimenting and validating them both privately and publicly. You don't mock, belittle, ignore, criticize, or undermine one another, but work to make your spouse feel special and significant. Rigorous respect involves courteous consideration of your spouse's individual identity, thoughts, feelings, and opinions—prioritizing and preferring your mate over others and at times over yourself.

Connected Communication. Connected communication is the lifeblood of a healthy marriage and is consistently deep, open, honest, and respectful. It involves intimately sharing and candidly discussing your personal problems, priorities, and pain as your spouse expresses a genuine interest in what you say by means of unselfish active listening. Couples who communicate clearly, closely, and candidly don't feel like they need to hide parts of themselves or pretend to be someone they are not in order to feel accepted by each other.

Fighting Fair. Constructive conflict is a normal and necessary process, which every marriage must embrace in order for spouses to better understand each other and grow closer together. Healthy spouses are not afraid of conflict, but instead are willing to face disagreements directly and talk them through in such a way that there is a win-win outcome where neither feels like a loser. You demonstrate a high degree of honor and respect even when you feel upset, misunderstood, and hurt, and you are ready to freely forgive and reconcile without resentment or holding grudges.

Routine Responsibilities. Regular domestic duties involve the administration of your life together and how you manage sharing the daily responsibilities of your home in a fair and equitable manner. Healthy couples recognize and respect each person's different strengths and backgrounds and work together as a team where neither partner feels taken advantage of or used. Humble household helpfulness happens in happy, healthy, harmonious, holy, hospitable homes.

Money Matters. Financial freedom is achieved by openly discussing major money matters while you support each other in reaching reasonable financial goals for your marriage. Because you realize that people are more important than things, you handle money and other resources unselfishly for your mutual benefit. Financial freedom results when you live responsibly within your means and are unencumbered by stressful debt.

Together Time. Together time means you enjoy and prioritize spending fun and relaxing time together. You like each other's company and look forward to meaningful and mutually beneficial experiences, which can be memorable and bonding. Though you may enjoy different activities and have different personalities, neither spouse feels neglected or devalued because you prioritize fun times to play together, recreate, and regularly date.

Attractive Appearance. Attractive appearance focuses on being appealing, alluring, and attentive to your spouse. You endeavor to remain physically healthy and try to reasonably cater to the likes, preferences, and desires of your spouse regarding physical appearance, hygiene, and dress. Spouses who value maintaining their appearance are flirtatious and seek to "turn on" and appeal to each other.

Sensational Sex. Sensational sex is developed when you share an exclusive, intimate, dynamic, and mutually fulfilling sexual relationship that is thrilling, vibrant, and uninhibited. You thoughtfully and considerately satisfy your spouse's needs for sexual pleasure and gratification, while you lovingly nurture growth, wholeness, and healing in your spouse regarding any painful past relationships or abusive experiences they may have suffered. You tenderly strive to cultivate an emotionally safe atmosphere of sacred trust and vulnerability, in which you intimately expose the depths of your soul to one another in a mutually affirming way that enhances and validates each spouse's personhood.

Additional Unique and Helpful   Features of *Making Magnificent Marriages*

Given that marriage was God's idea from the beginning, at the end of every chapter, specific **"Scriptural Searches"** relevant to each topic are recommended for your further growth and insight. These can be creatively used as a personal and/or relational biblical devotion in order to help build and strengthen your faith and understanding of marriage dynamics within that specific topic area. Furthermore, studying these passages can provide a springboard for growth and healing within and between each person.

There is also a brief section at the end of every chapter called **"Points to Ponder."** This set of tools will enable you to simply summarize and synthesize the main concepts contained in each chapter. As each spouse personally internalizes the information in each subject area, these discussion questions will give both of you a powerful opportunity to more deeply and directly know and understand yourself and each other.

Next, a personal application section called **"Activation Activities"** is designed to further assist you in putting into practice the information you have just received. These interventions are designed not only to give you food for thought about how you can heal, grow, and change, but also to gently challenge and stretch you in the process. Since there is no such thing as a perfect or ideal marriage, all of us can benefit from investing wisely in and working diligently on our closest relationships.

The final feature of each chapter is a list of **"Recommended Resources"** which will help further enrich your marriage in each of the specific topic areas, should you choose. There are zillions of books on marriage, and many of them are very useful. But for most people, to read them all would be unrealistic and possibly overwhelming. So, this section provides a brief descriptive summary of several of the most helpful resources in that particular area, from some of the best marriage experts.

As you can see, this is not just another garden-variety book on marriage. Extensive clinical training and working with thousands of couples over the past 36 years, as well as my own personal relationship experience, have taught me how hard, harrowing, and humbling the hurts, hassles, and heartaches of marriage can be.

> Perhaps nothing in all of existence can be as horrible as a bad marriage, yet nothing in the entire universe can be as heavenly as a good one!

Perhaps nothing in all of existence can be as horrible as a bad marriage, yet nothing in the entire universe can be as heavenly as a good one!

Much prayer, thought, study, and work have been invested in the creation of this book, *Making Magnificent Marriages*, its accompanying workbook, *A Marriage Maintenance Manual,* and the corresponding online *Relationship Health Score 1.0* inventory, for the expressed purpose of helping you make a truly magnificent marriage. These are designed to be fun, engaging, and interactive tools that can help you creatively customize your marriage relationship to become all that the original Designer intended it to be. No one wants to waste their time, money, and energy taking some unscientific magazine inventory or trying to read a simplistic "self-help" book that is dry, boring, and unhelpful. I believe you'll find these resources to be realistic, relevant, and redemptive.

Will your marriage become a clunker or a classic? The choice is yours. My hope and prayer is that you will decide to dedicate yourself to investing in your marriage by getting it running smoothly and efficiently and keeping it that way.

The journey ahead will prove to be an adventurous and hopefully scenic road trip. It is intended that this diagnostic mechanism and manual will provide direction, encouragement, and inspiration along the way. Your selection of these marital tools already indicates your interest in making your marriage at least manageable. Go ahead and dare to dream. Make it magnificent!

CHAPTER ONE

Spiritual Synergy

There is an old adage which says good marriages are made in heaven - but shucks, so are thunder and lightning!

"Jesus knew their thoughts and said to them, 'Every kingdom divided against itself will be ruined, and every city or house divided against itself will not stand.'"

—MATTHEW 12:25

L ife is relational. We were designed by the Creator in relationship, for relationship, and through relationship. Without the reality and reciprocity of relationships, life could not consist or continue.

But like life, relationships are far from easy or simple, and they possess many risks as well as rewards. When we experience stress, often the greatest toll is taken out on our closest relationships. Rather than turning *to* those with whom we are the closest, it is an almost built-in human reflex that we turn *on* them! Ironically but tragically, we tend to hurt the ones we love—just like the old country music song said.

Consider these complexities and complications: where are we taught (and by whom) how to make and maintain healthy and harmonious relationships? How close should we get to others and in what ways? And what about the real and potential dangers of relating to other people—after all, who hasn't experienced interpersonal hurt and heartache, frustration and failure, distance and disappointment, and/or crisis and conflict?!

Let's make this perfectly practical and personal. Realistically, no one is properly prepared at birth—or even by growing up in our society—to relate to other people in a fully functional way. No one enters into relationships expertly equipped with all the skills and tools needed to succeed at intimacy. We are all born dependent, selfish, fearful, needy, and... alone.

Creating

This painful, universal state of existential alienation is the only thing that God created that He did not declare to be "good." So what did God do to address this state of loneliness? Genesis 2:18 tells us that "The Lord God said, 'It is not good for the man to be alone. I will make a helper suitable for him.'" Voila! God performs the first surgery and Eve is created. (Some theologians actually believe the reason Eve was created was because God took one look at Adam, stepped back and thought to Himself, "I can do better!")

Still somewhat groggy from the anesthetic, Adam awakens and is absolutely awestruck and amazed. Depending on your perspective, he either exclaimed, "Wow!" or "Eureka!" Eve was certainly unlike anything he had experienced before. She was certainly no animal, but I'm sure he was tempted to become one at that moment!

In his profound book, *The Mystery of Marriage*, Mike Mason eloquently explains:

We may presume that we cannot know, as Adam did, what it is like to see another human being for the very first time, let alone a person of the opposite sex... secretly we long to perpetuate that one astounding moment in the Garden of Eden. We long to stand in awe of one another, just as Adam and Eve must have done when they first locked gazes. We long for our whole body to tingle with the thrill of knowing that this one fascinating being, this being of a different gender, has been created especially for us and given to us unreservedly for our help, comfort, and joy. Men and women ache for the heart with which to know this reality, and for the eyes with which to see one another (and therefore themselves) as the astounding miracles that they are (1985, p. 27).

Mason concludes:

This is what marriage is about. This is the one central experience it seeks to capture, to explore, and to exploit to the fullest. The encounter between the first man and the first woman is the archetypal stuff out of which marriage has been built. Marriage is made out of this encounter as the body is made of flesh, and it is the work of marriage continually to return to this encounter, to recapture it afresh and to feed upon it (1985, p. 27).

God's plan for marriage was, and still is, magnificent! But in order to be married well, each of us must first be able to be single well as a healthy, mature adult. Drs. Les and Leslie Parrott wisely describe this fundamental principle of relationship: "If you try to find intimacy with another person before achieving a sense of identity on your own, all your relationships will become an attempt to complete yourself" (1998, p. 20). In order to have healthy relationships, we must first become healthy individuals. We simply cannot give that which we do not have.

A healthy marriage is not so much about *finding* the right person as it is about *becoming* the right person.

You see, a healthy marriage is not so much about *finding* the right person as it is about *becoming* the right person. Our desperate search to fill the lonely, empty space inside often leads us to blindly seek out Mr. or Miss Right, hoping that they will somehow magically fill the aching void within, meet our deepest needs, and fulfill our greatest expectations. Destined to fail, this subconscious, sophisticated idolatry typically deteriorates into destructive and dysfunctional codependency. And given that one of the laws of physics is that nature abhors a vacuum, we are tempted at this point to medicate the pain of our aloneness with various compulsive self-destructive and addictive behaviors (e.g. alcohol, drugs, gambling, overeating, pornography, promiscuity, shopping, etc.).

Our culture often refers to a spouse as one's "better half." But relationally-speaking, two halves do not make a whole. *Instead, two individually whole people make a whole and healthy marriage.* Becoming whole and healthy in our sense of identity is each person's responsibility and is a lifetime process.

Identity is formed only through relationship. As infants, we only know *that* we are—and then *who* we are—in relationship to others. As we grow and develop, we progressively learn who we are as a result of and in context with relating to other people. In this interactive process, we express our individuality, test boundaries, acquire our value system, formulate our philosophical worldview, and thus become who we are.

To be relationally healthy really boils down to this: *to deeply know and to be deeply known.* In order to truly love and be loved, we have to be willing to risk knowing and being known. In this sense, to "know" one's spouse is much more than a biblical euphemism for intercourse. This kind of emotional transparency makes us feel intensely vulnerable. Down deep, we realize we will inevitably discover things about ourselves and the other person which we don't like or care for—just as they

24

will undoubtedly find things about themselves and us which they find displeasing or objectionable.

So let's get back to the first couple in the Garden of Eden. When you think about it, they really had some tremendous advantages: Adam never had to hear about her old boyfriends, and Eve never had to have her cooking be compared to his mom's! The Hebrew word in the creation account translated into English as "suitable," in reference to Eve as Adam's mate, means literally "corresponding to." God created the first marital couple to have complementary companionship—not contentious conflict.

Marriage was the crowning achievement of all of God's glorious creation. St. Augustine observed that in creating Eve, God did not take the bone from Adam's head for her to rule over him nor from his foot for him to trample on her, but from his side to be equal to him, under his arm to be protected by him, and near his heart to be loved by him. Pretty awesome, huh?

OK, that's a brief overview of God's original design for marriage. But what happens when one or both spouses do not buy into those basic beliefs? What is it like to try to drive down the road of life when each person wants to steer in a different direction? What occurs when one spouse has a radically different worldview or value system than the other?

Yoking or Aligning?

The apostle Paul wisely warns us, "Do not be yoked together with unbelievers. For what do righteousness and wickedness have in common? Or what fellowship can light have with darkness" (2 Corinthians 6:14)? The term "yoked together" is an agricultural word picture referring to the pulling efficiency and effectiveness of a matched team of oxen. The yoke was a wooden harness, which attached each ox to the other and enabled them to be driven in a straight line. If one ox was significantly larger or stronger than the other, or if it would try to go in

25

a different direction, both oxen's necks would rub against the yoke and chafe.

Now if you're like me, it's been a few years since I've hitched up my team of oxen to plow the south forty! For most of us city folk, a more contemporary analogy to illustrate the need for spiritual synergy in marriage might be the front wheels of an automobile.

Obviously, if both wheels of the car aren't pointed in the same direction, the steering, handling, and braking are going to be seriously impaired. If the camber or toe-in is off-center, the tread wear will be uneven. So too in marriage, when our goals, values, and beliefs are not compatible, the ride is bumpy, the steering is faulty, and the tires tend to squeal. However, even when our wheels are balanced and our front end is properly aligned, unforeseen potholes or obstacles in the roadway of life can cause us to wreck or end up in the ditch. Hence the need for ongoing and regular maintenance in our marriages.

> According to research on marital adjustment, the most consistently significant factor in marital happiness is having a similar or shared system of spirituality.

According to research on marital adjustment, the most consistently significant factor in marital happiness is having a similar or shared system of spirituality. In summarizing dozens of studies on marital adjustment, longevity, and satisfaction, Hood, Hill, and Spilka (2009, p. 162) report "... spouses with equivalent religious orientations/motivations expressed greater marital satisfaction. Spouses who consider their marriage a sacred covenant are happier with their union and are more devoted to each other than those who do not view their partnership in religious terms."

In their review of many other research studies on marriage, Markman, Stanley, and Blumberg (2001, p. 256) discovered that, "Couples who actively practiced their faith together—and who tended to view marriage as having a transcendent meaning—tended to be happier, to have less conflict, to work more as a team and to engage in less of what we have called the danger signs." In fact, their findings strongly suggest that the more faith-based activities a couple does together (e.g. church attendance, worship, prayer, Bible study, small group discussions, serving, etc.), the happier and more connected they are. It can be said with scientific validity that the couple that prays together stays together!

Among the many benefits of spiritual synergy to marriages are opportunities for socialization, service, sacrifice, and support. When a couple has a shared core belief system—including a mutual understanding of the meanings and values of life, death, and relationship—it's easier to develop a shared relationship vision unique to that couple. In turn, having a mutual relationship vision supports the long-term goal of keeping the relationship alive and vibrant by giving it hope, strength, and stability.

Conversely, married persons who do not share their mate's faith have been found to possess lower levels of marital satisfaction, personal fulfillment, and interpersonal health. Markman, et al. (2009, p. 263) concluded that, "When couples do not share their faiths or worldviews, the impact on the relationship can be devastating." Their research also consistently demonstrated that mixed faith couples or those who are 'unequally yoked' are much more likely to divorce.

Leaving, Cleaving, and Weaving

From the perspective of a Christian worldview, I find it fascinating that the three central characters of the Bible—Moses, Jesus, and Paul—all said two things in common. All three emphasized that the entire vertical dimension of relationship is summarized by saying that we are to love God fully and our neighbor as ourselves (Deuteronomy 6:5, Leviticus 19:18, Matthew 22:37-40, Romans 13:8-10), while the ultimate horizontal dimension of relationship is synopsized by commanding us to leave, cleave, and weave (Genesis 2:24, Matthew 19:5, Ephesians 5:31). Simply stated, marriage "is the contemplation of the love of God in and through the form of another human being" (Mason, 1985, p. 30).

My friends and former classmates in our doctoral program, Drs. Henry Cloud and John Townsend, point out that it is only when we love God first and fully that He empowers us to be able to love ourselves appropriately and then love each other. As they put it:

> When loving God is our orienting principle in life, we are always adjusting to what he requires from us. When things get tough in a marriage and when some change is required from us, we might not want to do it. We might feel that it is unfair that we have to change, or it might be too difficult or painful to change. At those moments, it is much easier to just please ourselves. But if we know that it's God with whom we ultimately have to deal, we submit to this reality and his higher calling to us to grow. In the end, the relationship wins (1999, p. 114).

Loving God with our entire being encourages and empowers us to love our spouse as we love ourselves.

The biblical concept of leaving is much more psychological than geographical. In Moses' day, to leave meant that a young man became emotionally, financially, and socially autonomous from his parents as he made his own tent, maintained his own flocks and herds, and traveled nomadically with his clan in search of grazing pastures. See, apron strings are remarkably elastic: they can extend exactly halfway around the globe in any direction! Some people may appear to be present with their spouse, but they are really stuck to their parents. It is extremely difficult for a young lady to respect, trust, and admire a husband who is still dependent upon his parents.

The somewhat antiquated word "cleave" means to permanently cling, adhere, or stick to like glue. Cleaving conveys the concept of catching someone by pursuit and clinging to them as a new rock of refuge and safety. Whereas the act of leaving is public, cleaving is private. It follows naturally that, after severing the primary parental attachment, when a couple secures their life with each other, it is based upon a powerful and permanent bond. Thus, "A marriage is not a joining of two worlds, but an abandoning of two worlds in order that one new one might be formed" (Mason, 1985, p. 91).

In their classic work, *The Intimate Marriage*, Howard and Charlotte Clinebell describe this marvelous mystery by declaring that:

> Intimacy is the interlocking of two individual persons joined by a bond, which partially overcomes their separateness. In the fullest expression of intimacy there is a vertical dimension, a sense of relatedness to the universe, which both strengthens the marital relationship and is strengthened by it. Quite apart from any churchy or churchly considerations, the spiritual dimension of marriage is a practical source of food for marital growth and health. No single factor does more to give a marriage joy or to keep it both a venture and an adventure in mutual fulfillment than shared commitment to spiritual discovery (1970, p. 179).

When a couple is committed to spiritual growth, their marriage will flourish and prosper. This leaving and cleaving results in the two becoming unified as one.

God designed this profound mystery of becoming "one flesh" to be initiated on the wedding night and to continue to become progressively integrated throughout the course of a couple's marriage. God designed the "weaving" together of the couple symbolized by sexual intimacy and fulfillment to be safely set within the sacred and sanctified security of marriage.

God commanded the first couple to be fruitful and multiply (Genesis 1:28). The Hebrew term first used in reference to sexual intercourse in Genesis 4:1 is *yadah,* which speaks of a profoundly intense intimacy, wherein two parties attain a deeply personal experiential knowledge of one another and see each other as they truly are. The depths, delights, and dimensions of this type of intimacy are impossible to achieve in premarital and/or promiscuous sexual relationships. No one can be "one flesh" with a bunch of different people without feeling internally fragmented in the process (Proverbs 6:23-35)!

But the multiplication process involved in weaving a married couples' lives together is more than just on the outside—it is also on the inside. In his clever book, *Men are From Dirt, Women are From Men*, Dr. Leo Godzich points out that, "The marriage, therefore, becomes an opportunity to show off the regenerative and reconciliatory power of God to blend two people created totally differently, so that the two can become one" (2006, p. 25). He concludes, "But marriage is about more than simply adding someone to your life. It is a union of two lives" (2006, p. 34).

Godzich observes that most people view marriage as addition: one plus one equals two. We typically think to ourselves, "I'm marrying someone who is adding to my life; who will complete and fulfill me." Instead, he notes that marriage is about multiplication: one times one equals one. This is truly what being "one flesh" is about. Since both spouses are imperfect people, we shouldn't look to fulfill each other but to unite. If you multiply a "better half" times ½, you get ¼! God did not design marriage for "½" spouses to complete one another, but for whole adults to complement one another. Everything God wants to do in and through our lives is to multiply us and magnify Him; everything Satan wants to do in and to our lives is to divide us and destroy Him.

Here is where much of our culture misses God's wondrous design for marriage: a healthy marriage requires two whole, maturely functioning adults.

Here is where much of our culture misses God's wondrous design for marriage: a healthy marriage requires two whole, maturely functioning adults. Marriage is neither a shortcut to nor a substitute for individual growth. The biblical prescription or pattern for being "one flesh" (which in the original biblical terminology means literally "one organism") in marriage is for two complete adults to become one. Fragmented, fractured people who codependently expect their mate to complete them are bound to be disappointed and probably miserable. As immature people who cannot freely give and receive love, they are too preoccupied with and/or limited by their own needs to be relationally-oriented. *Marriage was not intended to be the cause of maturity but the culmination of it.*

Gary Thomas further illustrates this mystical and beautiful weaving together process in his best-selling book, *Sacred Marriage.* He states, "A spiritually alive marriage will remain a marriage of two individuals in pursuit of a common vision outside themselves" (2000, p. 255). Such a jointly aligned mission—which focuses on loving God more pointedly and prominently than loving one's spouse—will ultimately cause us to be able to more fully love our spouse, as we reflect more of Christ's character in our personhood.

In other words, as each spouse seeks to become more holy instead of more happy, a true transfusion of and transformation by God's love and grace and mercy takes place in each person's heart. As Mason says, "Marriage for the Christian is a continuous sacrament, an act of praise and obedience, and a means of grace that is inherently every bit as 'spiritual' as anything that goes on in a monastery, or in any church or mission field for that matter, and every bit as important (or more so) as any other 'work' that one might do in the world" (1985, p. 20).

Home Building

Scripture has many important things to say about how to build a house. Perhaps that's due in part to the fact that the Son of Man's day job was being a carpenter. But more likely, this figure of speech powerfully symbolizes the place of permanence, protection, and privacy where couples and families live. So let's briefly explore some key passages utilizing this metaphor as they apply to marriage building:

> Proverbs 24:3-4: "By wisdom a house is built, and through understanding it is established; through knowledge its rooms are filled with rare and beautiful treasures."

Three significant features of both house building and marriage building arise from Solomon's astute observation. Solid homes and marriages are both constructed by intelligent, purposeful, and careful planning—from the architectural design to the actual construction process and finally to the interior decoration. Solomon repeatedly refers to these three virtues of wisdom, understanding, and knowledge as being precious, profound, powerful, and priceless (compare Proverbs 2:1-5, 3:13-15, 3:19-20, 4:5-9).

No one would want to live in a *house,* which was carelessly, casually, and cavalierly thrown together. Likewise, impulsively rushing into a marriage partnership without wisely knowing and understanding one's self, one's fiancé, and the dynamics of marriage systems will probably result in a *home* in which no one wants to live:

Matthew 7:24-27:   "Therefore everyone who hears these words of mine and puts them into practice is like a wise man who built his house on the rock. The rain came down, the streams rose, and the winds blew and beat against that house; yet it did not fall because it had its foundation on the rock. But everyone who hears these words of mine and does not put them into practice is like a foolish man who built his house on sand. The rain came down, the streams rose, and the winds blew and beat against that house, and it fell with a great crash."

When my wife, Linda's, and my oldest son, Jordan, was three years old, his favorite song from Sunday school was "The Wise Man Builds His House Upon the Rock." At that time we were in the process of building a new house. I had been told that there are three things which always occur when you build a house: it will cost more than you thought, it will take longer than you planned, and it will create many growth opportunities for your relationship! We found all three of these to be true in our situation.

We selected a beautiful, heavily wooded, picturesque lot, which backed up to a small lake adjoining a large regional park in a wonderful, close-in yet accessible subdivision. What we didn't know was that just a few feet under the surface of our property was an enormous vein of solid Bedford Falls limestone. The short version of the story is that it took a huge hoe-ram machine with a tungsten steel point ten hours per day for two weeks to chip out our basement from the solid rock. Needless to say, we did not anticipate this large cost overrun in our planning process, so it was a few years before we had all our draperies! But when we moved from that house 19 years later, there was not one small crack or fissure in the sheetrock. All of that difficult, time-consuming, and expensive work resulted in a solid, well-constructed home.

The parallels here to marriage building are obvious. The investment of time, money, and energy expended in digging for foundational truth is very well spent. In Luke's corresponding account of the above story, Jesus emphasized that the house builder "dug down deep" to lay the foundation on rock, but another person just built his house on the ground (Luke 6:46-49). On a beautiful, clear and sunny day, both houses will look the same from the street. The truth is that anybody can be married to anyone else under three idealistic conditions: richer, better, and healthier. But life has both literal and figurative storms and floods, some of which are predictable and some of which are not. Therefore, the deeper and stronger the foundation, the more likely that both the house and the relationship will endure:

> Psalm 127:1: "Unless the LORD builds the house, its builders labor in vain."

Marriage is probably the most humbling thing in the world. Think about it: you have two imperfect people who are selfish, immature, and demanding, each of whom expects their spouse to be perfect (although at least I realize that my dear, sweet, precious, lovely wife, Linda, isn't perfect because her mate selection capability is obviously flawed!). We want what we want when we want it because we want it! Submitting ourselves and yielding to the wishes and wants of another is unnatural. Human nature is inherently sinful and contrary to the will of God.

> **The naked, unvarnished truth is that in an intimate marriage no one has a deeper awareness of your faults, foibles, and failures than your spouse.**

The naked, unvarnished truth is that in an intimate marriage no one has a deeper awareness of your faults, foibles, and failures than your spouse. Plus, to be rather crass, your dirty laundry is normally done in the same machine as your spouse's! Because of this inherent vulnerability, *no one on this planet can potentially hurt us as much as our marriage partner.*

So, in our on-going attempts to avoid pain, we are naturally prone to become defensive and continue to hide—just like we have done since Genesis 3.

But God's blueprint for house and marriage building is radically different. The materials and tools with which God spiritually constructs lives and relationships consist of regeneration, redemption, restoration, and reconciliation. As Thomas (2000, p. 16) says, "A wedding calls us to our highest and best—in fact, to almost impossible—ideals. It's the way we *want* to live. But marriage reminds us of the daily reality of living as sinful human beings in a radically broken world. We aspire after love but far too often descend into hate. Any mature, spiritually sensitive view of marriage must be built on the foundation of mature love rather than romanticism." Thus we must continually strive to humbly do this marriage thing God's way instead of our own:

> Matthew 12:25: "Every kingdom divided against itself will be   ruined, and every city or household divided against itself will not stand."

Many years ago, I read a newspaper account of a man in Texas whose dearly loved wife had just divorced him. It was apparently a no-fault divorce wherein each party was to receive half of their personal property in the settlement. Deeply distraught, this man turned off the electricity to their house at the street, fired up his chainsaw and proceeded to cut his house in half right down the middle, offering his ex-wife first choice of the halves.

Whereas that story literally proves the validity of Jesus' explanation of the need for unity in family relationships, fortunately most household divisions are less dramatic than the Texan's. Again, when a couple's emotional, psychological, social, sexual, and spiritual wheels are not properly aligned, the stress and tension exerted on the front end can shake apart and eventually wreck the entire automobile. Insidious, internal division can destroy any marriage. Although the research consistently demonstrates that spiritual compatibility is the most important component of a marriage, it remains the least well-developed area of marriage for most couples.

Lovingly Leading

So what can you do as a married couple to increase your levels of spiritual synergy? Well, as with most things, you need to begin by simply talking about it. Both spouses need to recognize the enormous significance and multiple implications of getting your spiritual wheels properly aligned and attuned to one another. Then you need to acknowledge and itemize whatever barriers may impede your ability to be spiritually connected. Finally, you need to develop a proactive plan to intentionally nurture and develop this vital area of your marriage.

Many books have been written about gender and role differences in marriage, so we will not duplicate those efforts here. Simply stated, most experts agree that, from a biblical worldview, wives and husbands possess equal value in terms of their personhood, but have different roles in marital functioning.

Men, we husbands have been given an awesome opportunity as well as a gigantic responsibility to be the spiritual leader of our family.

Men, we husbands have been given an awesome opportunity as well as a gigantic responsibility to be the spiritual leader of our family. And it may feel like the hardest job you've ever had. In his hard-hitting book, *Why Men Hate Going to Church* (2011), David Murrow outlines how our culture has overly feminized faith and spirituality, and that because of this, men are caught in a horrible double bind. The concept of loving leadership may seem like an oxymoron—religious men have typically been either feeble and flaccid or autocratic and abusive.

In explaining this perplexing predicament to wives, Dr. Gary Rosberg says, "Being the spiritual leader of your family is the toughest job your husband will ever take on. Why? Because in order to do it, he must reject everything the culture teaches him about his masculinity" (2000, p. 178). Much of the traditional practice of Christianity has been disproportionately focused on addressing the needs of women and children. Thankfully, there has been an unprecedented outpouring of God's Spirit in the last several years, as evidenced by the Promise Keepers and other men's movements that have empowered men to embrace and exercise their God-given role in the home.

Meanwhile, some of the most common challenges to the development and exercise of loving spiritual leadership in marriage include the lack of healthy role models (few men have had the privilege of growing up with their dad being a loving leader—probably because his dad's dad wasn't—and we certainly didn't learn how to do this from John Wayne, Clint Eastwood, Mr. T, or Rambo!), being chronically busy, misguided priorities, inadequate or deficient training, unresolved relational conflict, a generalized sense of laziness or inconsistency, and/or a perceived lack of respect for and submission to his leadership by his wife. All of these need to be discussed as a couple and hopefully worked through to a mutual resolution.

Additionally, many people do not have a healthy understanding of what constitutes loving leadership. The concept of loving leadership is not that of a mighty potentate arrogantly sitting on his throne ruling over his cowering subjects with an iron fist. Furthermore, it is not like an officer commanding his army, a master lording over his slave, or even a computer analyst pushing all the right buttons. Actually, it is more like a conductor standing on his dais directing a symphony. Delicate, but definitive. Subtle, yet strong. Minimal, though masterful.

I believe Jesus was the toughest guy who ever lived. Contrary to flowery artistic depictions from the Middle Ages or from Hollywood of him being a strikingly handsome yet rather effeminate, passive, wimpy doormat, an accurate scriptural account portrays him as not only confident, courageous, cool, and collected, but also as an ordinary looking, rugged blue-collar worker, a fierce and mighty warrior, and a conquering King (see *The Jesus I Never Knew* by Phillip Yancey). Jesus was tough enough to be tender and strong enough to be gentle in the face of extreme social pressure, intense personal stress, excruciating heartache, and overwhelming conflict. As we emulate his excellent example, we can learn to lead like he loved.

The final part of achieving spiritual synergy in our marriage involves intentionality and application. Spiritual intimacy requires spiritual growth. And spiritual growth rarely happens by accident. It must be maturely motivated and deliberately designed.

Though no one ever thinks of starting up a business without a definitive business plan, most couples do not have any sort of formalized purpose about how they will grow together spiritually. When asked directly, most couples wish they were closer with their spouse spiritually but rarely even talk about it. So how do we develop a plan to align ourselves spiritually with our spouse?

To borrow from the hilarious old movie, *What About Bob?*, it's probably best done with "baby steps." It is unrealistic for a relationship to move from being a spiritual wasteland to a lush spiritual garden overnight. In order to reap a bumper crop of spiritual intimacy, the couple must first take the small steps to prepare the seedbed, sow the seed, water, wait, weed, fertilize, water, wait, prune, water, weed, prune, fertilize, water, wait, weed, water, and wait some more. After all that, you can begin to harvest!

The first step in planting the seeds of spiritual growth in your marriage is to lead by example. A wife is naturally inspired to grow herself by witnessing her husband's own personal spiritual growth.

Second, a husband must take initiative for the growth and development of the couple's mutual spiritual health. It is on this point that many men feel discouraged and defeated due to erroneously believing that the leader must do all the work. On the contrary, effective leaders delegate much of the work to others for their good and development. It's not the husband's role to personally do the work, just to make sure that it gets done.

The third step in achieving spiritual synergy is to develop regular, meaningful, and mutually fulfilling times of and opportunities for prayer (for some practical pointers on how to effectively pray together in a nonthreatening way, see the section entitled "Conversational Prayer" in Chapter 6), worship, service, devotional study, and small group activities in which to invest.

There is no universal template or cookie-cutter approach to spiritual intimacy that works for every marriage. What is most important is that each couple develops and then works a plan for growth. I would encourage you to be as creative as possible in customizing what works for you and your marriage relationship. Finding a healthy church in which both spouses can be spiritually nurtured, experience vibrant corporate worship, contribute to its operation, and sacrificially serve others is an important starting place. Many people have been wounded and disillusioned by previous hurts from a church or by people calling themselves Christians. Don't let that distract, discourage, or deter you from all the many blessings and benefits we can both give and receive in a healthy church. There is no such thing as a perfect church—I know my church isn't perfect because I go there! A healthy church should be a hospital for sinners, not a museum for saints.

Some couples find it very helpful to be involved in a monthly marriage mentoring relationship in which to be discipled and then to disciple others. Many couples find books for daily prayers and devotionals along with systematic Bible reading helpful to structure their spiritual times. Likewise, regular or periodic times set aside specifically for spiritual interaction such as prayer retreats, fasting, conferences, missions trips, or elongated reading/study times can also prove to be very beneficial in keeping us rolling down our life's roadways in a balanced, straightforward manner.

In conclusion, "It takes time, open communication, humility, grace, and a desire for spiritual growth for any couple to grow together spiritually. Even then, there are major blocks we must overcome to achieve it... Growing together spiritually is not our natural bent" (Burns, 2006, p. 154). Like anything else, the marital foundation of spiritual synergy requires an investment of time and commitment. It will never happen on its own. You have to *make* your marriage magnificent!

Scriptural Search

1. Genesis 1:26-28
2. Genesis 2:18-25
3. Genesis 3:1-24
4. Ephesians 5:1-33
5. 1 Peter 3:1-12

Ponderable Points

1. What is your core belief system or worldview? In what do you believe most deeply? What do you value the highest, or what is most important to you?

2. How did you acquire or develop these beliefs and values? What or who was most influential in the process of forming your worldview?

3. What were your beliefs growing up? How were these beliefs practiced in your family of origin? What was your parents' worldview or value system?

4. How have your beliefs and values changed since you have been married? How would you like to change your worldview or core beliefs in the future, if at all?

5. What would you most like to change about your spouse's belief system and/or spiritual practices? What do you think your spouse would most like to change about your personal values and how you live them out?

Activation Activities

1. Write down a personal plan about how you want to develop or improve your own individual beliefs and faith practices. This may include spiritual disciplines such as Scripture reading/study, prayer, worship, fasting, ministry or service to others, small group involvement/Bible study participation, discipleship/mentoring, and devotional/spiritual growth reading.

2. Consider sharing this plan with your spouse and request that they do the same with you. Concentrate on creating an emotionally safe environment in which to communicate these personal beliefs, focusing on actively listening to your mate's heart without making them feel uncomfortable, threatened, or defensive. Give them space and permission to be their own unique person and accept them with empathy and understanding and without judgment. Implement grace and mercy.

3. Taking into account the inevitable individual differences which exist between your and your spouse's worldviews and faith practices, discuss how you are willing to adapt to, perhaps compromise about, experiment with, and integrate your differences and preferences in an effort to harmonize and balance the belief systems in your marriage.

Recommended Resources

The Mystery of Marriage, Mike Mason (1985).
Sacred Marriage, Gary Thomas (2000).
The Love Dare, Stephen and Alex Kendrick (2008).
Men are from Dirt, Women are from Men, Leo Godzich (2006).

Night Light: A Devotional for Couples, James & Shirley Dobson (2008).

CHAPTER TWO

Concrete Commit-ment

Did you hear about the couple who broke up because of illness in the family? Yep, they just eventually got sick of each other!

"...for the LORD your God goes with you; he will never leave you nor forsake you."

—DEUTERONOMY 31:16

hen I was a little boy, my father worked as a concrete finisher with a large construction company for several years. At a young age I learned that a good concrete floor, wall, or roadway required a lot of skilled and difficult work and concerted planning. Engineering the design, preparing the site, digging the holes, constructing the forms, tying together the rebar, mixing the gravel, sand, water, and cement, pouring and then finishing the concrete, and properly curing the surface is a fascinating but laborious process.

Consequently, concrete is a very expensive yet durable construction material which possesses excellent properties of strength and stability. Precisely because concrete is such a costly commodity and involves such a labor-intensive process, unethical contractors can be tempted to scrimp on ingredients or take shortcuts to minimize their outlay. But if the site isn't properly graded or prepared, the forms aren't precisely fabricated, an insufficient amount (or inferior quality) of steel reinforcing rods or mesh are utilized, the mix contains too low a percentage of cement, it is poured too thinly, and/or not enough time is taken to carefully finish and correctly cure the surface, concrete can be worthless. It can buckle, heave, flake, crack, and break apart at the first signs of stress.

In many ways, marriages are a lot like concrete. They require a lot of hard work and a significant investment, but if the proper procedures are followed, they can become a permanent foundation upon which a strong and enduring home can be built. Or, without proper preparation and construction, they can collapse under pressure.

When it sets up, hardens, and dries, wet cement conforms to the parameters by which it is formed. Several years ago, when our four sons were much shorter, I built a patio on the lower level of our backyard. After I finished the surface, but before it completely dried, each boy permanently preserved his handprint and initials on the edge of the concrete. Perhaps many of you have preserved fond familial memories for posterity in a similar way. *In marriage, it is the vows we make on our wedding day which permanently define and direct the nature and future of our marriage.*

In his excellent book, *The Heart of Commitment,* Christian marriage researcher, Dr. Scott Stanley, states, "Wedding vows, taken seriously, embody the essence of the commitment made on the wedding day" (1998, p. 5). He asserts that a wedding vow is basically making the choice to give up other choices. Someone once humorously described a wedding ring as a small gold band that cuts off your circulation!

Never is a person more fully free than when he or she is completely committed.

Paradoxically, never is a person more fully free than when he or she is completely committed. As Mike Mason puts it: "Adherence to the vows is not a confining so much as a delimiting discipline, a marking of the natural boundaries of our human abilities. Far from being trapped, we are actually set free, set free and consecrated for the performing of a task which turns out to be the most vital work in the world: the work of covenant, of loving relationship" (1985, p. 104).

Let's define terms. Webster describes a vow as a solemn promise, pledge, or personal commitment. It involves not only intentionality but also a determination and individual involvement to fulfill our word irrespective of the circumstances. It furthermore conveys the meaning of initiating and swearing to a personal oath based upon one's own individual identity and integrity. It is this profoundly powerful act of the will that is involved in responsibly choosing to keep one's vow to love another person perpetually and exclusively.

The sacred rite of holy matrimony constitutes the most popular set of vows in history. However, these vows have become so commonplace that most people don't even consider them to be sacred promises at all, but simply a sort of warm and fuzzy folk ritual or social custom. Many couples at the altar seem to mindlessly recite whatever the preacher tells them, somewhat like a glorified exercise of Simon Says, without seriously considering and contemplating their meaning as a holy, sacramental event.

As a minister, over the years I have had the wonderful privilege of officiating at several weddings. I always encourage couples to invest themselves deeply and meaningfully into their marriage ceremony by writing and exchanging their own personalized vows. Reciting these holy pledges only takes a few seconds, but keeping them takes a lifetime.

"Marriage is to human relations what monotheism is to theology" (Mason, 1985, p. 81). Just as we commit to loving one God with all our heart, soul, mind, and strength, and serving Him only, in marriage we commit to loving one other human unconditionally for the rest of our life. Mason asserts, "For most people, in fact, marriage is the single most wholehearted step we will ever take toward a fulfillment of Jesus's command to love one's neighbor as oneself" (1985, p. 91).

But when we actually consider the constitution and content of these sacred vows, it is simply sobering and staggering. We are basically telling our spouse in front of God, a preacher, and a bunch of people that we will love them altruistically, on days that end in "y," as long as we are breathing—no matter what. Thus, "In purely human terms the marriage vows are impossible: impossible to keep, and impossible to walk away from" (Mason, 1985, p. 92). So what are we to do with this personal perplexing predicament? To try to keep an unconditional promise as a sinful human being seems to be a cruel and perverse hoax, somewhat like telling an innocent child to sit in the corner of a round room!

The truth is if people were faithful by nature, vows would not be necessary!

The taking of one's vows is actually an act of faith. *The truth is if people were faithful by nature, vows would not be necessary!* It is precisely because we are not inherently faithful nor honest nor loving that we must stand up in front of our family and friends and declare that we will be. This public declaration of accountability does not automatically transform us into mature stalwarts of virtue and integrity who will always and perfectly keep our word. To keep a vow doesn't mean that you won't break it, because everyone does. Again, Mason tells us that keeping a vow means, "… to devote the rest of one's life to discovering what the vow means, and be willing to change and grow accordingly. It might almost be said that the sign that a vow is being kept is the realization of how far one is from keeping it. In a very real way it is the vow which keeps the man [or woman] rather than vice versa" (1985, p. 94).

Obviously we need to look to the Lord at this point. The Bible frequently likens human marriage to an earthly picture of God's heavenly covenant with his church. And it is this incredible concept of covenant which inspires hope for our human dilemma and limitations.

God's amazing love for His children is absolutely unconditional and altogether unilateral. Romans 5:8 reveals that God demonstrates His love for us by the fact that when we were undeserving, unrepentant sinners, Christ nonetheless died for us. First John 4:10 definitively declares, "This is love: not that we loved God, but that he loved us and sent his Son as an atoning sacrifice for our sins." This good news is unmistakably finalized in the realization that "We love because he first loved us" (1 John 4:19).

Just as God's love for us is unconditional and intrinsically motivated, our love for our spouse cannot be dependent on our changing emotions or contingent on their inconsistent behavior. The truth is that commitment just doesn't sound or seem very romantic. We will never see its praises sung on any Hallmark card or in any Hollywood movie. But it is absolutely essential for any marriage to be successful. According to Dennis and Barbara Rainey, "There is only one way to make marriage and romance last: *a renewable commitment to each other that has no escape clauses and hopes only in God and not in each other*" (2004, p. 47).

It is this hope in God and in His unconditional love for us on which our imperfectly loving commitment to our sinful spouse must be founded. In their book, *The Love Dare*, popularized by their heart-hitting movie, *Fireproof*, Stephen and Alex Kendrick discuss the necessity of this covenantal love at length. They believe, "Every marriage is called to be an earthly picture of God's heavenly covenant with his church. It is to reveal to the world the glory and beauty of God's unconditional love for us" (2008, p. 198). Realizing that God is the supply source for this kind of love motivates us beyond the limitations of our human intentions and sense of duty. In making a marriage vow we are doing what the Lord Himself did with Abraham: making an unconditional promise of love to one individual.

If all this is true, then why do half of all marriages—even Christian ones—fail legally and most cf the rest fail functionally? I believe this is due in large part to the widespread belief in our culture that marriage is a merely a contract instead of a covenant. Many people in our society believe that a marriage certificate is just a piece of paper, and therefore they are not unconditionally committed to the relationship. But I believe there at least 10 basic differences between a contract and a covenant, and if we really understand them, they will impact our ability to fully commit to our covenant.

Contract vs. Covenant

1. Conditional vs. Unconditional

The key characteristic of a contract is that it spells out a list of conditions and contingencies upon which the agreement between the parties is based. In other words, there is always an escape clause or loophole in case one changes their mind. But in a healthy marriage, divorce is never an option. Marriage liturgies do not mention the possibility of a breach; there are no qualifiers or disclaimers. *I believe the "D" word should be permanently banished from every couple's vocabulary!* Ruth Bell Graham many years ago was interviewed about what it was like to live with such a famous and godly husband. While sitting on the porch of the log cabin in Montreat, North Carolina where Billy took her on their wedding night and where they had lived together ever since and raised their five children, she was asked if she had ever contemplated divorcing him. Instantly, she famously replied: "divorce no, murder yes!"

But what, you may ask, of the loophole given in Scripture regarding adultery? Or what about abuse? Careful analysis of both chapters 5 and 19 of Matthew reveals the contentious doctrinal debate in which the hypocritical religious leaders attempted to entrap Jesus over the divorce issue (in Matthew 19:1-12 the conservative school of Shammai was feuding with the liberal camp of Hillel over the interpretation and application of Deuteronomy 24: 1-4). Jesus wisely refocused the discussion to God's original and unchanging design for marriage: in the beginning they were to become one flesh. He then stated authoritatively in verse 6, "So they are no longer two, but one. Therefore what God has joined together, let man not separate." In response to their question as to why Moses then permitted divorce, Jesus replied in verse 8 that it was simply because of their "hard hearts"—strongly intimating that although forgivable, divorce can never be God's original intent or perfect will.

If we want a clear and specific example of how God truly desires a person to deal with their mate's chronic infidelity, just read the horrible, obscure little book of Hosea (many people who have done so are tempted to rip it out of their Bible!). Briefly, the story was that God told His holy prophet to marry a promiscuous woman who ended up prostituting and degrading herself so extensively that Hosea was eventually able to buy her back for about half the price of a typical slave. How horrible, humbling, and humiliating! But Hosea's faithfulness and forgivingness singlehandedly redeemed, restored, and reconciled their marriage relationship—which allegorically represents how our loving heavenly Father faithfully forgives our perpetual waywardness from Him.

Malachi 2:16 declares that God **hates** divorce. Though certainly not an unforgivable sin, God's will is that we always love and forgive our spouse as He loves and forgives us unconditionally. At the same time, please let me emphasize that I have seen situations where divorce can be the lesser of two evils. Although God hates divorce, Proverbs 6 lists seven additional things that God hates, detests, and abhors. We all definitely need God's wisdom, love, mercy, and grace—certainly none of us is qualified to judge anyone.

When I speak at marriage conferences or conduct marriage seminars or workshops, I usually make a statement that I know many people will take as controversial: I firmly believe that adulterations of various forms occur in all marriage systems at one time or another—and they are all destructive. Now sometimes when I say this, I don't get invited back, but that's okay because number one, it's true, and number two, I have another job! I know it's offensive to be accused of this horrible sin if you have not had an inappropriate physical relationship with someone to whom you are not married. But before you throw this book into the trash or fireplace, please allow me to define terms.

The dictionary defines adulteration as: "watering down the purity of or diluting the intensity of a given state, property or entity." I think "adultery" is much like the antiquated term "idolatry" (which functionally means "anything or anyone we put before God," or "anything or anyone that has us instead of us having it or them"—which also practically defines an addiction. All addictions are idols, and all idols are addictive!). Therefore, I believe *adultery means simply, "anything or anyone, besides God, that comes in between me and my spouse."*

Think about how you prioritize your mate.

Think for a moment about how you prioritize your mate. Does she or he come right after God in your heart, checkbook, and daily calendar? Adultery is actually a very broad, far-reaching phenomenon. The most common forms or patterns of marital adulteration in this country are typically completely asexual. They are, respectively, husbands' over-emotional identification and preoccupation with work and wives' over-emotional identification and involvement with children. Both are God-given gifts and blessings (see Ecclesiastes 3:13, Psalm 127:3-5), but when we permit them to slip out of their proper level of prioritization, they can functionally and dynamically adulterate a marital union just as deleteriously as having a sexual relationship with someone else.

Furthermore, as was His custom, Jesus elevated our sin to an even higher (or deeper) level. He stated that when we lust in our heart about someone else (Matthew 5:27-28), then the unrealistically idealized and decidedly perverted and distorted depictions of pornography and romance novels and soap operas become the equivalent to having full-blown intercourse with them. And just to add icing to the proverbial cake, the Bible cranks up the notion of adultery even more intensely and broadly when God uses the sexual metaphor of adultery to describe His chosen people's repetitive waywardness from Him (see Ezekiel 6:9, 16:32, Hosea 1:2, Matthew 12:39, Mark 8:38, James. 4:4). I realize this teaching messes with our self-righteousness, but now do you see what I mean when I say we have all committed adultery? *Keeping our marriage vows, just like being a Christ-follower, means that we are completely committed to being all in, all the time.*

As to abuse issues, I don't believe scripture teaches us that we're to live without healthy self-respect or firm, clear boundaries (see *Love Must be Tough* by Dr. James Dobson for further guidance on these difficult and complex issues of spousal affairs, neglect, and abuse). God never intended us to be a human punching bag—verbally, emotionally, and/or physically. But even if we are experiencing those often heartbreaking, lonely, nightmarish situations, it doesn't automatically mean we are to divorce.

> **Remember that everyone enters marriage counseling hoping their *spouse* will change.**

I realize this is a very controversial issue in some circles, but we are called to *make every effort to live in peace* (Colossians 3:15, 1 Thessalonians 5:13, Hebrews 12:14, 1 Peter 3:11). Sometimes those efforts can feel lonely and exhausting, but that's when we need to reach out for help. And if the first course of marital therapy doesn't "work," try, try again. Remember that everyone enters marriage counseling hoping their spouse will change. Instead, it may be helpful to consider what you might change about the person who uses your toothbrush. Your attitude of openness and humility could be the catalyst that motivates and empowers your mate to also cultivate humility, which would allow God to change them, too!

Still, many challenging and complex marital entanglements call for an informal or even formal legal separation as per the guidelines contained in 1 Corinthians 7. Proverbs 4:23 insists that above all else we guard our hearts so that our emotional and physical safety is ensured in extreme situations. And there are many important distinctions between the forgiveness which God commands and the reconciliation process which He prefers (and which will hopefully be the topic of a future book!). Some of these differences are that forgiveness is unilateral/intrapersonal but reconciliation is mutual/interpersonal, forgiveness is unconditional/idealistic while reconciliation is conditional/realistic, and forgiveness does not require an apology or trust whereas reconciliation does.

Think about it this way. When someone breaks a bone, it is excruciatingly painful—especially if it is a compound fracture with slivers of bone protruding through the skin. To bring about healing, the broken bone must be set and then immobilized by placing it in a protective cast. Though the pain level may be so high as to tempt the person to instead amputate their limb, apparently few people choose to do so.

In this illustration, when the marriage vows have been fractured, legal separation—and hopefully marital therapy—symbolizes the protective, healing potentiating cast, whereas divorce is tantamount to amputation. What we know from physiology is that a broken bone, if properly set and casted, becomes stronger than it was before the break occurred. This incredible miracle is an amazing demonstration not only of God's awesome healing power, but also of His undeserved grace and unfailing mercy. But broken bones—and broken relationships—are excruciatingly painful. And admittedly, orthopedists do have an advantage which marriage therapists do not: it's called anesthetic!

Again, our love to our spouse can only be unconditional and therefore covenantal because of God's consistent love, grace, and mercy to us. God never designed or intended marriage to be contractual or conditional. Or ever broken.

2. Mutual vs. Unilateral

Early on in our marriage, I was often immaturely more focused on how I thought Linda should be more effectively keeping her marriage covenant than on how I was frequently failing to keep my own. Foolishly, I would even occasionally offer her nuggets of wisdom on how she could better accomplish that! Then, of course, it hit me like a ton of bricks one day that her marriage covenant has absolutely nothing to do with mine, and vice-versa.

Marriage vows are completely one-sided.

Actually, Linda has nothing to do with my marriage covenant one way or the other. The yellow piece of metal with some shiny little rocks in it that I wear on my left hand has nothing to do with her, either. It has to do with me. It has to do with what I promised God and her in front of my good friend, Rev. Bill Newby, (and a bunch of our family and friends) that I would do. No matter what. Marriage vows are completely one-sided.

To state the obvious, this is, of course, completely unfair. But then after I got over my little temper fit, the Holy Spirit impressed to me that this is the only way a healthy marriage can ever work. Oh, and by the way, that's how God's consistently transmitted and one-sided love to me operates, as well. Even if I could successfully manipulate, coerce, or even brainwash Linda into loving me, I wouldn't ever want to. This is because not only would my manipulation constitute an abusive violation of her free will, it could never make me feel secure, since I would never know if she loved me freely of her own accord or not. Thus, just as drinking salt water when thirsty intensifies and exacerbates one's original thirst, it would ironically make me more insecure.

In other words, commitment must by nature be entirely one-sided. *We can never fully and freely say "yes" unless and until we are able to fully and freely say "no."* Marriage works only when both people choose to keep their covenant whether their spouse does or not. In her wonderfully empowering book entitled *How to Act Right When Your Spouse Acts Wrong* (2001), Leslie Vernick provides many helpful character-building examples of how to unilaterally keep your marriage covenant, especially when your spouse does not seem to be keeping theirs.

Although the language of a contract typically alternates between the duties and responsibilities of each party, both people must agree to all of the conditions. A covenant still exists from one person to the other in a one-sided fashion whether or not the other person keeps theirs, much like a powerful radio beam transmitting a signal is in the air whether anyone tunes into it or not. God's covenantal love is like that—it's always being sent; we just have to open up in order to receive it.

3. Reactive vs. Proactive

So many times over the years in my practice I have seen a spouse engage in an extramarital relationship simply because they learned about their spouse's infidelity and wanted to get even with them. Obviously, this immature and foolish act of revenge at best compounds a person's original grief and heartache; they destroy themselves in addition to retributively, reflexively, and regrettably hurting their mate (see Proverbs 6:20-35). A "get back" affair can never "get even." This kind of unforgiveness is like drinking poison in an effort to hurt the other person.

Our spouse's failures to keep their covenantal commitment should in no way motivate us not to keep ours. In fact, doesn't our spouse need to be loved the most when they are the *least* loving, lovely, and lovable? Shucks, anybody can love anyone who is loving, lovely, and lovable. Jesus said even the heathens do that (Matthew 5:46)!

Our Hollywood-ized culture has subtly but systematically brainwashed us into believing that interpersonal love is an ethereal, elegant enterprise into which we just passively and oftentimes helplessly fall. But the truth is no one "falls" in love. Gravity is just simply not that powerful! *Anyone who falls in love can just as easily fall out of love, because both are reactive in nature.*

What we typically fall into is romantic infatuation. And while romantic warm and fuzzy infatuatory feelings are wonderful, they are just icing on the cake of what true love entails. And if all you eat is icing, after a sugar high you will eventually die of malnutrition! There is nothing substantive or sustaining in a concoction of sugar and artificial flavorings and colors. Although the cake itself may not be as glorious and glamorous as the icing, the eggs and flour have much more nutritional value to the consumer.

The decision to marry is designed to represent the height of a person's adulthood, self-definition, autonomy, and individual maturity. This is why there aren't supposed to be any loaded firearms at weddings! Hopefully both people proactively chose their spouse.

I believe that the more psychologically healthy people are, the less reactive they are. When I study the Gospels and analyze Jesus' personality and patterns of interpersonal relationship, I never find one example where He reacts to anything or anyone. He is always and exclusively proactive. In the listing of the fruit of the Holy Spirit (Galatians 5:22-23), I don't believe it is coincidental that self-control comes last. Of all Jesus' outstanding personality features and exemplary character traits, this one impresses me perhaps the most. This means He would've never honked or made inappropriate gestures in traffic, been rude to a customer service representative, or impatiently snapped at His wife. Oh wait—He never got married!

4. Distrustful vs. Trusting

The entire rationale for a contract is based upon the underlying assumption and potential reality that the other party is not to be trusted. Thus, a written agreement outlines the conditions and consequences that will ensue if the agreement is broken. In contrast, a hundred years ago a person's word was their bond and a handshake sealed any gentleman's agreement. Sadly since then, many law schools have sprung up!

A marital covenant is written on our hearts and lived out daily.

58

A covenant is a verbal agreement based entirely and exclusively on trust. This verbal assurance guarantees someone else that your promise is unconditional and irrevocable. Perhaps that sounds old-fashioned or outdated, but nothing generates and engenders trust more than a solemn pledge fulfilled. It is a tribute or testimony to one's maturity, character, dignity, and integrity.

The problem of distrust is crucial to relationships. Without trust, no relationship—much less the most intimate relationship of all, marriage—can be safe, secure, or successful. Trust is the basic building block of all healthy relationships. We will address this fundamental topic much more fully in the next chapter.

5. Adversarial vs. Advocational

Without trust, an ally becomes an adversary. At their core, all contractual relationships are philosophically if not procedurally adversarial. Ergo, it is precisely because one or both parties do not believe the other party is unilaterally and unconditionally on their side that they think they have to have a legal document to protect themselves and/or their interests.

Every marriage is called to be an earthly picture of God's heavenly covenant with His church that He loves unconditionally. *Every marriage was designed to reveal to the world the glory, majesty and beauty of the complete and concerned commitment with which God continuously cares for His creation.* Unconditional commitment is a gloriously beautiful thing.

The Bible declares authoritatively that Jesus Christ is our personal advocate in the spiritual warfare against our adversary. His job is to defend and protect us from attack, accusations, and antagonism. Simply stated, He is on our side. Actually, because He loves us more than we love ourselves, He

MAKING Magnificent MARRIAGES

is even more on our side than we are! So too, we are to be on our mate's side in like manner.

When a married person compliments and praises their spouse, it is a wonderful sign of support. Conversely, when someone criticizes and derogates their mate, it is a horrible indicator of betrayal. Standing up for those whom we most love in any and all situations is a result and an expression of covenantal love and commitment.

6. Static vs. Dynamic

When we think about it logically, the very idea of making a lifelong, unconditional covenant with someone seems foolhardy and ill-advised. None of us is omniscient (or even clairvoyant!) and knows what the future may hold. What if our spouse changes? What if they become grossly overweight? What if they become chronically ill or disabled? What if they become unable or unwilling to work anymore? What if they lose their physical attractiveness as they age? What if they do something evil or shameful? Are we still to love them?

The truth is not only do we not know who our spouse will become; we really don't even know who they are when we marry them! I know this sounds crass and perhaps caustic, but in my opinion, dating and courtship in our culture are based primarily on two faulty foundations: fraud and deception.

Think of it this way. A healthy marriage dynamic consists of a mutual teaching and learning process wherein we progressively learn about our spouse to the point of becoming the world's expert on knowing and understanding who they are, while at the same time we try to teach them to become the world's expert on knowing and understanding who we are.

Let's say two 20-year-olds meet and then decide to date and court for two years before they get married. What has to be crammed into two years of time is 22 years' worth of teaching and learning and learning and teaching. Well, let's be realistic.

That simply cannot happen. So what we end up with is at best something like a *Readers Digest* condensed version of the other person that frankly has been fluffed up and slicked over. The proverbial honeymoon ends abruptly when we start to read the unabridged version of our spouse.

If what we have is just a contract, then when the other person doesn't meet our expectations or turn out like we hoped, we can just return them to their parents and get our money back! We got baited and switched. They misrepresented themselves. This was not what we signed up for. We never expected them to turn out like this. See what I mean? Fraud and deception.

In all fairness, I really don't believe most of us intentionally try to deceive one another—we so want to be accepted by the other person that we try to put our best foot forward in order to sufficiently impress them. This happens innately in all other realms of God's creation. Birds sing sweetly and strut their feathers, animals grunt and roar, and even fireflies turn on to try to turn each other on!

People change. If a legal contract could ever be written to cover all of the anticipated and unanticipated changes people could possibly make over the course of their lives, the earth would rapidly run out of trees due to how voluminous such a contract would be. Reality suggests that we all marry several different people over the course of our marriages—but hopefully with the same name and Social Security number! Just as God expanded and renewed His covenant with His people, perhaps we need to periodically revise and adjust our covenant in order to deeply and directly love our mate according to their changing needs.

> **A legal contract is written on pieces of a dead tree.**
> **It has no life, energy, or vitality.**

A legal contract is written on pieces of a dead tree. It has no life, energy, or vitality. In contrast, *a marital covenant is written on our hearts and is lived out daily* as we decide to faithfully love one another, warts and all. Whether we feel like it or not.

7. Egocentric vs. Heterocentric

A contract exists purely for self-serving and self-protective reasons. It limits one's liability, focuses on one's rights and de-sires, and establishes a timeframe which outlines expectations for certain deliverables to be fulfilled or accomplished. But a covenant is for the benefit of others and comes with unlimited responsibility. It has no expiration date or conditional contin-gency clauses.

Functionally, true (agape) love is defined as an unconditional commitment for the good and to the betterment of an imperfect person, to the point of self-sacrifice. There is no way to legis-late love. There is no way to force or coerce love. God simply loves us for our good out of the majestic and glorious richness of His heart. It has been said that He accepts and loves us just as we are—but He loves us too much to leave us this way!

A marriage vow says nothing about being loved back. A marriage vow only declares how the lover will love the beloved. The vow is not only for the speaker; it benefits the listener, as well.

Everyone longs to know that at the core of their soul they will be loved at their deepest level of pain, their deepest point of vulnerability, their greatest time of failure, their loneliest experi-ence of shame, and their strongest sense of fear. To be loved like this, regardless of all of our human shortcomings, allows both partners in a marriage to feel secure.

Down deep, we all realize that the perfect person and the perfect life is a myth or fairytale. But when we exercise faith in the God of love to fill us with His love even though we are always unworthy of receiving it, giving out that love to our spouse becomes much easier. We both know that neither deserves to be loved. But it sure does feel good to hear from our spouse, "I love you and I will always love you no matter what," and, "If I had it to do all over again, you are the one with whom I would choose to spend my life."

8. Negativistic vs. Positivistic

A contract always implicitly presumes the worst case scenario. This concept obviously stands in stark contrast to a loving vow which always protects, always trusts, always hopes, always perseveres, never fails (1 Corinthians 13:7-8), and is determined to maintain a positive mental attitude (see Philippians 4:8). Furthermore, the fundamental nature of a contract is such that it is specifically looking at what can go wrong with the agreement or fulfillment of the conditions contained therein. A marriage vow doesn't operate like that. Whereas a contract focuses attention on what one is *not* going to do, a covenant emphasizes what one *is* going to do in the relationship. It is always looking for how the relationship can be supported and benefited. It looks forward, not back. It is proactive, not reactive.

In other words:

...While love must certainly be present if a marriage is to continue and be successful, practically speaking (and the practical level is always the deepest and most mystical) it is the vows which really hold the thing together, undergirding love itself. Of course this is just another way of saying that love is not an emotion or an experience, but a promise, a resolve, an act of the will... Marriages which are dependent on love fall apart, or at best are in for a stormy time of it. But marriages which consistently look back to their vows, to those wild promises made before God, and which trust him to make sense out of them, find a continual source of strength and renewal (Mason, 1985, p. 95).

Covenants are life-giving entities which support and sustain the marriage.

Marriage has long had a pretty bad name in much of our culture. Sarcastic jokes about losses of freedom such as being led around by a nose ring (which started way before body piercings were popular! Here is another "ring" joke, which I think is actually pretty funny: Did you know that marriage is like a three ring circus? First you have the engagement ring, then the wedding ring, and then the suffering!) and caustic references to one's spouse as being the "old man" or the "old lady" (or even less flattering nicknames) are destructive, degrading, and derogatory. These insidious generalizations and various other criticisms of married life have caused us to lose much of the magnificent mystery and marvelous majesty of marriage with which God originally blessed us and which He intended us to enjoy.

9. Temporary vs. Permanent

A contract is designed to be time-limited, whereas a covenant is intended to be both unending and unbreakable. Pastors frequently use beautiful and flowery language in a wedding ceremony to describe the rich and vivid symbols of committed love signified by the unending circle and tremendous value of the rings. *A marriage covenant is firm, filial, and final; it cannot be terminated—only violated.*

Here, we once more draw inspiration from God's covenantal love to us. Repeatedly, to make us feel secure in His steadfast commitment, He assures us that, "I will never leave you nor forsake you" (Deuteronomy 31:6, Joshua 1:5, Hebrews 13:5). And in Psalm 27:10, King David reports that even when our parents reject us God will accept us.

The Spanish explorer Hernando Cortez landed his troops at Vera Cruz Mexico in 1519. In order to ensure that his over 6000 men were irrevocably committed to their task of conquering the new land for the mother country, he dramatically set fire to the ships anchored in the harbor that had brought them there—which made for a pretty long swim for them to get back home! That kind of wholehearted, no-retreat commitment in marriage is the essence of a leaving, cleaving, and weaving relationship foundation. Said another way, "Marriage is a covenant intended to cut off all avenues of retreat or withdrawal. There is nothing in all the world that should sever what God has joined together. Your love is based on covenant" (Kendrick & Kendrick, 2008, p. 198).

As many things (actually most things) do, this reminds me of a joke. One day, while a chicken and a pig were out taking a walk in Farmer Jones' field, they noticed a new billboard that had just been put up along the highway, advertising a delicious traditional eggs and ham country breakfast. The chicken excitedly commented that this publicity should be good for Farmer Jones' business. When the chicken noticed that the pig did not seem to share as deeply in her enthusiasm, she asked why. The pig replied, "Well, for you that breakfast involves meaningful participation, but for me it requires total commitment!"

Marriage vows are like that: irrevocable (or should I say "whole hog?"). Mason concludes:

> One thing that is very important to know in marriage is that there is always a way out. And the way out is not divorce! No, the way out in marriage (no matter how bad things may get) is simply to put everything we have back on the line, our whole hearts and lives, just as we did the moment we took our vows. We must return to an attitude of total abandonment, of throwing all our natural caution and defensiveness to the winds and putting ourselves entirely in the hands of love by an act of the will. Instead of falling into love, we may now have to march into it (1985, p. 95).

10. Legalistic vs. Spiritual

Finally, another major distinction between a contract and a covenant is that one is a reflection of human ordinances, and the other is an expression of supernatural principles. Human nature is such that we can stubbornly and grudgingly uphold the letter of the law while completely violating its intent or spirit. Feeling stuck in a bad marriage or feeling resigned to go through the motions of marriage due to obligation is very far from what God intends.

The problem with a duty-bound constraint is that such a person's heart is not invested in the relationship.

The problem with a duty-bound constraint is that such a person's heart is not invested in the relationship. Furthermore, their motivation for maintaining this misery or monotony is usually fear and/or guilt, rather than liberating love. Their heart just isn't in it. *Far too many couples, even Christian couples, just go through the motions.*

In God's kingdom, motivation is almost everything. Throughout the Gospels, Jesus seems to be much more focused on the "why" of what people do than on what they do. Doing the right thing for the wrong reasons never works. The self-righteous religious leaders of Jesus' day proudly proclaimed all of the "right" things which they did, yet He didn't seem to be very impressed with their wondrous works. Actually, He usually yelled at them and called them a bunch of names—"whitewashed tombs" is my personal favorite.

In the New Testament, God *never* motivates us by fear and/or guilt. He only and always motivates us by love. Just as God wants us to serve and obey Him with a happy heart filled with joy and delight, He wants us to experience the benefit and blessings of reaping what we sow in our marriages when we "love one another deeply, from the heart" (1 Peter 1:22).

Jesus taught us that where our treasure is our heart will be also (Matthew 6:21). Our heart simply follows our investment.

Whatever you pour your time, money, and energy into will draw your heart toward it. Before you were married, you probably wrote letters (now texts and emails), cards, and love notes, bought gifts, spent wonderful times together as a couple, and presto—your heart followed. But when you stopped investing as much in the relationship and started investing yourself into other things, your heart naturally followed you there. *If you are not in love with your mate today, it may be because you stopped investing in them yesterday!*

Let's go back to our original theme in the introduction section: if your marital vehicle isn't running smoothly, how long has it been since you changed the oil or tuned it up? Remember, preventative maintenance is always much better, easier, and cheaper than an overhaul.

Scriptural Search

1. Matthew 19:1-12
2. Hosea 1-3
3. Malachi 2:16
4. 1 Corinthians 7
5. Hebrews 13:5

Ponderable Points

1. Did you "fall" in love with your spouse? If so, when? What was it that made you feel that way?

2. What makes you feel most like loving and respecting your spouse?

3. What makes you feel least like loving and respecting your spouse?

4. To what degree is genuine and enduring love influenced by or based upon feelings, circumstances, and/or situational conditions?

5. Define and discuss the meanings of the word "vow." What examples of a vow have you witnessed or experienced in your life?

Activation Activities

1. Think about what it means to be fully faithful. Research examples (in Scripture, history, etc.) of people who have demonstrated the fruit of faithfulness in a relationship. Write down what you believe to be the basic components of what faithfulness looks like, how it responds, and what, if anything, influences it in a marriage.

2. Write down what for you is most challenging about the concept of making an unconditional, permanent, "concrete" commitment to your spouse. Think about any previous hurts, disappointments, fears, and/or other unmet expectations you have experienced in close relationships that may contribute to your present difficulty. Consider devoting yourself to intensive, introspective prayer regarding these past injuries.

3. Consider asking your spouse about what you do or do not do that makes it difficult or challenging for them to concretely

commit their love to you. Try to listen non-defensively and keep in mind that this is about them, not you. Prayerfully consider asking the Holy Spirit how you can learn to be their helpmate—not "hurtmate"—in these areas of your spouse's life and relationship with you.

Recommended Resources

The Heart of Commitment, Scott Stanley (1998).
The Marriage Masterpiece, Al Janssen (2001).
Covenant Marriage, Gary Chapman (2003).
I Promise You, Willard Harley (2006).
Rekindling the Romance, Dennis and Barbara Rainey (2004).

CHAPTER THREE

Total Trust

Sign on the wall behind the cash register of the old-fashioned "mom-and-pop" hardware store: "In God we trust—all others pay cash!"

"It [love] always protects, always trusts, always hopes, always perseveres"

—1 CORINTHIANS 13:7

Trust is the cornerstone of any healthy relationship. Yet trust seems to be an enigma which is characterized by several paradoxes and apparent contradictions.

While no relationship commodity is as potentially strong and foundational as trust, it is perhaps the most easily damaged of all properties of interpersonal relationship. Trust can take years to build yet can be destroyed in an instant. In some ways trust must be given freely, but in other ways it clearly needs to be earned. Furthermore, we can love someone we do not trust and trust someone we do not love.

According to pioneer developmental psychologist Erik Erikson, the capacity of an infant to trust its caregivers lays the groundwork for all future relating. This quality of being able to rely safely on others while in a state of helpless dependency creates a deep sense of security within a baby. Erikson believed our initial formation of identity is solidified when we can develop a belief in the reliability of our parents to consistently meet our basic needs. Conversely, if our caregivers are not consistently trustable and we cannot surely and securely depend upon them, it is very difficult to form a positive bond or attachment to them, or later to others.

In a marital context, Drs. Cloud and Townsend define trust as, "...the ability to be totally real, authentic, and unguarded with your lover. It means being able to bring all parts of yourself to him [or her], good and bad, strong and weak, without fear of condemnation or judgment" (2005, p. 198-199). This sense of emotional nakedness is reminiscent of what it must've originally been like in the Garden of Eden, where both people were able to safely relax, peacefully share, and naturally interact without anxiety, shame, or defensiveness.

Many people are by nature very skeptical and mistrustful (although some of you may not believe that!). Due to unhealed hurts from the past, the thought of risking vulnerability or being openly intimate like Adam and Eve seems terrifying, foolish, and unrealistic. Although we inwardly long for relational closeness, the thought of risking further hurt, rejection, and/or betrayal can often keep us internally conflicted, emotionally paralyzed, and painfully lonely.

So how do we start to trust? Should we trust others blindly? Is anyone completely trustworthy? Can broken trust ever be rebuilt? Though it may be difficult to see at first, keep in mind that behind everyone's wall, mask, façade, and defense mechanisms hides a wounded person who doesn't feel safe. Everyone has suffered pain and rejection in this fallen world. Consequently, the wisest man who ever lived poignantly warned us to, "Above all else guard your heart, for it is the wellspring of life" (Proverbs 4:23).

Nothing is to be more important than guarding our heart!

Let's briefly consider some profoundly insightful implications for our lives from this simple admonition. Think for a moment about how incredibly significant those first three words are—*nothing* is to be more important than guarding our heart! The Bible refers to our heart nearly 1000 times, not as a fist-sized pump in our chest, but in reference to the innermost core of our being and personhood. The Hebrew word for "guard" here is a militaristic term for a big, tough, fully battle-dressed warrior whom no one is getting by without expressed permission. God considers our heart to be precious and priceless, and He wants it to be perpetually and personally protected.

Furthermore, we typically fail to grasp the life and death intensity of this passage in its original meaning, because most of us do not live in the desert, and we have access to many different methods of hydration. But 3000 years ago, there was no such thing as plumbing. And especially in a desert climate, without available access to a clean water supply, one would have only a few hours to live. If your water supply was poisoned, polluted, or purloined—you were in serious trouble. Finally, the word "wellspring" encompasses the totality of both deep and surface sources of water, suggesting the embodiment of all that is life-giving for us.

To disclose and devote our heart to our spouse requires that we do so cautiously and judiciously, not casually or recklessly. We need to feel safe. We need to make certain that our mate will be interested in and receptive to what we have to share. We need to feel confident that they will listen with an open mind to our thoughts and feelings without offering unsolicited advice, criticism, judgment, ridicule, shame, or disrespect.

Exactly how does this kind of relational confidence develop? As with most things of value, acquiring trust requires a considerable investment. "It's true that a measure of trust is built during courtship and in your commitment to the wedding vows, but complete trust is established over time and under the pressure of daily life" (Rosberg & Rosberg, p. 121).

Issues of trust are in a relational category all their own, because trust underlies and supports the entire foundation of the relationship. When trust is broken, it's as if the foundation of one's home is cracked, making it no longer a hospitable, or perhaps even safe, place in which to live. As we can see, the relational cornerstone of trust is built squarely upon the foundation of commitment and is progressively constructed over the life of a marriage. But what are the building blocks of trust? What does trust in a healthy marriage look like?

Traits of Trust

Trust is relational: it is heterocentric, altruistic, and prioritizes the other person first.

We all want to know that we are deeply loved. We want to know that our feelings, desires, and preferences matter to our spouse. The seeds of trust will not sprout in the selfish soil of indifference, disinterest, or disaffection. Trust grows best when we feel unconditionally cared for and highly valued by our spouse. It's horribly lonely to be married to someone for whom everything seems to be about them and they are only focused on themselves.

Trust grows best when we feel unconditionally cared for and highly valued by our spouse.

Trust is reliable: it is faithful, loyal, and fundamentally honest.

It is impossible to place our trust in or be able to count on someone who is not dependable. For someone to be trustworthy, they must demonstrate the character traits of honesty, loy-

74

alty, and faithfulness. Simply stated, "A faithful spouse is one who can be trusted, depended upon, and believed in, and one in whom you can rest" (Cloud & Townsend, 1999, p. 130). We must be able to believe them and believe in them. When someone does not keep their promises or fails to follow through with their commitments, they prove themselves to be unreliable and therefore untrustworthy. According to Dr. Willard Harley, dishonesty and deceit are major "love busters" in marriage relationships (2002). Truth transmits trust.

> Trust is responsible: it is competent, nondefensive, and consistently dependable.

To be responsible means that one is able to respond. The elegant word picture contained in Ecclesiastes 4:9-12 dramatically describes our basic human dependencies. Solomon wisely observed that, "Two are better than one, because they have a good return for their work: If one falls down, his friend can help him up. But pity the man who falls and has no one to help him up! Also, if two lie down together they will keep warm. But how can one keep warm alone? Though one may be overpowered, two can defend themselves. A cord of three strands is not quickly broken." There will be times in life when we all need to be helped up, warmed, and/or defended and are unable to meet these needs in our own ability. It is particularly during times of weakness and vulnerability that we need a strong, capable, and dependable partner upon whom we can confidently rely. We need a person of integrity who will be unafraid to accept liability and accountability for their actions and who will follow through without making excuses. Drs. Archibald Hart and Sharon Hart Morris say we all need "a trustworthy person to whom you can turn, knowing that person will be emotionally available and respond to you in a caring manner" (2003, p. 1).

We need a person of integrity who will be unafraid to

accept liability and accountability for their actions and who will follow through without making excuses.

Trust is respectful: it is courteous, considerate, and honors the other person as valuable.

A spouse who ignores, dismisses, or invalidates their partner's feelings, thoughts, or needs is betraying marital trust. Furthermore, it is difficult for us to place our trust in someone who is rude, critical, judgmental, controlling, demanding, manipulative, abusive, and/or calls us disparaging names. Trust is also violated when partners breach privacy boundaries by expressing grievances to or embarrassing a mate in front of others. We all long to be supported and sustained through all of life's satisfactions and successes as well as its sorrows and setbacks. We all need someone to appreciate our differences and honor our individuality by accepting us just like we are—whether they agree with us or not.

Trust is realistic: it is accepting, tolerant, and doesn't expect perfection.

Only God is totally trustable. The exchange of marriage vows is an act of faith not so much in our self or our spouse but in God. Once again, Mason masterfully explains:

If people were faithful by nature, the vows would not be necessary; their yes would be yes and their no would be no. But it is because people are neither inherently faithful, honest, nor loving that they must stand up and declare that they will be. The public declaration does not automatically transform them into marvelous creatures of virtue that will always keep to their word. On the contrary, it only makes more obvious and public their complete lack of personal virtue... emphasizing their dependence upon resources that are utterly beyond human strength (1985, p. 97).

Many times, well-intended spouses subconsciously and codependently place their mate on a pedestal. But when gravity inevitably takes effect, the idol typically crashes down upon the worshiper, crushing their illusions and unrealistic expectations. Only God is perfect.

> Trust is responsive: it is attentive, compassionate, and sensitively cares for the other.

When someone reaches out to us in a concerned and caring way and puts themselves in our shoes, we experience the amazing Christ-like quality of empathy. When a person is genuinely responsive to us in a compassionate manner, it facilitates trust in a deep and enduring way. Because they are there for us, we know we are being attended to and cared about. It is easy to be trusting of someone who has demonstrated that they are trustable.

> Trust is redemptive: it is gracious, merciful, and forgiving of faults and failures.

Ideally, you cannot trust too much. Marriage was meant to transmit light and grace to every part of you through your helpmate, so that you can safely know and be known and grow from that. But white lies, financial indiscretions, public betrayals, and sexual infidelities are violations of trust. As was discussed earlier, a breach of the marital covenant is much like a broken bone. It hurts like crazy, requires external support for reconciliation, takes a long time to heal, and can produce a dull ache when there are changes in the atmospheric pressure. But I believe broken bones and broken marriages can powerfully illustrate God's miraculous healing and redemptive power at its best. If the break is properly realigned, protected, and therapeutically strengthened, the focused calcified bonding around the brokenness of both the limb and the relationship can be stronger than they ever were before the break! Restoring broken trust requires the appropriation of God's grace, mercy, and forgiveness.

Transformation of Trust

Everyone who is not living alone on a mountaintop or on a desert island has experienced the pain of broken trust. Our natural reactions to these hurts are typically to fight or to take flight. We lash out angrily or pull in protectively because unless we are really masochistic, we don't relish the opportunity to be reinjured.

> **One of the biggest challenges in making and maintaining a magnificent marriage is how to rebuild trust when—not if—it is broken.**

One of the biggest challenges in making and maintaining a magnificent marriage is how to rebuild trust when—not if—it is broken. When the cornerstone of the foundation cracks and crumbles, the rest of the house can easily collapse and crash. It is tempting to address cracks in the sheet rock and leaks in the roof by means of superficial or cosmetic repairs. But spackling and shingles will never fix a foundational problem. So how do we dig down to the footings and rebuild?

Trust is not some sort of a vague, mysterious, ethereal, or abstract concept. Rather, it typically exists in varying degrees and in varying forms throughout the course of a relationship. It's not an "all or nothing" kind of thing. The truth is that trust can be healed, developed, and nurtured, and it is well within your power to do so. Here are some tools to help keep trust operating smoothly in your marriage.

1. Trust God

Among others, David, Solomon, and Isaiah repeatedly declared their absolute reliance upon God alone. Some of the manifold blessings and benefits of entrusting ourselves to God include never being forsaken, salvation, security, freedom from shame, fulfillment of our heart's desires, righteousness, deliverance, freedom from fear, refuge, protection, stability, help, blessing, unfailing love, divine direction, strength, and perfect peace (Psalm 9:10, 13:5, 22:4-5, 25:2, 37:3-6, 40:1-4, 56:4, 62:8, 91:1-16, 125:1, 143:8, Proverbs 3:5-6, Isaiah 12:2, 26:3-4). That's a pretty awesome list!

It is fascinating to me that the most trustworthy person in the history of the universe did not demand blind trust from others. In John 10:37- 38 Jesus said, "Do not believe me unless I do what my Father does. But if I do it, even though you do not believe me, believe the miracles, that you may know and understand that the Father is in me, and I in the Father." Jesus was always directing our faith to be placed in our Heavenly Father. Though our loved ones will inevitably disappoint us, God's faithfulness is great and His compassions never fail (Lamentations 3:22-23).

2. Become Faith-ful

To be faithful means to be full of faith. When our faith is placed in God instead of in ourselves or in our spouse, it changes everything—beginning with us. Faithfulness is a character trait that has to do with one's own integrity. According to the old sermon definition, integrity means how we act when no one else is around. Our responsibility is to remain steadfastly loyal to our marital commitment and be consistently dependable to our marriage partner. It is not our job to fix our spouse or get them raised right (as tempting as that may be!). We are accountable before God for our own attitudes and actions. Not those of our mate.

Faithfulness is a character trait that has to do with one's own integrity.

For broken trust to be restored, you must become both trusting and trustworthy—whether your spouse does or not. For us to be trusting requires that we responsibly risk (about which we will speak more in a minute); for us to be trustworthy requires that we become relationally real. To be worthy of trust means that your spouse can believe in you; in your heart for them, your motives, your words, your intentions, and your actions. Trustworthiness means to recognize and respect the inherent value, virtue, and vulnerability of the other person and to treat them accordingly.

3. Take Time

One of the most common mistakes couples make is failing to realize how much time is involved in building trust. When I practiced for over 22 years in Kansas City, Missouri, my office was located in a beautiful area of town known as the Country Club Plaza, overlooking a renowned, picturesque little park with majestic fountains. One day I noticed a huge construction project being started directly across the park. It took nearly two years for workers to remove the dirt and rubble and dig down to bedrock to pour the foundation. Then it took another year to build the rest of the twin 20-story American Century Towers office buildings, which are reputedly both tornado proof and earthquake proof. It impressed me that twice as much time, money, and energy were invested into that construction project below ground on things that no one could see. But more than 20 years later, those magnificent buildings still look brand-new. The relationship parallels are obvious: developing a deep, abiding trust is a lengthy and gradual process, and the result is well worth the wait.

First Corinthians chapter 13 reminds us that love is patient... and always trusts, always hopes, always perseveres. When trust has been broken in a marriage, it gives both partners a divine growth opportunity (for which they probably never asked!). It takes time to heal, time to grieve, time to forgive, and time to grow. For these elements to develop, there is neither substitute nor shortcut.

I have observed over the years that only mature people recognize divine growth opportunities for what they are and welcome them into their lives as such. Our flesh is by nature impatient and immature because we want what we want when we want it the way we want it because we want it! To many of us the word "wait" is a four-letter word. But those who wait upon the Lord will renew their strength (Isaiah 40:31). His timing may seem slow, but it is never late.

4. Consider Risks

Risk management experts and life insurance agents all recognize the inescapable mortality of our lives. In perhaps his most relationally-oriented book, *The Four Loves*, C.S. Lewis wisely warned us: "There is no safe investment. To love at all is to be vulnerable. Love anything and your heart will certainly be wrung and possibly broken. . . The only place perfectly safe from all the dangers of love—and it is a horribly cold and lonely place—is hell" (1971, p. 121). Hip hip hooray! Those inspirational words will certainly brighten up our day! But at a deep level of our soul they intuitively resonate, don't they? To love means we will certainly be hurt.

Breaches of trust can penetrate and damage the core of our being. When our spouse is untruthful, uncaring, unreliable, and/or unfaithful, it wounds the most fragile and delicate parts of our heart which we exposed and entrusted to them. And so we naturally flinch—if not recoil—from the possibility of re-injury. But couples who refuse to risk because they are afraid

MAKING Magnificent MARRIAGES

of the painful consequences are actually not protecting the relationship; they are destroying it.

> **Breaches of trust can penetrate and damage the core of our being.**

Recall the miserable, mean, miserly monster of Charles Dickens' classic story, *A Christmas Carol.* Ebenezer Scrooge's heart was broken as a young man when his fiancé cheated on him. His narcissistic, tyrannical abusiveness was certainly understandable, but not acceptable. He decided he was never going to risk being hurt again. It was not until the dramatic intervention from the ghosts of Christmas past, present, and future that he decided to risk and therefore relate again.

5. Assume Responsibility

Another hallmark of individual maturity is to take appropriate responsibility for one's part in a relationship. In dealing with matters of trust, both people's responsibility is absolutely paramount. We must confront violations of trust head-on and talk about them candidly. In the face of trust violations, we need to learn how to properly set and maintain healthy boundaries. The injured person must no longer codependently enable their spouse to live in an irresponsible way. Additionally, we must resist the temptation and perhaps the familiarity of playing the victim role. We need to assertively stand up for ourselves (without knocking the other person down) so that we no longer feel walked on. And finally, when we have been betrayed, we need to learn how to give up our right to hurt back and genuinely forgive. *Remember, never does an offender control us more than when we do not forgive them. And never are we more like God than when we truly forgive.*

When we have broken our mate's trust, we need to be absolutely honest, speaking the truth in love, while we confess what we have done to be hurtful to our spouse. We must non-defensively listen to, genuinely attempt to understand, and sensitively empathize with our spouse's hurt. Without dismissing or minimizing how our spouse feels about the betrayal's affect upon them, we need to apologize and express remorse without making excuses. Then we need to change.

> **Submitting to a process of healing and growth in order to repair the damaged trust is worth the investment.**

The foregoing is part of the process which the Bible calls repentance. To repent is to turn away from what we were doing and do the opposite. We must become accountable to others and perhaps relinquish certain freedoms and rights in order to be trustable. Perhaps we need to seek treatment for an addiction. Maybe we need to get into individual therapy to deal with old baggage from previous relationships. We may need to perform plastic surgery by cutting up our credit cards and giving our spouse access to all our financial accounts. We might need to change our cell phone number and give our mate our passwords to all of our electronics. If all of these necessary restrictions seem extreme, it's because they are. They cost us something. They are hard, hurtful, and humbling. But submitting to a process of healing and growth in order to repair the damaged trust is worth the investment. It takes a lot of effort and expense to dig down to bedrock. Without doing this, deep reconciliation is highly unlikely.

The somewhat obscure Old Testament prophet Malachi provided us with a distinct and definite description of the damage done when we break our spouse's trust. He asked rhetorically:

> Have we all not one Father? Did not one God create us? Why do we profane the covenant of our fathers by breaking faith with one another?... Another thing you do: you flood the LORD's altar with tears. You weep and wail because he no longer pays atten-

> tion to your offerings or accepts them with pleasure from your hands. You ask 'why?' It is because the LORD is acting as the witness between you and the wife of your youth, because you have broken faith with her, though she is your partner, the wife of your marriage covenant. Has not the LORD made them one? In flesh and spirit they are his. And why one? Because he was seeking godly offspring. So guard yourself in your spirit, and do not break faith with the wife of your youth. 'I hate divorce,' says the LORD God of Israel... So guard yourself in your spirit, and do not break faith (Malachi 2:10, 13-16).

Breaking faith or trust dishonors God, disrupts prayer, and destroys families.

Cohabitation and Prenuptial   Agreements

Both of these relatively recent developments—couples living together prior to marriage and the signing of legal documents to protect their property—have one important thing in common: they both stem from and ironically perpetuate a lack of trust in the relationship. Due to the astronomic divorce statistics in their parents' generation, many younger couples today have decided to "try before they buy." Fearful of divorce themselves, the rationale is that the couple will determine their compatibility levels before they make a lifetime commitment to one another.

To me, this concept has all the wisdom of choosing to put a live round in the starter's pistol and shooting oneself in the foot as one begins to race a marathon. Basically, both people are telling the other, "I don't trust you—so will you live with me?" This ill-advised but wildly popular distortion of relationship in our society is tragically hurting far more people than anyone ever could have imagined.

It is a fundamental maxim of God's universe that sex without commitment cannot work. Without the exclusivity, permanence, and unconditionality of a mutual vow, nothing exists to create the security, stability, and strength, which a relationship requires in order to be supported and sustained. There is a continuous threat of fear, comparisons to others, and performance pressures to keep the relationship hanging by the precarious mood of the moment. You cannot be one flesh casually or consensually—just committedly.

No wonder these superficial relationships are so trying and temporary. And the numbers bear this out. Whereas about 40% of all first marriages in this country end in divorce, 80% of all cohabitations break up! Again, the irony is striking. Relationships motivated by fear create even more of the mistrust about which they were originally concerned: "I'm afraid to trust that you won't leave me, so I'll just basically double the odds of you hurting me since I don't trust you!" Generally, after the first major relationship storm, houses hastily built on such scenic, sandy beaches are blown down and washed away.

Another increasingly common example of relational mistrust in our culture is even more ironic and anti-relational than cohabitation. Prenuptial agreements are an absolutely unabashed and unapologetic declaration that, "Not only do I not trust you, but I love my stuff more than I love you. Will you marry me?" Wow! Talk about romantic! No wonder I have never once seen a couple with a prenuptial agreement not eventually end up divorced.

As our society becomes progressively more affluent and materialistic, there has been a corresponding increase in people paying lots of attorney's fees so they won't get ripped off financially by a new spouse. Please understand, I realize that people need to responsibly protect their assets and their children's inheritances. Furthermore, I get that people often get taken to the proverbial cleaners in a nasty divorce settlement and so are fearful of being vulnerable to that again. So I am all in favor of a couple creating a legal trust (ironic name, huh?) wherein it is decreed that Aunt Mabel's cedar chest will be passed down specifically to one's granddaughter, thus insuring that it stays in the family lineage. There is certainly nothing wrong with guaranteeing that the couple's premaritally held assets will be distributed according to each person's desire. That's not only fair and prudent; it's just plain, common sense.

But that has nothing to do with the marriage. I know this is controversial to some people, but a prenuptial agreement is intrinsically and essentially *adversarial* not *advocational*. I have never seen prenuptials help a marriage; in fact, as I previously stated, they have undermined and destroyed every single one I have ever seen. At the end of the day, or at the end of our days, people simply *must* be more important than things!

> **To trust our spouse can be the most glorious or the most gruesome experience in life.**

To trust our spouse can be the most glorious or the most gruesome experience in life. The transparency and vulnerability of opening our hearts to one another is an awesome privilege and a sobering responsibility. Healthy couples consistently report that trust is the single most important marker of lasting happiness (Rosen, 2002, p. 1). I trust your trust will deepen and grow!

Scriptural Search

1. Psalm 37:3-7
2. Psalm 40:1-4
3. Psalm 91
4. Proverbs 3:5-6
5. Lamentations 3:22-23

Ponderable Points

1. What are the positive benefits or outcomes of being able to completely and confidently trust another person?

2. Who is someone other than your spouse that you've been able to trust deeply in the past? What qualities about their personal character made them trustable to you?

3. Who is someone that you do not trust? What is it about their personal character that makes it hard for you to trust them?

4. What are some key components of what makes a person emotionally safe?

5. How is trust developed? Is it reasonable or realistic to blindly demand trust of someone?

Activation Activities

1. What can you do to strive to become a generally more *trustworthy* person?

2. What can you change so that your spouse can safely trust you to be more reliable, responsible, and responsive to their heart?

3. What can you do in order to rebuild areas of trust which have been strained, damaged, fragmented, eroded, or broken in your spouse's heart?

Recommended Resources

Safe Haven Marriage, Archibald Hart and Sharon Hart Morris (2003).

I Promise, Gary Smalley (2006).

Rescue Your Love Life, Henry Cloud and John Townsend (2005).

Boundaries, Henry Cloud and John Townsend (1992).

Slaying the Marriage Dragons, Douglas Roseneau (1991).

CHAPTER FOUR

Compassionate Caring

It has been said that marriage is like a game of cards: it starts off with a diamond and a couple of hearts, but many times it ends up with the couple wanting a club and a spade!

"...love one another deeply, from the heart."

—1 PETER 1:22

*E*veryone longs to love and be loved. It has been said that love is the universal human language; it is the expression of caring for someone beyond ourselves. Unlike anything else, the rosy and romantic topic of love has inspired poets, playwrights, and philosophers down through the ages, as they have extolled its virtues and vicissitudes.

It is intriguing that the epic saga of the Almighty Creator of the universe's intimate disclosure of Himself to His creation—the Bible—begins and ends with marriage. From the first chapter of Genesis (1:27) to the last chapter of Revelation (22:17), God's love story unfolds within the context of marriage.

This profound mystery (Ephesians 5:32) of the marriage relationship in many ways expresses the essence of God's Kingdom. It should be no surprise that the Giver of Life chose to express Himself to us, His beloved Bride (Revelation 21:2, 9) by means of the greatest love story ever told—and use the paradigm of marriage to illustrate it. Love, the deepest yearning and need of the human heart, mirrors the magnificent expression and reflection of the Creator's heart!

Clearly the Almighty Sovereign God—who is love personified (1 John 4:7-12)—designed us in love, for love, to love (Luke 10:27; 1 Peter 1:22; 1 John 4:16-21) out of His everlasting love for us (Jeremiah 31:3). As Christ followers, love is to be the definition of our identity, the declaration of our intentions, and the demonstration of our integrity (John 13:34-35, 15:10-12).

It's actually pretty easy to love someone who is lovable, lovely, and loving. As a matter of fact, that just seems to be reflexive human nature. The conditionality of this quid pro quo dynamic was illustrated by the ancient Greek poet, Ovid, when he concluded, "If you would be loved, be lovable." It seems sort of like the rich getting richer—the easier you are to love, the more you are likely to be loved.

But Jesus turned this natural tendency of human nature upside down when He asked rhetorically, "If you love those who love you, what reward will you get? Are not even the tax collectors doing that?" (Matthew 5:46). Obviously if even IRS agents can love those who love them, Jesus doesn't sound very impressed!

What's harder—and therefore requires an unconditional covenant—is to care for and love someone who isn't always lovable, lovely, and loving. It is at this level of depth that actually and actively loving one's marriage partner becomes realistic instead of romantic. It's easy to pontificate poetic platitudes; it's hard to relate regularly and relevantly.

Now, admittedly I feel pretty hypocritical as a husband on this point because my dear, sweet, precious wife, Linda, is extremely lovable, lovely, and loving. It's very easy for me to naturally love her. But several years ago the Holy Spirit hit me between the eyes with a profound and powerful realization: she needs me to love her the *most* when she is the *least* lovable, lovely, and loving! The first is simply an immature *reaction* borne of my flesh; the latter is a mature *response* activated by the Word and Spirit of God. And this is precisely how God loves us: when we were at our very worst and least lovable, He loved us His very best (Romans 5:8—perhaps the best line in the whole Book!).

> **God loves us because of His *lovingness*, not because of our *lovability*.**

This is an incredibly significant principle for both theology and psychology: God loves us because of His *lovingness,* not because of our *lovability.* God is proactive, not reactive. One of the most impressive things to me about Jesus' character is that He never immaturely reacted to anyone or any situation. Unlike me, He was entirely and exclusively self-controlled and therefore always and only proactive (John 10:17). God loves us because of who and how *He* is, not because of who or how *we* are. No matter what we do or don't do, Jesus cannot love us any more—or any less—than He does right now! It's really not about us; our being loved by God is all about Him. In the same way, I believe that in our marriages **true love is more about the character of the lover than the characteristics of the beloved!**

This concept is both radical and revolutionary. It is radical because it is counter to and in conflict with everything that our culture teaches us about love, and it contradicts the natural reflexes of our flesh. It is revolutionary because it has the potential and the power to permanently transform marriages like possibly nothing else can.

As Stephen and Alex Kendrick explain in their fantastic instruction manual about how to proactively love someone who is not necessarily being loving or lovable, "The truth is this: love is not determined by the one *being* loved but rather by the one *choosing* to love" (*The Love Dare*, 2008, p. 46). As has already been established, mature love is not only volitional; it is unconditional. Again, let me emphasize: love has to do with the character of the lover, not the characteristics of the beloved.

Whenever someone comes into my office and says, "I just don't have feelings for him/her anymore," or, "I have fallen out of love with them," or, "they just don't make me happy any more," it makes me question the nature, depth, and quality of that person's love in the first place. This is because, "No matter whom we fall in love with, we sooner or later fall out of love if the relationship continues long enough. This is not to say that we invariably cease loving the person with whom we fell in love but it is to say that the feeling of ecstatic lovingness that characterizes the experience of falling in love always passes. The honeymoon always ends. The bloom of romance always fades" (Peck, 1978, p. 84-85). However, loving feelings can be regenerated and rekindled. We'll look at how to do so later on in the chapter.

> The truth is that mature love is not based on feelings, fancy, or fickleness. Warm and fuzzy loving feelings are the *result*, not the *cause* of love.

The truth is that mature love is not based on feelings, fancy, or fickleness. Warm and fuzzy loving feelings are the *result*, not the *cause* of love.

You see, Hollywood and Hallmark have taught us over the years (perhaps *brainwashed us* is more accurate!?) that romantic love is generated by the other person and is focused on us. We have been conditioned to expect the other person to initiate the first move and then meet our needs to fulfill us and make us happy. That is the stuff of which romantic fantasies, novels, pornography, and chick flicks are made.

But the exact opposite is true. *Mature "agape" love is both self-generated and other-focused.* We are to love our spouse no matter what, and we are to be committed to doing what is best for their welfare no matter what it costs us. Genuine love always has an altruistic attitude and agenda. In his magnificent exploration of personal spiritual growth, Dr. Scott Peck defines love as, "the will to extend one's self for the purpose of nurturing one's own or another's spiritual growth" (1978, p. 81). It is *our personal character,* which should internally motivate us to love our spouse, not *their personal characteristics.*

Thus we can see that genuine love consists of stretching ourselves toward altruistic attitudes and actions (1 John 3:16-18). But:

> Romantic love has no elasticity to it. It can never be stretched; it simply shatters. Mature love, the kind demanded by a good marriage, must stretch... A wedding calls us to our highest and best—in fact, to almost impossible—ideals. It is the way we want to live. But marriage reminds us of the daily reality of living as sinful human beings in a radically broken world. We aspire after love but far too often descend into hate. Any mature, spiritually sensitive view of marriage must be built on the foundation of mature love rather than romanticism (Thomas, 2000, p. 15-16).

When we expect the other person to love us and make us happy, we are eventually bound to be disappointed.

When we expect the other person to love us and make us happy, we are eventually bound to be disappointed. By expecting our spouse to make us happy, we subconsciously idolize them in the place of God. As with so many other things, we are unintentionally and unwittingly tempted to worship and adore the creation instead of the Creator. We confuse the vehicle (marriage) with the destination (God's will for our lives).

Therefore we expect more from marriage than God intended it to provide. God meant for us to find Him *through* marriage— not *in* marriage! No matter how winsome and wonderful a marriage partner may be, no spouse is worthy of worship all day every day. *The inevitable hurts, hassles, and heartaches of marriage should drive us to divinity—not to divorce.* Our spouse is not our ultimate source; God is.

I realize this one-sided notion of marital love seems decidedly unfair and definitely unpopular. Yet as Leslie Vernick reminds us, "God has called you to love your spouse as no one else on this earth will" (2001, p. 169). This is a love which can be practiced by either partner in a marriage relationship, and which when done, will radically revolutionize the marriage system.

As Thomas states, "If we viewed the marriage relationship as an opportunity to excel and love it doesn't matter how difficult the person is who we are called to love; it doesn't matter even whether that love is ever returned. We can still excel at love. We can still say, 'Like it or not, I'm going to love you like nobody ever has'" (2000, p. 266). Loving our spouse like this truly is a test of and testimony to our own integrity. At our wedding I promised my wife in front of God and our families and friends that I would love her on days that end in "y," no matter what, as long as I am breathing. Plain and simple... period.

Distinctions Between Infatuation and Love

Most of us got married to *be* loved like this; not to learn *how* to love like this! In all fairness, I believe this is true not only because we are all selfish, fallen sinners, but because our culture has not adequately and appropriately educated us as to the nature and dynamics of a healthy, maturely developed love which focuses on what is best for the other person to the point of self-sacrifice.

Instead, we are typically taught unrealistic, overly romanticized notions of infatuation (mere "icing" on the proverbial cake, as was mentioned in Chapter 2). The more robust ingredients of caring love are what provide nutrients for sustenance and growth over the lifespan of your marriage.

As you read through the following lists, think about which characteristics or traits describe the way you typically love your spouse. But also keep in mind the fact that there has never been and never will be such a thing as a perfect marriage. (Remember that the only guy who was ever capable of perfect love chose to remain single!) So please resist the temptation to feel guilty or put yourself down as you compare the way your spouse gets loved by you with the way they need you to love them.

Infatuation	Love
Conditional	Unconditional
Egocentric	Heterocentric
Born at first sight	Develops, deepens, and grows over time
Naked bodies	Naked personalities
Blindly idealistic	Objectively realistic
Based on feelings	Based on commitment
Possessive of the other	Affirmative of the other
Exclusive	Inclusive
Traps/restricts/smothers	Frees/liberates/emancipates
Narcissistic	Altruistic
Exploits	Protects
Objectifies	Personifies
Focuses on self-gratification	Focuses on pleasing the other

Demands one's rights	Nurtures other's growth
"Need-love" (codependent)	"Gift-love"
Irresponsible	Responsible
Now-oriented	Future-oriented
Attitude of taking	Attitude of giving
Stagnates during separation	Grows during separation
Conflict separates	Conflict unifies
Holds grudges/seeks to get even	Forgives/releases the right to hurt back
Competitive	Cooperative
Defensive	Vulnerable
Immature	Mature
Exerts disorganizing and destructive effect upon one's personality	Exerts organizing and constructive effect upon one's personality

How well did you do? If you're like vast majority of us, the forces of both our flesh and our socialization process have combined to cause our relationships to begin in the left-hand column for the most part. We all know the right answer: our marriages need to be lived out in the right-hand column. The 64 zillion dollar question is, how do we get there from here?

Characteristics of Compassionate Caring

Most people feel truly loved when they are cared about in an active, personal, and emotionally meaningful way. Caring connotes compassion. Compassion cultivates caring.

The etymology or meaning of the word "compassion" is fascinating. The prefix "com" means "with," and the suffix "passion" means "deep feeling." When one demonstrates compassion to another person, they are expressing their heart to them in a deep and personal way.

As with everything else in the Christian life, Jesus' life example and relationship patterns offer to us as Christ followers both an inspiration and a prescription for how we are to live and love. Many times in the Gospels we see Jesus motivated to minister and reach out to hurting people because He was compelled by compassion for them (Matthew 9:36, 14:14, 15:32, 20:34, Mark 1:41, 6:34, 8:2, Luke 15:20).

Compassion is heartfelt and visceral. Jesus was not afraid to become personally involved and literally get His hands dirty, bloody, or infected. Neither should we—especially if we are to care and love like He cared and loved. Caring compassion both involves and requires risk, as well as reward.

> **True love does not happen spontaneously, casually, or automatically.**

True love requires our focused *intention*, emotional *investment,* and personal *initiative.* True love does not happen spontaneously, casually, or automatically. True love is a self-determined discipline, which requires expenditures of our effort and energy directed toward the benefit and betterment of the other person. Furthermore, true love like Jesus' is action-based and honestly motivated (1 John 3:11-18).

True love expresses itself by means of caring, compassion, concern, consideration, compliments, companionship, communication, comfort, courtship, and closeness. Specifically, these components of caring are manifested in the following seven "A's":

Acceptance

Perhaps nothing in human relationships hurts more than rejection. To not be accepted reinforces our most painful relationship experiences and confirms our most condemning self-doubts. Down deep, we all have a powerful longing to be accepted—warts and all. When we are accepted, it creates a heartfelt sense of worth and value. Actually, acceptance is a distinctly divine commodity. In its purest form it is only available from God, and we must receive it from Him for ourselves before we can give it to others (Romans 15:7).

> **In essence, love is an unconditional commitment to an imperfect person.**

In marriage, acceptance is one of the most difficult concepts with which people struggle. In order to unconditionally love another fellow sinful mortal, we must learn how to accept one another's differences and imperfections without judgment or discrimination. In essence, love is an unconditional commitment to an imperfect person.

However, acceptance doesn't mean condoning sinful behavior; it involves looking past the other person's fault and seeing their need. Acceptance looks beyond differences/disagreements/disputes, irritations/imperfections/idiosyncrasies, and faults/foibles/failures— not to excuse them, but to see value and worth in your spouse in spite of them. Genuine acceptance is never based upon blind, idealistic denial; it is grounded firmly in the liberating truth that our spouse is an amazing creation who is made in the image and likeness of the perfect Creator, but who is also unfortunately marred by sin (just like their mate!).

Attention

Everyone loves to be noticed and thought well of. Once, a little boy was attending a conference reception with his parents in a large hotel ballroom. Feeling rather bored and neglected, he noticed a microphone up on the stage. Climbing up to the podium, he grasped the mic and said loudly, "May I have your attention please?" Many people quieted down, but others were still talking, so he repeated his question. Finally, the huge room was at a hush, and hundreds of eyes were riveted on him. Looking out over the crowd, after a few seconds, the little boy then announced, "Thank you. All I wanted was some attention!"

> **It is a fundamental human need to be noticed and attended to.**

It is a fundamental human need to be noticed and attended to. Being ignored is a terribly painful and lonely feeling. Having someone else's undivided attention is intensely personal and is necessary to create a secure emotional attachment. Developmentally, caretaking forges a bond of closeness when the infant's dependency needs are met in a nurturing, caring way.

All Little Leaguers, recital soloists, and soccer players want their parents to notice their endeavors and exploits. Similarly, we feel valued and cared about in a deeply intimate way when we receive compassionate attention from our loved one. There's an old joke which says, "When I was growing up I was so poor I couldn't even pay attention!" (not to be confused with all of those of us who have ADD or ADHD!). Indeed, the cost of not paying priceless attention to our spouse is enormous; it makes them feel worthless, unimportant, and unloved.

Admiration

To esteem and commend another person highly makes them feel valued and cared about. Everyone likes to be complimented because it is honoring. Especially in a marriage, that special look or loving expression of your spouse's eyes conveys a profoundly personal and powerful validation of your identity. When you are either privately or publicly admired by your spouse, you can't help but feel good about yourself and deeply cared for by them.

In his landmark research on the predictors of divorce in marriage, Dr. John Gottman found the importance of expressing admiration to our spouse to be absolutely crucial to a long-lasting and mutually rewarding romance. Not only does admiration generate an abiding sense of fondness in both the giver and receiver of admiration, but without it, any marriage will become cold and contemptuous. In fact, Gottman warns, "If your mutual fondness and admiration have been completely extinguished, your marriage is in dire trouble" (1999, p. 65).

> **The more you express admiration to your spouse, the more lovingly you will feel toward them.**

But happily, the more you express admiration to your spouse, the more lovingly you will feel toward them. And the more you admire them, the more likely they are to admire you in return. A heart that is filled with admiration cannot help but express itself with intimate eye contact, loving touches, verbal statements, and written love notes which convey your approval and commendation for them. Praising your spouse for who they *are* (in terms of character—unconditionality) rather than for what they *do* (in terms of behavior—conditionality) is especially validating at a deep level. Admiring and complimenting your spouse will make them feel special and build their self-esteem.

Appreciation

After several years, most spouses tend to gradually feel taken for granted in their marriages. The tender, thoughtful, and considerate gestures and actions naturally expressed during the romantically exciting dating process are typically forgotten or become mere afterthoughts once the honeymoon ends and the duties and drudgeries of married life take over.

Just as well-toned muscles can become fatty, flabby, and flaccid if not exercised regularly, relational laziness and complacency can make loving feelings lose their fire and wane cold. This can cause the relationship to get out of shape. At best, a lack of appreciation can make us feel unimportant or overlooked; at worst, it can make us feel used and resentful. Complaints, criticisms, contempt, cattiness, contentiousness, and condemnation are the antithesis of appreciation and are toxic to marriage systems.

Appreciation can help invent and invigorate intimacy.

Adopting an attitude of gratitude toward life in general and toward our spouse in particular can transform us from being a normal, self-absorbed narcissist to being a healthy, maturely loving relater. More than just the good manners of nicely saying "please" and "thank you," showing genuine appreciation for your mate helps them to feel valued and cared about at a deep level. Expressing appreciation focuses on and thereby creates even more of the blessings and benefits in your marriage that you may otherwise naturally overlook. I encourage you to begin by finding even little things about which to sincerely express thankfulness to your mate. Appreciation can help invent and invigorate intimacy.

Approval

Human beings have a deep innate need to gain approval from others. To approve of someone is to make them feel affirmed, endorsed, and blessed. In their best-selling book, *The Gift of the Blessing* (1993), authors Gary Smalley and John Trent suggest that a deep-seated yearning for parental approval is both universal and timeless, dating back thousands of years to patriarchal practices in the old covenant. The devastatingly painful effects upon us when we do not receive this essential parental approval are revealed by our vulnerabilities to peer pressures in everything from fashion to normative cultural practices, gangs, and even cults. Everyone wants and seeks approval.

In marriage, we really can't demonstrate our love effectively to our spouse through approval unless we thoroughly know them through their attributes, attitudes, and actions. For a sense of approval to have power and meaning, it must be not only sincere but realistic. Telling our spouse how proud we are of the way they breathe, blink, or swallow for example, will probably not do much to enhance their self-esteem!

But the more deeply we know who our spouse is and what they're about, the greater impact our affirmations will make, and the greater emotional security they will provide. Giving approval to our spouse will provide powerful and precious deposits into what some authors have called their love bank or love tank. Attitudes and actions expressing basic thoughtfulness, kindness, and consideration of your partner are not only honoring and respecting, they demonstrate acceptance in a powerful and personal way. A simple smile and affirming look can be very approving and therefore energize and motivate loving thoughts, feelings, and actions.

Affection

Perhaps one of the most natural forms of conveying caring and compassion to our spouse in a loving way is by means of affection. Fond and fuzzy feelings freely follow friendly forms of fraternization and fellowship!

Affection creates the environment of the marriage in which the event of sex occurs.

At the same time, it is important to distinguish the many forms of expression of physical affection in a healthy marriage from those which are sexual. Whereas I realize that some of you have already peeked ahead to read Chapter 12 on Sensational Sex, this means of expressing marital love is not about sex (but we will get to that!). Rather, affection creates the environment of the marriage in which the event of sex occurs.

On this point, Dr. Willard Harley believes that, "A woman's need for affection is probably her deepest emotional need" (2001, p. 46). Furthermore, he observes that most of us men are poorly suited and inadequately trained for supplying our wives with this vital relationship nutrient, because we tend to view affection as a means to an end (i.e., sex), whereas women find affection important in its own right. While it is not that men do not desire or need affection, it is that, "From a woman's point of view, affection is the essential cement of her relationship with a man" (ibid, p. 39). It is a husband's nonsexual affection, which ironically and paradoxically activates his wife's sexual response.

There are many methods of being healthfully affectionate in marriage. In his classic book, *The Five Love Languages* (1988), Gary Chapman helped us to realize that everyone experiences and expresses love in different ways, including words of affirmation, quality time, receiving gifts, acts of service, and physical touch. Although affection can be displayed in all of these ways, nonsexual physical touch is probably the most common and natural means of expressing this particular type of caring to your mate.

All societies have some form of physical touch as a basic means of social greeting. Almost instinctively, during a time of crisis we hug one another. Nonsexual, appropriate, tender, and thoughtful touches can mean a great deal and can make one feel deeply cared about. Holding hands, warm embraces, affirming pats on the arm or shoulder, and similar forms of giving affection to our spouse will also make interest-generating deposits into their love bank or tank. In fact, the ubiquitous "Love Doctor," Leo Buscaglia (1988), famously declared that we all need at least 12 hugs per day to maintain our physical-emotional-relational health!

Advocation

In healthy marriages, we function as our mate's staunchest advocate—not their strongest adversary. Unfortunately, in dysfunctional relationships it's the other way around. It's important that we strive to become our spouse's "helpmate," not their "hurtmate." When we realize and are secure in the knowledge that the person we married is on our side no matter what, it makes us feel genuinely cared about like nothing else can.

> **No one on this planet can potentially help—or hurt—us as thoroughly as our marriage partner.**

The more deeply we get to know each other, the more power we have to either help heal, or further hurt each other. In fact, no one on this planet can potentially help—or hurt—us as thoroughly as our marriage partner. Consequently, this very practical, but admittedly somewhat sadomasochistic definition of love really makes sense to me: *True love is knowing how to deeply hurt the other person, but choosing not to.*

It is at this point of incredible interpersonal vulnerability that we once again see how Jesus is our example and encourager, demonstrating how we are to compassionately care. As our Advocate, He continuously stands in the gap created between us and the Father by our sin (for which He paid or atoned), and He pleads our case (or intercedes) to God on our behalf (Isaiah 53, Hebrews 7:25). He is resolutely and relentlessly on our side and wants nothing but our Father's best for us.

Another wonderful way in which Jesus models advocation is through empathy (Hebrews 2:18, 4:14-16). Among all the components of caring, empathy is perhaps the strongest and most significant. It not only makes us feel deeply cared about, it makes us feel understood. The classic "pickup" line in the bar supposedly is, "My spouse doesn't understand me." Everyone needs to feel cared about and understood. Empathy is defined as "the ability to identify with another person's experiences, feelings, and thoughts." When we listen to our spouse without judgment and sensitively attend to their heart, they will experience compassionate caring from us and feel validated and understood. Think how you can apply the saying "random acts of kindness and senseless acts of beauty" to your wife or husband. They will definitely feel your advocacy and support.

> **Without ongoing, regular and routine reinvestment in to the relationship, most couples' feelings of love decline and deteriorate.**

Love is the strongest force in the universe. The wise King Solomon said, "... love is as strong as death, its jealousy unyielding as the grave. It burns like blazing fire, like a mighty flame. Many waters cannot quench love; rivers cannot wash it away... " (Song of Songs 8:6-7). Love is unquestionably the highest calling to which any person can aspire, and it is the fulfillment of all biblical mandates. But like anything else, love can wither and atrophy if it is taken for granted and/or neglected. It is a natural law of physics (entropy—the second law of thermodynamics) that things by themselves tend to wind down or lose their momentum. Without ongoing, regular and routine reinvestment into the relationship, most couples' feelings of love decline and deteriorate.

Consequently, our marriages, like our vehicles, suffer greatly when they are not well cared for. A used car that has been treated with tender loving care is much more valuable than one that has been neglected or treated roughly. In a similar way, our spouse's sense of worth is greatly enhanced when we care for them by giving them the seven "A's" of acceptance, attention, admiration, appreciation, approval, affection, and advocation.

A decidedly unromantic, but nonetheless profound old saying reminds us that it is far more important to love the one you marry than to marry the one you love. Hopefully the following tools can help you more effectively love the one you married, so that you can be marvelously married to the one you love! God has personally called and commissioned you to have the privilege to love the person you married like no one else on Earth ever can, or ever will.

Scriptural Search

1. Proverbs 10:12, 16:6,17:9, 19:22
2. Hosea 2:19-23
3. Matthew 5:43-46
4. 1 Corinthians 13:1-13
5. 1 John 4:7-5:3

Ponderable Points

1. What do you have to sacrifice about yourself in order to truly want and provide the best for your spouse? What makes this so difficult or challenging for you?

2. When your mate is hurting, lonely, afraid, and/or vulnerable, what do they need most from you? What makes this most difficult for you to provide? In what ways can you become more generous in lavishing this type of love on your spouse?

3. What personality or character traits are required in order for you to reach out to your mate with deep feelings of caring

and concern? How does your spouse need those to be expressed?

4. What are your primary love languages? How can you more effectively teach your spouse to become fluent in them?

5. What are your mate's primary love languages? How can you more effectively learn to become fluent in them?

Activation Activities

1. Ask your spouse to tell you times in their life when they have felt most deeply cared about: cherished, valuable, worthwhile, validated, precious, and priceless. Learn what it was that made them feel that way. Commit yourself to encourage and support your mate to nurture and further develop those experiences for them.

2. List and describe 10 things you can do to make your mate feel more deeply cared about. Ask yourself what makes it difficult for you to extend yourself for their benefit in these ways. Develop a plan to change *yourself* to make sure you commit yourself to do them.

3. Various authors have established that marriage is not designed to make us happy and that our spouse is not responsible for our happiness—we are. Since growing people tend to be attractive and appealing to others, what are some ideas you can pray about to help yourself to grow spiritually, emotionally, and relationally?

Recommended Resources

The Five Love Languages, Gary Chapman (1988).

The Five Love Needs of Men and Women, Gary and Barbara Rosberg (2000).

Bold Love, Dan Allender and Tremper Longman III (1992).

Making Love Last, Glenn Egli and Jennifer Carroll (1993).

Building Your Mate's Self-Esteem, Dennis and Barbara Rainey (1986).

CHAPTER FIVE

Rigorous Respect

*It's true that I married my wife for her looks... just not for
the ones she's been giving me lately!*

*"Be devoted to one another in brotherly love. Honor one
another above yourself."*

—ROMANS 12:10

e live in a culture of progressively increasing disrespect. Within the last generation or two, we have
witnessed an unabashed and unprecedented de-
cline in the value and virtue of relationships. The way down this
societal slippery slope has been led by a degeneration and decline of morality primarily popularized and promulgated by mass
media and the entertainment industry. The corrosive cumulative effect of this widespread lack of respect of personhood in
general and marriage relationships in particular has been both
assaultive and atrocious.

The inherent strength and honorability of the traditional masculine leadership role and identity as the provider, protector,
and progenitor of the family unit has been ridiculed, disparaged,
and weakened by sitcoms and permissive philosophy. Likewise, the inherent worth and dignity of traditional feminine roles

and relationships has been marginalized, diminished, and exploited by pornographic perversions and teenybopper fashion magazines. Finally, the inherent value and innocence of children has been damaged, polluted, and violated by means of epidemic abuse and widespread victimization, tragically typified by the socially acceptable violent destruction of unborn human life.

As always, the Bible calls us to live on a much higher plane. The priority and prominence of giving universal respect is illustrated by the apostle Peter who tells us to, "show proper respect to everyone: Love the brotherhood of believers, fear God, honor the king" (1 Peter 2:17). Furthermore, we are instructed to respect the elderly (Leviticus 19:32), authority figures and bosses (Ephesians 6:5, 1 Timothy 6:1, 1 Peter 2:18), spiritual leaders (1 Thessalonians 5:12), unbelievers (1 Peter 3:16-17), parents (Leviticus 19:3, 1 Timothy 3:4), and spouses (Ephesians 5:33, 1 Peter 3:1-7). Quite unlike the nature and practice of our contemporary culture, isn't it?

The meanings of the words "respect" or "reverence" from the original Greek texts in these last two passages (which refer to marriage relationships) are both profound and powerful. Literally, they mean we are to honor, revere, esteem, appreciate, defer to, prize, notice, prefer, be devoted to, deeply love, enjoy, and in a human sense, adore, admire exceedingly, and praise our marriage partner. Wow! Read those relationship principles again, and meditate on them for a moment. Talk about awesome! God's plans, pleasure, and purpose for marriage relationships are exquisite, excellent, and extraordinary.

A Respect Story

Although this phenomenal sense of mutual respect and honor is God's design and desire for us, as humans we often fall short of His calling and commands. A dramatic Old Testament narrative poignantly illustrates the nature and dynamics of marital respect by outlining both the negative and positive examples of it.

The book of Esther tells of the elegant celebration given by King Xerxes (cool name, huh? In college, I bet he had "Double X Man" stitched on the back of his intramural jersey!), who was the potentate of the Persian Empire. As the grand finale to a six-month long party, he threw an opulent, week-long banquet for the entire capital city of Susa. (I can't imagine how much that catering bill was!) At the end of the banquet, Xerxes called for his gorgeous wife, Vashti, to be honored, "...wearing her royal crown, in order to display her beauty to the people and nobles, for she was lovely to look at" (Esther 1:11).

But instead of respecting her husband's request, Queen Vashti acted with contempt toward him by refusing to come. Publicly humiliated by her showing him up by not showing up, in accordance with the custom of the times, Xerxes removed her from her position of honor. A search was immediately launched for a new queen who would be more worthy.

From among the most beautiful women of the kingdom, Esther is eventually selected to become the new queen. As the story continues, we discover that Esther's beauty is more than just skin deep, though it is recorded that she "...was lovely in form and features..." (2:7). Her godliness, wisdom, and mature character are revealed by how deeply she respects her new husband, as the tale suddenly turns from romantic to dramatic.

Soon after becoming queen, Esther learns from her uncle, Mordecai, of a sinister political plot to murder all those of her native Jewish descent who are living in the kingdom. Mordecai urges Esther to go to the king and plead with him on behalf of her people. Esther is suddenly confronted with a terrible dilemma—what we refer to in marriage and family therapy as a "double bind." She knows that palace protocol dictates that no one can approach the king without being summoned (4:11), and she is keenly aware of the fact that her predecessor was deposed for massively disrespecting her husband. On the other hand, she is courageously compelled to risk her position and power in order to do the greater good of advocating for her people (4:14-16).

In her decision to approach Xerxes, several things are apparent about Esther's relationship with her husband, the king (besides the obvious fact that they did not know one another well enough for Xerxes to even be aware of her nationality...they definitely would have benefited from premarital counseling!). First, she did not act in a presumptuous, arrogant, or entitled manner. Although Esther came before him with all the elegant trappings of royalty, it was not her jeweled crown or regal robes which made her a true queen; her healthy and respectful attitude did. She didn't just barge unexpectedly into the throne room and interrupt her husband's busy schedule with her personal demands. When Xerxes saw her standing patiently in the entrance to his throne room, he called her in and excitedly received her. Esther's display of humility, honor, and respect for her husband delighted him.

> Selfish people use others and love things; whereas mature people love others and use things.

Second, she respected not only her husband's personhood, but also his position. As she approached the throne, she touched his golden scepter in acknowledgement of his authority. Before she ever said a word to him, she directly exhibited her high regard for him twice. Although he immediately offered her up to half of his kingdom (5:3, 5:6, 7:2), she demonstrated that simply being with him was more important to her than what he could do for her. Before she ever made her personal request, she spent meaningful time with him and served him dinner three times. In this regard, Esther powerfully proved the principle that selfish people use others and love things; whereas mature people love others and use things.

Third, in every recorded conversation between this king and queen, Esther prefaces her remarks to her husband by saying, "If it pleases the king..." (5:4, 5:8, 7:3, 8:5). This was not just an expression of unofficial formality, but a genuine expression to Xerxes of her overall honor, caring, and respect to him as her husband. Consequently, not only did Xerxes change his mind and reverse his decision to exterminate her people, but his response to Esther proved his personal love and devotion to her. Esther's mature attitude and actions of respect not only healed her husband's broken heart, it changed the entire destiny of God's chosen people.

> **When we respect someone, we give that person a highly honored position in our lives.**

This beautiful story proves that when we respect someone, we give that person a highly honored position in our lives. According to Gary Smalley, "Honor is to any growing and loving relationship as diamonds are to jewelry" (1996, p. 134). This high value or esteem which we place on the relationship is a powerful expression of our love and devotion to our spouse, and it typically generates the same response in kind from them to us. Relating respectfully results in being both respectable and respected.

Unfortunately:

> The sad truth is that comparatively few Christians think of giving respect as a command or a spiritual discipline. We are obsessed with being respected, but rarely consider our own obligation to respect others... All of us have a visceral desire to be respected. When this desire isn't met, we are tempted to lapse into a self-defeating response. Rather than work to build our own life so that respect is granted to us, we work to tear down our spouse in a desperate at-

tempt to convince ourselves that their lack of respect is meaningless. Spiritually, this becomes a vicious and debilitating cycle that is extremely difficult to break (Thomas, 2000, p. 54-55).

Marital Disrespect

So what about disrespect? What happens when we are not responding respectfully to our spouse? Or what about when they "diss" us? Here are some excruciating examples of what disrespectful attitudes and actions look like, not only in marriage but in all relationships:

Criticism
Humiliation
Blaming
Insults
Second-guessing
Contempt
Lecturing
Abuse
Ignoring
Condescension
Scolding
Arrogance
Interrupting
Bossiness
Labeling
Controlling
Judgment
Nagging
Ridicule
Hostile teasing
Sarcasm
Unsolicited advice

Rudeness
Over-functioning
Neglectfulness
Shaming
Mocking
Name-calling
Usurping authority
Violation of personal boundaries
Disdainful nonverbal expressions (e.g., rolling of the eyes, making faces, etc.).

Obviously, this is a horrible list! These arrogant, antagonistic attitudes and actions will damage any relationship. No marital seeds or plantings can possibly survive and grow, much less thrive and prosper, in the toxic dump of this kind of deleterious and destructive disrespect.

But as we carefully re-examine these distasteful details of disrespectful attitudes and actions, they all seem to have a common root or denominator: *self-centeredness*. Think about it—parents don't have to teach an infant how to be egocentric; they are just naturally selfish due to their primitive state of immaturity and their inherent propensity to sinfulness. (By the way, these innate tendencies are genetically transmitted! Kids inherit them from their other parent. ☺) Tiny infantile fingers will instinctively curl around and tightly grasp whatever is placed in their innocent hands. What parents have to progressively teach their child is how *not* to be selfish.

The quality of respect originates from deep within our soul.

You see, the quality of respect originates from deep within our soul. Just as you cannot love your neighbor better than you love yourself, you cannot give respect to others unless you first possess self-respect. It is a logical truism that we simply cannot give that which we do not have. So for many people, the reason they engage in the above disrespectful behaviors to others is that they do not adequately respect themselves.

In addition, many times people lack self-respect because as children, they themselves were not treated with respect and dignity. As was mentioned previously, not only do children see relational disrespect practiced routinely in our society— including toward them—there is a decided lack of positive and healthy role modeling displayed as to how they should respect themselves and others. It is true that values are caught more than they are taught.

Nonetheless, at some point in our Christian growth process we are challenged to put childish things behind us (1 Corinthians 13:11). Furthermore, throughout the New Testament, we are consistently commanded to transform these disrespectful attitudes and actions of our sinful nature and learn to walk in the Spirit (Romans 8:1-14, 12:1-2, Galatians 5:13-25, Ephesians 4:22-24, Colossians 3:5-10). But it's usually easier to see and focus on which of the above manifestations of disrespect our spouse messes up with than to see how the person who uses our toothbrush needs to change.

As Thomas explains, "As our partners and their weaknesses become more familiar to us, respect often becomes harder to give. But this failure to show respect is a sign of spiritual immaturity more than an inevitable pathway of marriage" (2000, p. 57). When we focus on our own disappointed expectations and our spouse's failures, we fight to *receive* respect. But when, out of a deeply appreciative attitude of thanksgiving, we focus on the liberating reality of God's grace and mercy, we strive to *give* respect.

When we naturally and normally focus on the hurt our spouse has inflicted upon us by their disrespectfulness, it is often very difficult to maintain a Holy Spirit-motivated sense of self-control. When rejected, we realistically and routinely react with resentment. Resentment is relationally regrettable and can cause us to retaliate; reflexively requiring revenge, retribution, reprisal, and recompense. But when we selfishly, stubbornly, and stupidly give our personal power away like that and allow our spouse or the situation to control us, we are first diminished personally, and then the marriage relationship suffers.

> **This is typically when couples are prone to "fall" out of love.**

This is typically when couples are prone to "fall" out of love. Or they may still love one another, but no longer like each other. The Plexiglas walls go up, they emotionally disconnect, and the proverbial cold war ensues. Those warm, fuzzy, fond feelings gradually grow cold, and the formerly passionate couple no longer looks forward with excited anticipation to spending magical and meaningful moments together. Crass contempt gradually outweighs and overtakes loving longings.

Many times these couples just settle. For various reasons—such as for the children, because of religion, or just for the sake of appearances—they may remain legally married, but not emotionally bonded. This pitiable yet pathetic pathological degeneration is often caused by a basic lack of respect. Listen to how Jim and Sally Conway describe this terrible tragedy: "Isn't it strange that a husband will open the car door for a woman guest who is riding with the couple, but he won't normally open the door for his wife? It's sad that we withhold common courtesy and respect from each other. We interrupt, badger, put down, ignore or condemn our mates, when we would never think of doing that to another person" (2001, p. 138). It is strange and sad indeed.

Marital Respect

In Ephesians chapter 5, the apostle Paul eloquently elaborates the longest and most comprehensive teaching about marriage relationships contained in Scripture. Concluding with verse 33, Paul teaches that a husband "...*must* love his wife as he loves himself, and the wife *must* respect her husband" (italics mine). Note the (four-letter!) word preceding both love and respect: "must." There are no ifs, buts, or other qualifiers. Both are to be given to the other without reservation or condition.

> **So, how do we unconditionally respect our marriage partner on days that end in "y?"**

So, how do we unconditionally respect our marriage partner on days that end in "y?" In his outstanding book, *Love and Respect*, Dr. Emerson Eggerichs offers groundbreaking insights into the key dynamics of how couples are to treat each other with the power and principle of unconditional love and unconditional respect. Simply put, "A husband is to obey the command to love even if his wife does not obey this command to respect, and a wife is to obey the command to respect even if the husband does not obey the command to love" (2004, p. 15-16).

But let's be realistic. How many husbands do you know who unconditionally love their wife? Similarly, how many wives do you know who unconditionally respect their husband? Are these commands just simply too difficult to implement? Surely not, because after all, the Bible does declare that God's commands are not burdensome (1 John 5:3). Yet, since love and respect seem to be so universally lacking, what makes these commands so hard to actually put into practice?

To begin with, it seems to me that we just generally resist being told what to do. We are naturally prone to argue, rationalize, justify, protest, defend, and often ultimately disobey commands given to us by authority figures, due to our rebellious and sinful nature. (And if you would contend that isn't the case, that would just illustrate the point!) We all want to be in charge. I always smile to myself when I hear a client allege that their spouse is "controlling." To me, that simply proves they are hitched to one of those *Homo sapiens* critters.

> When a husband feels disrespected, it is particularly difficult to feel like loving his wife. And a wife who feels unloved finds it difficult to be motivated to respect her husband.

Additionally, it is a natural reflection of our human nature to justify to ourselves, "I will think about loving my wife after she respects me," or, "I will consider respecting my husband after he loves me." This is because when a husband feels disrespected, it is particularly difficult to feel like loving his wife. And a wife who feels unloved finds it difficult to be motivated to respect her husband. Certainly, "No husband feels fond feelings of affection and love in his heart when he believes his wife has contempt for who he is as a human being. Ironically, the deepest need of the wife—to feel loved—is undermined by her disrespect" (Eggerichs, 2004, p. 4).

Furthermore, Eggerichs points out that, in our culture, there is an enormous difference between each gender's typical perceptions of how they are expected to obey the complementary commands to love and respect. Although they rarely seem to do it well, in general, men at least theoretically understand that they are to unconditionally love their wives to the point of self-sacrifice. No wife is ever expected by our culture to take a bullet for her husband, if necessary, but most men do grasp that grand concept of nobility and ultimate dedication. They get that love is not to be earned, but to be actively demonstrated. (Did you hear about the guy whose wife asked him if he loved her? He replied, "Yes dear. You know I love you." Then she asked, "Do you love me so much that you would be willing to die for me?" He wisely responded, "No darling; my love for you is an undying love!").

In contrast, Eggerichs found in his research that most women intuitively believe that respect for their husbands should be "deserved." He discovered that for most wives, the phrase "unconditional respect" is basically an oxymoron. And whereas most women felt that respect should be earned, they were outraged to have suggested to them that if that is true, then it follows that love should be conditionally deserved, as well.

Therefore, when a wife believes her husband needs to earn her respect before she gives it to him, she leaves him in a horrible double-bind or lose-lose predicament. Now he's responsible for being the cause or initiator of both love and respect in the marriage. That is, he must unconditionally love his wife, as well as somehow merit her respect. This is about as challenging as trying to sit in the corner of a round room! In the face of this absolute impossibility, many men just shut down, disconnect, and leave.

According to Eggerichs, when men stonewall their wives who confront them about feeling unloved, that emotional detachment and abandonment makes their wife feel even more unloved, such that the last thing they want to do is grant their husband respect. Thus, what he called the "Crazy Cycle" is ironically yet unintentionally created and self-perpetuated in most marriages: "Without love from him, she reacts without respect; without respect from her, he reacts without love" (ibid. p. 6).

So what is a wife to do? In her excellently written guide for wives to better understand their husbands, Shaunti Feldhahn advises, "Just as you want the man in your life to love you unconditionally, even when you're not particularly lovable, your man needs you to demonstrate your respect for him regardless of whether he's meeting your expectations at the moment" (2004, p. 26). She goes on to emphasize that although it is a completely foreign concept to many women, men need unconditional respect from their wives just as much as women need unconditional love from their husbands.

Arlene Pellicane wisely advises wives on this crucial point:

> If someone were to repeat all the things you say to your husband, would it be 'news that's fit to print?' Are you heaping on praise, encouragement and honor?... Treasure your husband's efforts to please you and provide for your family. Don't trash what he does either to his face or behind his back. Your words matter more to him than anyone else's... Does your husband know from your words—not the words you spoke on your wedding day, but the words you speak to him today—that you respect him (2012, p. 54)?

It is not that men don't necessarily enjoy being loved or that women don't have a need to be fundamentally and freely respected. It is just that according to research, men place a higher value on feeling respected than on feeling loved. Studies show that about 75% of men, if given a choice, would rather feel alone and unloved in the world than be disrespected, whereas for women the opposite is true. It is as if, on the hierarchy of human needs, for men respect is like water and love is like food. Conversely, for women love is like water and respect is like food. Both are essential, it's just that the one is more primary.

At the same time, I find it very interesting that Scripture never once specifically commands wives to love their husbands. Believe me, I've looked—it's not even in Hezekiah, 2nd Confusions, or 1st Whale! What the Bible does teach is for older women to, "... train the younger women to love their husbands and children" (Titus 2:4). However, the Greek word translated "love" in this passage is the word *phileo*, not the word *agape,* which is what husbands are commanded to demonstrate to their wives. This implies that a woman will naturally *love* her husband in an altruistic way; but not necessarily *like* him in a friendly, filial, and familial fashion. Obviously there can be a big difference between loving someone and liking someone. The first is apparently automatic for women; the other is learned on the job.

One day, while pondering this apparent discrepancy, it suddenly hit me. I noticed that the Bible never once commands me to breathe, blink, or swallow, either. Due to the automatic function of my parasympathetic nervous system, I seem to be hardwired from the factory to do that stuff pretty naturally. Then it occurred to me that, perhaps in the same way, the reason why the Bible doesn't command women to love their husbands is because they already do love intrinsically. Plus, this dynamic has been at work since the first couple's disobedience, when God said to Eve in Genesis 3:16, "Your desire will be for your husband..."

(Interestingly, this is one consequence of the Fall which is rarely discussed, particularly by traditional male preachers. Of course when you really think about it, at first glance, this doesn't seem to be particularly complimentary to men. The implication is that unless wives are somehow coerced to want their husbands, they won't desire them at all. This is kind of like being so homely as a little kid that your mom had to tie a bone around your neck just to get the dog to play with you!)

Men do not naturally love, but they do normally have an inherent sense of respect for others. While there is certainly no love lost on a football field, after three hours of trying to bash each other's heads in, psych each other out, and gain a hard-fought competitive advantage, at the end of the game a curious phenomenon occurs. After the whistle blows, both teams line up and shake hands. There is an implicit and often explicit message of mutual respect communicated regarding the others players' skill, strategy, and sportsmanship.

It is axiomatic that women naturally give and need love while men naturally give and need respect.

Thus, it is axiomatic that women naturally give and need love while men naturally give and need respect. And just as we have already established that people need to be loved the most when they're least lovely, loving, and lovable, perhaps it is also true that *people need to be respected the most when they're least respectful, respecting, and respectable!*

I realize that concept initially sounds completely outrageous. Giving respect without condition seems completely counterintuitive and countercultural. We think that respect surely must be earned in some manner or deserved to some degree. How can someone possibly even slightly respect a person who is disgusting, degenerate, and deplorable? And while there are many greeting cards which extol the virtues of love (which, by the way, has its own holiday celebrated by lovers every February), I would challenge you to find a greeting card which says, "I respect you," much less an entire holiday devoted to creative and caring expressions of it. So much for equity and equality!

Well, just as Hosea teaches men how to love their wife no matter what, Peter instructs women how to treat a husband who is a completely heathen reprobate. He counsels such wives of unbelievers to display an honoring and yielding attitude so, "… they may be won without a word by the behavior of their wives, as they observe your chaste and respectful behavior" (1 Peter 3:1-2, NASB). This is a superb functional description of how to unconditionally respect, just as Hosea demonstrated a fantastic example of how to unconditionally love.

The New Testament epistle of James clearly challenges us to live what we learn. Jesus' half-brother issues this directive:

"Do not merely listen to the word, and so deceive yourselves. Do what it says" (1:22). We have seen that respecting our mate is difficult, yet demanded. Let's now consider some practical principles regarding how to respect our mate on a regular, ongoing basis.

How to Show Respect: L.A.S.H.

To briefly review, a biblical operational definition of respect involves consistently giving high value, esteem, and regard to the other person in an unconditionally honoring way. Obviously, this involves consistently treating our mate with dignity, kindness, thoughtfulness, and consideration on a daily basis.

One place where these values and virtues are still taught is within various scouting programs. For many years I have been a commander in Royal Rangers, a Christian scouting and discipleship program now operating in 86 countries, whose purpose is to mentor future men. Two very fun and useful merits for boys (of all ages!) are Ropecraft and Lashing. Teaching boys how to tie knots seems to be a great symbolic precursor for learning how to tie the marital knot!

In Ecclesiastes chapter 4, verses 9 through 12, the wisest man who ever lived said, "Two are better than one, because they have a good return for their work: if one falls down, his friend can help him up. But pity the man who falls and has no one to help him up! Also, if two lie down together, they will keep warm. But how can one keep warm alone? Though one may be overpowered, two can defend themselves. A cord of three strands is not quickly broken."

Several fascinating relationship principles jump out from this familiar passage. To begin with, in all three couplets, the person functioning at the lowest level is restored to equivalency with the person functioning at a higher level. At the same time, the person who reaches out a hand, warms the other's cold feet in the middle of the night (Solomon must also have taught the

Winter Camping merit, because he knew that the best treatment for hypothermia is skin to skin contact!), and has the other person's back is not threatened, regressed, or diminished in any way. Often, people are afraid to reach out and risk extending themselves in relationship for fear that getting involved will cost them something and they will somehow get burned.

Once, while speaking at a Valentine's banquet, I spontaneously referred to this passage (which was not in my notes) and was struck by the apparent discrepancy that Solomon seemed to get into here; he talks about two, two, two, and then boom: three. I wondered where that "three" came from, and then it occurred to me that perhaps this was sort of like the fourth guy in the fiery furnace with Shadrach, Meshach, and Abednego. Jesus proclaimed, "… where two or three come together in my name, there I am with them" (Matthew 18:20). Could it be that whenever a couple is unified and co-operating, no less than the third person of the Trinity shows up to strengthen and support them? Incidentally, I find it fascinating that several thousand years later, regardless of its diameter or composition, every good rope has three cords or strands which weave it together.

The craft or practice of weaving two ropes together to make something durable and useful is known as lashing. Square, diagonal, shear, round, and continuous forms of lashing can be used to create primitive implements, camping furniture, and other helpful tools. Using analogies from Ropecraft and Lashing, I want to tie together several relationship principles, which can teach us how to show respect in our marriages. Using the acronym L.A.S.H., I want to suggest that respect is definitely and duly demonstrated when we Listen, Affirm, Support, and Honor our spouse.

Listen

Down deep, everyone wants to be heard. Having someone's complete and undivided attention with direct eye contact and no

125

interruptions makes one feel important and cared about. Men often lament that their wife doesn't understand them, and women often complain that their husband never talks to them. Perhaps these two classic components of miserable marriages are functionally and circularly related.

As has already been established, most men tend to shut down when they feel judged, criticized, or demeaned. Conversely, when a woman experiences the corresponding silent treatment from her husband, she will often express the pain of her feelings of abandonment and rejection in a fairly vocal and unmistakable way. For many women, meaningful and intimate conversation is their greatest relational need. Thus, when a husband shuts down emotionally because he feels attacked in some way by his wife, and when her response to him is then intensely and/or loudly emotional, the resulting scenario is not exactly a potentially fertile breeding ground for relationships replete with rigorous respect.

While we will talk much more about the communication process in the next chapter, let's briefly consider how important the dynamics of active listening are to conveying unconditional respect to our spouse. To really listen means that we will never ignore or interrupt our spouse. We will try our very best to understand them. When we listen, it's not about us—it's about the one who is speaking. They are (or once were) very special to us, and they are worth being heard. When someone deeply and directly listens to us, we will not feel disregarded, dismissed, or discounted.

> **When we listen, it's not about us—it's about the one who is speaking.**

Affirm

A crucial aspect of respect is to be valued and validated for who one is as a person. Your marital partner will feel priceless and precious when you prize and praise them. Most couples affirm each other freely and frequently during the dating and courtship process, but typically and tragically end up neglecting to nurture each other through the ongoing ruts and routines of life.

A sense of affirmation is indispensable for feeling respected.

A sense of affirmation is indispensable for feeling respected. According to Gottman, "By simply reminding yourself of your spouse's positive qualities—you can prevent a happy marriage from deteriorating. The simple reason is that fondness and admiration are antidotes for contempt. If you maintain a sense of respect for your spouse, you are less likely to act disgusted with him or her when you disagree" (1999, p. 65). Compliments make anyone feel good.

In her research, Feldhahn discovered that men in particular have a deep need to be respected in the public arena. Women may   understandably think of this as constituting male pride or egoism, but it isn't. Ladies, without trying to be pedantic or preachy, please allow me to give you a brief primer on deeply understanding the masculine mindset. Men will do almost anything to avoid experiencing what I call the "unholy trifecta"—feeling inferior, inadequate, and/or incompetent.

Men will do almost anything to avoid experiencing what I call the "unholy trifecta"—feeling inferior, inadequate, and/or incompetent.

In our culture, these feelings start for us as boys when we strike out with the bases loaded in Little League, and progres-

127

sively escalate as we get taller and the stakes get higher. Public humiliation and shame erode and destroy the foundation of masculine identity. Teasing can be torturous. But in a positive vein, Feldhahn points out that "just as your man will be hurt and angry if you disrespect him in public, he will think you are the most wonderful woman in the world if you publicly build him up... Trust me—from the women I talked to, that will be the equivalent of his coming home to you with a dozen roses and a surprise date night without the kids. He will feel *adored*" (2004, p. 45). Affirmation is absolutely awesome.

Scripture speaks repeatedly about the importance and impact of communication, about which we will study much more in the next chapter. Careless comments in casual conversation can come across as cold, critical, calculating, or caustic. Therefore "... we should make every effort to filter our words through a 'disrespect meter' before they pass our lips" (Feldhahn, ibid. p. 40).

Support

It has been said that behind every successful man stands a proud wife and a surprised mother-in-law! Though it may seem vain or egotistical to a woman, *secretly every man down deep wants his wife to be his personal cheerleader throughout life*. Her ongoing support is invaluable to his level of self-confidence and critical to his level of self-esteem. Her expressions of encouragement enthuse and energize him enormously.

For a woman, the need for support may take many forms. A husband can communicate respect and worth by providing for her emotional, spiritual, financial, co-parental, and domestic needs. Much more about these significant topics is discussed elsewhere in this book. Expressions of assurance and a continuing commitment to responsibly and responsively be there for our spouse are incredibly securing. It feels great to know that our spouse will always be there for us and is on our side and in our corner, no matter what.

> **Respect is undermined when we do not feel supported in what is important to us and to the achievement of our own personal identity, goals, and dreams.**

For both spouses, respect is undermined when we do not feel supported in what is important to us and to the achievement of our own personal identity, goals, and dreams. Furthermore, when our spouse makes incorrect assumptions about us and fails to believe the best about us, we feel unsupported and disrespected. In unhealthy marriages, couples ironically become each other's adversary, not their advocate. Strive to become your spouse's helpmate—not their hurtmate.

Honor

> **We can make our mate feel taken for granted, used, and unimportant when we fail to consistently honor them.**

To show honor to someone about whom we care deeply is to show the utmost respect. But unfortunately, the opposite is also true. Ironically, many married people often feel as though their knowledge, opinions, and decisions are actively appreciated and respected everywhere else and by everyone else except at home and by those who live there. We can make our mate feel taken for granted, used, and unimportant when we fail to consistently honor them.

The concept of honor is a fairly rare one in our culture. We do not have good role models in our society for examples of how to demonstrate or display it. But biblically speaking, "...honoring someone involves viewing him [her] as a priceless treasure and treating him [her] with loving respect" (Smalley &

Trent, 1987, p. 280). Giving honor is connected with and conveys the essence of both love and respect.

Conversely, "The lower the value we attach to a person, the easier we can 'justify' dishonoring them by yelling or treating them with disrespect" (ibid. p. 286). But we should "build contempt for contempt. Give honor to those who deserve it—beginning with your spouse" (Thomas, 2000, p. 71). Angry tones and loud decibels can damage, if not destroy, marriages. Verbal and emotional abuse is dishonoring and dishonorable.

Showing respect, like showing love, is a choice.

Clearly we can see that showing respect, like showing love, is a choice. It is an intentional act of our free will. In this way, a healthy marriage is about continuously deciding to place your spouse's needs above your own (Romans 12:10). When we intentionally initiate showing unconditional respect to our mate, it benefits us by increasing our integrity, and it blesses them by improving their identity. After all, "Without the fundamental belief that your spouse is worthy of honor and respect, where is the basis for any kind of rewarding relationship?" (Gottman, 1999, p. 65).

As Christians, we are called to spiritual maturity. Remember, respect is not something that is earned or deserved. It is an essential spiritual discipline which provides daily opportunities for our personal growth. No spouse is perfect—you know that yours isn't because they chose you! We are to humbly respect our fellow fallen, flawed, fickle friend with all their faults, foibles, and failures. Rigorously demonstrate respect to your spouse by the way you Listen, Affirm, Support, and Honor them!

Scriptural Search

1. Leviticus 19:3, 32
2. Proverbs 11:16
3. 1 Thessalonians 4:11-12
4. Titus 2:1-3
5. 1 Peter 2:13-25

Ponderable Points

1. Is giving respect to your spouse something that is to be earned or deserved, or is it an attribute and reflection of your own character, maturity, and devotion to God?

2. What do you believe makes the concept of unconditional respect so difficult to grasp and apply in our culture? When have you seen unconditional respect demonstrated, or what role models have shown you examples of how to do this?

3. What makes it difficult to give someone unconditional respect? List and discuss some obstacles or challenges to doing this.

4. Does anyone ever truly and fully "deserve" unconditional respect? Why or why not?

5. What do you think of the research which says about 75% of men would rather feel alone and unloved in the world than disrespected? Do you (husband) or does your husband agree with this for yourself/themselves?

Activation Activities

1. Read 1 Peter 3:1-12 together, preferably in several different translations or versions. Specifically think through and discuss with your spouse your understanding of what unconditional respect for each other means and what it looks like in practical terms.

2. What do you need to change about yourself in order to more fully and effectively give unconditional respect to your mate?

3. When wives feel unloved, it is not natural for them to show respect. When husbands feel disrespected, it is not natural for them to show love. Since it is easier for us to see what our spouse has/has not done to us, instead of what we have/have not done to them, what biblical principles or passages will help a wife show unconditional respect when she does not feel like doing it, and which ones will help a husband demonstrate unconditional love in the face of feeling disrespected?

Recommended Resources

Love and Respect, Emerson Eggerichs (2004).
For Women Only, Shaunti Feldhahn (2004).
The Gift of Honor, Gary Smalley and John Trent (1987).
How to Have a New Husband by Friday, Kevin Leman (2011).
31 Days to a Happy Husband: What Every Man Needs from His Wife, Arlene Pellicane (2012).

CHAPTER SIX

Connected Communication

I know you think you believe you understand what I said,
but I'm not sure you realize that what you heard is not
what I meant!

"Let your conversation be always full of grace, seasoned
with salt, so that you may know how to answer everyone."

—COLOSSIANS 4:6

Communication is the lifeblood of any healthy marriage. Just as in real estate, where the three most important things are location, location, and location; in marriage the three most important things are communication, communication, and talking! Communication is the means by which interpersonal relating takes place. Communication is the process through which we share life with one another. Communication is the primary vehicle that couples use to connect with each other. Communication is the pathway to intimacy.

Sounds simple, doesn't it? Actually nothing could be farther from the truth. Although humans have been communicating with their loved ones from the very first moment of their arrival on this planet, most of us experience difficulty understanding and being understood by those about whom we care most. The number one complaint marriage therapists encounter is communication problems.

According to Drs. Les and Leslie Parrott, "... a couple's ability to communicate is the single most important contributor to a stable and satisfying marriage" (2004, p. 31). Conversely, a couple's inability to communicate is the single most important contributor to divorce. Dr. Jim Burns concludes, "The trait that is most closely linked to the success or failure of your marriage is your ability to communicate" (2006, p. 71).

> ### Effective communication involves much more than mere talk.

This should not be surprising to us. Effective communication involves much more than mere talk. In fact, I believe it is impossible to overestimate the complexities, consternations, and conundrums of the human communicative process. But it hasn't always been this way.

In Genesis chapter 11, verse 1, Moses remarked, "Now the whole world had one language and a common speech." Think about that for a minute—what a great idea! When you consider that the 500 most common words in English have over 1400 collective meanings (and this doesn't even take into account additional potential subtleties and nuances of meaning, like regional colloquialisms, double entendres, idiosyncratic inferences, intuitive idioms, and the like), speech can become absolutely mind-boggling. They must have really had it easy.

But those ancient Babylonians really messed up the communication process for all of us (this is even worse and more unfair than when back in the third grade some troublemaker threw a spit wad or shot a rubber band while the teacher's back was turned, so everyone in the whole class had to stay in for recess because he or she wouldn't fess up to it!). Because of their overwhelming pride, arrogance, and egotistical attitude resulting from this universalized singular language, God saw that He needed to intervene in order to prevent the ultimate self-destruction of humankind.

Here we see God's consistent, loving discipline in action. He declares, "Come, let us go down and confuse their language so they will not understand each other. So the Lord scattered them from there over all the earth, and they stopped building the city. That is why it was called Babel—because there the Lord confused the language of the whole world" (Genesis 11:7-9). He is always about saving us—usually, as in that case, from ourselves.

Well, communication certainly is confusing all right. Now we have thousands of different languages and dialects, and I'm not sure that anyone understands anybody. Does that make sense (just kidding)? This ironic legacy of Babel was not lost on Jesus, either. In His Sermon on the Mount, as He is teaching us how to communicate with Him, he sardonically notes, "And when you pray, do not keep on babbling like pagans, for they think they will be heard because of their many words" (Matthew 6:7). Banished Babel begat baffling, brainless, banal babbling behavior!

Several years ago, on my first mission trip to Iceland, when I was complimenting the excellent English spoken by an elderly gentleman who was fluent in five different languages, he asked me if I wanted to hear a joke. If you know me, that's like asking if I want a double scoop ice cream cone! He asked, "What do you call someone who can speak three languages?" I replied, "I dunno." He stated knowingly, "a tri-linguist." Then he said, "What do you call someone who can speak two languages?" Catching on, I confidently answered, "a bi-linguist." He nodded and then said, "Now what do you call someone who can speak one language?" After I shrugged, he grinned and exclaimed, "an American!" Ouch.

Communication Concepts and Components

The science of conversing is indeed incredibly complex and convoluted. Communication experts estimate that the average adult spends approximately 70% of their waking hours communicating with other people. More than virtually any other human activity, we are almost constantly interacting with others. Actually, we cannot not communicate. Even silence can speak volumes. Let's briefly consider some of the manifold methods, mysterious mechanics, and multiple messages involved in the communication process.

> **The average adult spends approximately 70% of their waking hours communicating with other people.**

To begin with, communication is more than just simply speaking words. In fact, the majority of interpersonal communication is completely nonverbal. Research suggests that between 55 and 80% of all communication is expressed through body language. A flirtatious wink or disdainful roll of the eyes, the gentle touch of a hand, a warm smile or a disgusted frown, an arched eyebrow, eagerly outstretched or defiantly folded arms, plus hundreds of other facial and bodily gestures convey messages that can be clearly understood by those who observe them. All of these serve to reinforce the maxim which literally says that actions speak louder than words. Yet speech classes and communications courses largely ignore or at least underemphasize this vital and vibrant part of human expression.

Also, much more important to the communication process than the specific words we use is our tone of voice. Communications experts believe anywhere from 12 to 35% of our communication is comprised of *how* we say what we say. For example, there is a huge difference in meanings conveyed by someone saying, "I love you," while acting bored and stifling a yawn, and saying, "I love you," loudly and harshly in the midst of an angry confrontation, and saying, "I love you," to your darling spouse in a sweet, endearing manner while walking arm in arm along an exotic beach as you enjoy a beautifully romantic sunset together.

Last, and definitely least, there are the specific words we actually use, which, along with grammatical structure and punctuation, comprise the remaining 8 to 10% of the communication process. English is a great language—at least we don't have to draw pictures like in Mandarin! I mean, where else can you park on a driveway and drive on a parkway or play at a recital and recite at a play? I recall teasingly telling my sixth grade teacher, Mrs. Leonard, during an English lesson that, "I ain't never been no good at grammar no-how" (which can also be taken as, "I ain't never been no good at grammar know-how!"). She, like no doubt many of you, just rolled her eyes and groaned.

However, having a command of and being able to adequately articulate the English language does not necessarily mean that we can effectively communicate with another English-speaking individual. Perhaps you heard about the woman who went to see a divorce lawyer, adamant about her desire to end her marriage. The attorney asked, "Do you have grounds?" "Yes," she said, "about 5 acres." The attorney responded, "No, I mean do you have a grudge?" She stated, "No, just a carport." Then the lawyer inquired, "Well, does he beat you up?" "No," the woman replied, "I always get up before that lazy bum does." Getting exasperated, the attorney finally demanded, "Madam, then why do you want to get divorced from your husband?" She retorted, "Because it is impossible to communicate with that man!"

Not only do words themselves describe and convey meaning; let's consider the prominence of punctuation. Take the lowly comma for example. There is a huge difference in saying, "Woman, without her, man is nothing," or saying, "Woman without her man, is nothing." My personal favorite is the huge difference between saying, "Let's go eat, everyone," or saying, "Let's go eat everyone." One tiny punctuation mark can mean the difference between a gracious social invitation and a grandiosely ambitious cannibal!

In addition, personality and perception play a huge role in the communication process. Consider the following exercise as you try to decipher this message:

Love
isnowhere

What did you see? Some people see, "Love is now here," whereas other people read this as, "Love is nowhere." Then there are a few Northerners who somehow read "Love I snow here!" Our brains can perceive and process the same information in very different ways. Obviously, a message can be received in an entirely different way than it was intended.

> **Communication is not just sending a message or even sending and receiving a message.**

Another enormous barrier to connected communication involves the exceptionally tedious and technical nature of the beast itself. Communication is not just sending a message or even sending and receiving a message. Whenever you attempt to communicate with someone, what is actually involved are the following eight separate and distinct mechanisms:

1. What you intend to say

2. What you actually say

3. What the other person hears

4. What the other person says to themselves about what they have

   heard

5. What the other person intends to say back to you

6. What the other person actually says to you

7. What you hear them say

8. What you say to yourself about what you heard

Whew! Talk (get it?) about complicated! Whenever we open our mouth, there is the potential for all kinds of misunderstandings and misconceptions. Growing up, we hear different sayings like "loose lips sink ships" and "talk is cheap but you can't buy it back," but how often do we really apply those truths to our relationships? Communicating is difficult, and tone, non-verbal expressions, and words do matter.

> No wonder King Solomon wisely warns us so frequently about the potential pitfalls of mouthing off.

No wonder King Solomon wisely warns us so frequently about the potential pitfalls of mouthing off. A few of the dozens of Proverbs pertaining to our speech include, "When words are many, sin is not absent, but he who holds his tongue is wise" (10:19); "A man of knowledge uses words with restraint, and a man of understanding is even-tempered. Even a fool is thought wise if he keeps silent, and discerning if he holds his tongue" (17:27-28); "He who guards his mouth and tongue keeps himself from calamity" (21:23); and "Do you see a man who speaks in haste? There is more hope for a fool than for him" (29:20). And just to reiterate: Les and Leslie Parrott predict that, "Your love life will sink or swim according to how well you communicate" (2004, p. 19). Wow, no pressure!

Levels of Communication

To continue to compound and complicate conversational concepts, communication consists of consecutive converging categories. These move along a continuum from superficial to intimate.

Communication on the first level consists of sharing facts and information. Conversations at this surface level are much like exchanging newspaper stories or speaking in social clichés. While the information can be interesting, it is often considered to be small talk or polite, superficial social interplay (e.g., "Hi, how are you? Fine, how are you? Nice weather, huh?"). Consequently it isn't very meaningful or of enduring value to building a relationship. Though shallow, it's safe, and therefore couples who are fearful of intimacy or conflict spend a lot of time conversing here.

The second level of communication centers on sharing the ideas, activities, and opinions of others. Conversation at this level is a bit more interesting (and often degenerates into gossip), yet it involves negligible self-disclosure or emotional vulnerability. Very little intimacy can be developed between two people when the discussion is focused on persons, places, or things outside the relationship.

At the third level of communication, we begin to state our own opinions, thoughts, and ideas. As we began to disclose some of our own personal views, there is a moderate risk of vulnerability and potential for intimacy, but we have yet to reveal who we really are. Though most couples do progress to this stage, the vast majority of marital conversation rarely goes beyond it to the deeper degrees of intimacy.

The fourth level of communication is where we begin to share our personal preferences, beliefs, concerns, and experiences. Opening up like this can be frightening, but it is the only way for us to know and be known, as well as to love and be loved. Paradoxically, the only way to become understood and accepted is to risk judgment and rejection.

> **The fifth level of communication involves the deepest sharing of our soul.**

The fifth level of communication involves the deepest sharing of our soul. This is where we feel safe and secure to share our deepest personal feelings, needs, and preferences. About 20 years ago, a client shared with me a wonderful functional definition of intimacy. *Intimacy means "into—me—see!"* Isn't that fabulous? When we allow ourselves to be seen into deeply by someone else, we experience intimacy. This is the most awesome—but unfortunately also the rarest—level of communication achieved in the average marriage.

Gender Differences

Another built-in obstacle to effective communication in marriage has to do with biological gender differences. Because of these, wars between the sexes have been waged for millennia. More recently, various authors have characterized basic male/female distinctions in terms of us being from different planets (John Gray: *Men are from Mars, Women are from Venus*), made from different materials (Leo Godzich: *Men are from Dirt, Women are from Men*), or being different foods (Bill and Pam Farrell: *Men are Like Waffles, Women are Like Spaghetti*). It's actually quite a bit more complicated than that.

Neurologists discovered that between the 16th and 26th week of pregnancy, the brain of a male baby is bathed with testosterone and other sex hormones that destroy some of the corpus callosum, the connective tissue that exists between the right and left hemispheres of the brain. Therefore, the right side of a boy baby's brain recedes slightly so that he becomes more left-brain oriented and dominant. This hormonal activation provides a specialization to the male cognitive functioning capacity (which focuses predominantly on logical reason and thought processing) that females don't chemically receive.

The right side of the brain is characteristically intuitive or emotionally oriented and controls linguistic processing and communication skills. Since a girl baby's brain is not subjected to this chemical metamorphosis, she develops normally without being 'dain bramaged!' Consequently, women tend to be more adept at and suited for conversational and emotional processes and functions than men. It is not that women are incapable of logic or that men are incapable of feeling; it's that their brains are naturally hardwired from the factory more predisposed respectively to the one than the other.

Given these intrinsic differences, we can clearly see that either God is naturally sadistic, cruel, and perverse, or that He intentionally designed males and females with complementary strengths. Thus, if a woman truly expects to have meaningful and rewarding conversation with her husband, it is *imperative* that she activate the right side of his brain. And if a man truly wants to communicate with his wife, he *must* enter into her world of emotionality. That is the way for us to connect. It is a law of physics (God's natural laws of the universe) that polarized opposites naturally attract.

Unfortunately, when we finally find someone totally different from us and are attracted to them, we automatically and unconsciously spend the rest of our lives trying to change them to become like us! This is an ironic yet universal dynamic of male/female relationships. Husbands think to themselves, "Why can't she just be logical?" and wives think to themselves, "Why won't he just open up and talk to me about his feelings?" But guess what? Everyone naturally resists external efforts to change themselves, no matter how well-intended the other person is. (One wise lady observed that the only time a woman can ever successfully change a male is when he's a baby!)

These factory-installed genetic differences in conversational style become clearly apparent to even the most casual observer of children on a preschool or elementary playground. From the outset, little girls place a premium on talking with a few other girls and sharing secrets with them in order to make friends and be close. Feminine language is relationally oriented with a definite focus on the process of developing intimacy. Given how difficult and daunting that is, perhaps that's why the average woman speaks about 25,000 words per day, while the average man has just 12,500 words per day in his verbal reservoir.

Meanwhile, little boys are much more likely to play competitively in large groups—with an emphasis on activity, aggression, accomplishments, and achievements—than talk. One study conducted in a nursery showed that girl babies exhibited more lip movement than male babies, and a Harvard study, which wired a playground for sound, discovered that 100% of vocalizations from little girls were recognizable words. In contrast, only 63% of the boys' sounds were words. The rest of their masculine language consisted of monosyllabic utterances such as "ugh" or "mmm" or sound effects such as "varoom" or "zoom" (McDonald and McDonald, 1994). I know, ladies, I know—we just get taller!

These basic language differences and approaches to the communication process naturally carry over into adulthood. As the Farrells explain, "When a man starts a conversation, it is generally because he perceives there is some sort of problem that needs to be addressed. If there is no perceived problem, he feels no particular need to talk" (2001, p. 28). Hearing no problems, the average husband assumes all is right with the world and typically reaches out to connect with his wife in a side-by-side type of activity, rather than the face-to-face discussion which she prefers.

Most wives tend to be the emotional caretakers of the marriage. Generally, they are more attuned than their husbands to their own feelings, as well as to the shifting tides or changing barometer of their relationship. Therefore, they tend to notice and bring up problems more often than men do. Again, in the Farrell's words:

His wife, on the other hand, has a constant desire to talk with her husband. She wants to connect him to everything in her life and assumes he wants to connect her to everything in his life. When she begins a conversation, he assumes she's bringing up a problem that needs to be resolved. Generally she is starting the conversation because it seems natural to talk about whatever is on her mind. While she is in conversational mode, he turns on the "fix it" mechanism and the conflict begins. She gets her feelings hurt because he is trying to figure her out rather than just visit with her. He gets impatient because there seems to be no point. What started out as a hopeful moment for drawing closer together becomes another nagging defeat (ibid.).

She's left feeling ignored and uncared for; he's left feeling criticized and emotionally wrung out.

So, irresistible force meets immovable object: women yearn for their husbands to be a sounding board or to lend a sympathetic ear so they can discuss their feelings and hash out problems, whereas men want action and feel rejected and nagged at when their wives don't seem to want or need the solution they propose. She's left feeling ignored and uncared for; he's left feeling criticized and emotionally wrung out.

Many couples remain stuck in the muck and mire of miserable mutual misunderstanding for 30 or 40 years. The confusion, hurt, and frustration of being unable to communicatively connect with the person they care about more than anyone else on the planet (or any other planet!) leaves them feeling lonely, sad, and empty. No one signs up for deep disappointments, horrible

hurts, and continuous conflicts. We seem to be set up for failure. It's like our spouse is speaking Greek or Swahili. Marriages often seem to be like a nightmarish reenactment of Abbott
and Costello's comedy routine "Who's on First?" (if you haven't
seen it, Google it—it's hilarious), except that neither spouse is
laughing.

In fact, many marriages become chronically embroiled in
constant back-and-forth bickering reminiscent of a tense tennis
volley at match point. Other couples engage in regular arguments and power struggles rather akin to an epic tug-of-war
contest. Still other spouses, in their efforts to avoid the resentment and bitterness of strife and dissension, attempt to avoid
conflict at all costs, engaging in the frustrated stalemate of a
never-ending Cold War. We can do better than this—and we
must. In the next chapter, we will discuss some tools to use in
order to constructively cope with conflict.

> **Healthy, mature couples have discovered that their
> marriage relationship is designed to be *complementary*
> not *competitive*.**

Healthy, mature couples have discovered that their marriage
relationship is designed to be *complementary* not *competitive*.
It's only by recognizing, accepting, and embracing one another's differences that two separate, unique, and autonomous individuals can fulfill the "profound mystery" (Ephesians 5:32) of
God's ultimate design for marriage. But to do so, we must first
understand and become proficient at bridging these gender
gaps and successfully meeting the challenges of connected
communication.

What follows is a very exciting and practical set of conversational principles, which have proven to be powerful and productive with real-life couples in the trenches of clinical practice.
Although I do not have enough faith to believe in magic, I do

believe in miracles. As a clinician, I am not very impressed by lofty sounding theory; I am pragmatic and simply want to know what works. I have seen God use the following steps to wondrously transform many couples' communication processes over the years. These tools have been forged in the fiery furnace of intensive interpersonal interventions. I encourage you to apply them directly and diligently. I believe if you do, you'll experience a discernible and definite difference in your daily dialogue.

> I have seen God use the following steps to wondrously transform many couples' communication processes over the years.

"Soul Sharing:" Six Simple Steps for Connected Couples' Communication

Goals: mutual understanding, closeness
Requirements: emotional safety, willing and cooperative attitudes
Processes: active listening, clear boundaries, direct and intimate sharing

	Speaker:	Listener:
1.	Ask if this is a good time for your spouse to listen; extend your hands.	Focus exclusively on them; reach out and grasp their hands with yours.
2.	Be aware of your nonverbal messages—tone, volume, intensity level, facial expressions, etc.	Face them directly for eye contact; prepare your heart to be open.

3.	Prayerfully choose to speak about one topic briefly (try to condense your statements to one paragraph).	Listen for emotions expressed in addition to content.
4.	Use "I" language; do not use "you" language or inflammatory speech (e.g., exaggerations, accusations, generalizations, etc.). Do not blame, shame, name-call, criticize, belittle, or threaten; inform them about you.	Monitor your temptation to become defensive; remember this is about them. They have the floor, so do not interrupt; try your best to empathize.
5.	Pause and allow the listener to give feedback.	Paraphrase (in your own words) what you heard the speaker say; respectfully ask clarifying questions in order to understand.
6.	Clarify and if necessary amplify your message; gently restate and politely reword your statement.	Don't rebut or argue; patiently summarize what you understand the speaker to have said. Don't try to apologize, problem-solve or change the subject; ask if they feel understood.

Let's briefly go through each of the six steps in order to offer training tips for each technique. As you go through this exercise with your mate, don't be surprised if you feel a little bit awkward or uncomfortable at first. The structure may feel somewhat artificial or mechanical, but it is necessary in order to ensure an atmosphere of emotional safety, and to guide the practice of self-discipline and patience required to address potentially threatening issues in the marriage relationship. Most couples probably don't need the safety and structure of "Soul Sharing" techniques to make a decision about where to go out to eat, but they may benefit from them to effectively work through emotionally charged issues around hot-button conflicts or sensitive topics.

- Speaker: Ask if this is a good time for your spouse to listen; extend your hands.
- Listener: Focus exclusively on them; reach out and grasp their hands with yours.

This first step is probably the most important, yet it is likely the least practiced one in the average marriage. Human nature simply suggests that when we have something to say, we just automatically and casually say it. But that may be extremely unwise.

Not only is it patently disrespectful to the other person when we blurt out something impulsively, we are often hurt as a consequence because we have not thought to guard our own heart in the process (Proverbs 4:23). The other person simply may not be ready, willing, and/or able to devote their full and undivided attention to us at the instant we demand it. Timing is important because there is definitely "…a time to be silent and a time to speak" (Ecclesiastes 3:7). Therefore, we should "… be quick to listen, slow to speak and slow to become angry" (James 1:19).

When the speaker requests their spouse's time and attention, many couples find it helpful to use a real object to designate who has the floor. Since I really like puns, it's a no-brainer to me to recommend that couples keep a piece of ceramic tile, carpet square, or linoleum on their lap for this purpose, so it's easy to see who has the "floor." This literal reminder of who is to be the speaker and who is to be the listener can be a helpful reminder to both parties of the purpose, nature, and process of this communication exercise. (Other people prefer to use a soft, stuffed animal or even a heart-shaped object to symbolize their soul somewhat literally).

After asking your spouse if this is a good time for them to hear what you want to say to them, sitting down and reaching out your hands to them is not only non-threatening, it symbolizes your attempt and motivation to reach out to and literally connect with them. When you agree to hear your spouse out and sit down across from them and take their hands in yours, you have completed the connective loop and have made them feel accepted before they have shared anything verbally—plus it's harder for them to hit you when you're holding their hands!

. • Speaker: Be aware of your nonverbal messages—tone, volume, intensity level, facial expressions, etc.
   • Listener: Face them directly for eye contact; prepare your heart to be open.

In step two, recall that the majority of the communication process is nonverbal and has to do with body language. It is absolutely crucial that—before you say a word to them—you monitor how your spouse is likely to perceive you by the nonverbal messages, facial expressions, and tone of voice you use. The way you look and sound can completely override the content of what you say. In this respect, *the metamessage* (underlying meaning) *is always more important than the spoken message.*

In addition to becoming more self-aware of what our body language communicates, it is important to think through and carefully plan what we intend to say. In Colossians 4:6, the apostle Paul gives us this recipe for successful communication: "Let your conversation be always full of grace, seasoned with salt, so that you may know how to answer everyone."

151

What we say—and how we say it—impacts our mate.

Not only are we to be mindful and intentional about what we *want to say*, we also need to be thoughtful and considerate of how what we *actually do say* is likely to impact our spouse. In Ephesians 4:29 we are commanded, "Do not let any unwholesome talk come out of your mouths, but only what is helpful for building others up according to their needs, that it may benefit those who listen." Even when it's about us, it's not *only* about us. What we say—and how we say it—impacts our mate.

Meanwhile, the listener needs to be prepared to devote their full and undivided attention to hear—really and deeply hear—their spouse. Early in our marriage, I was watching a baseball game on TV one evening when Linda came in the room and shared something with me. Instead of turning off the television or at least muting the sound, I selfishly kept watching the game while she was talking. She understandably felt as though I didn't listen to her, and she walked off feeling hurt and uncared for. Even though I got up and followed her into the next room and accurately repeated word for word what I heard her say, it didn't help. My nonverbal behaviors had completely ignored her and had not made her feel listened to, even though I was certain I had heard every word she said. Stubbornly, I tried to convince her that I really did hear her even though I was watching the game. To proudly and immaturely prove to her that I actually could do two things at once, I announced to her that the next night I would watch one game on TV with the sound off while I listened to another game at the same time on the radio—and keep accurate box scores on both games. By the way, it shouldn't be surprising that I was by myself that evening!

I'm ashamed to admit that I actually did follow through with that plan in order to prove my point to her. Needless to say, she wasn't impressed when I showed her the box scores—

which were flawlessly corroborated by the newspaper the following morning. I sort of won the battle, but I definitely lost the war. There's a big difference between hearing and truly listening; now, when I'm smart, I turn off the TV or put down whatever I'm doing or reading so I can make her feel deeply listened to and hopefully understood.

> **The Lord probably knew what He was doing when He created us with two ears and only one mouth!**

My former graduate school classmates, Henry Cloud and John Townsend, put it this way: "Listening has occurred only when the other person *understands that you understand*" (2005, p. 153). Much more than just hearing the other person, listening deeply is completely unselfish and an ultimate act of love. In fact, it has been said that, "Listening is the language of love" (Burns, 2006, p. 92). The Lord probably knew what He was doing when He created us with two ears and only one mouth!

- Speaker: Prayerfully choose to speak about one topic briefly (try to condense your statements to one paragraph).
- Listener: Listen for emotions expressed in addition to content.

Adhering to this principle is paramount for productive communication. Just as a good sermon does not preach the entire Bible, good communication is brief, descriptive, and to the point. Sometimes we are tempted to believe that if a little is good, then more is better. In gardening, a little bit of fertilizer is growth producing, but too much burns the roots. Similarly, it's tough to drink from a fire hose. Don't dump the whole truck load—use the K. I. S. S. principle: keep it short and sweet.

Solomon furnishes us with an elegant example of how to do this when he says, "A word aptly spoken is like apples of gold in settings of silver" (Proverbs 25:11). What Solomon so beautifully uses here is an excellent illustration of a very powerful relationship device: an emotional word picture. According to Smalley and Trent, "An emotional word picture is a communication tool that uses a story or object to activate simultaneously the *emotions* and *intellect* of a person. In so doing, it causes the person to *experience* our words, not just hear them" (1988, p. 17).

The goal of "Soul Sharing" is mutual understanding and closeness.

Using emotional word pictures takes a lot of work, forethought, and consideration about how the other person is likely to hear us. But remember, the goal of "Soul Sharing" is mutual understanding and closeness. Again Solomon reminds us, "... though it cost all you have, get understanding" (Proverbs 4:7). As with most things in a healthy marriage relationship, putting this into practice effectively requires patience, wisdom, self-control, intentionality, and experience. In the words of business management guru, Stephen Covey, begin with the end in mind. Formulate what you want to accomplish before you say a word—in other words, engage brain before putting mouth into gear.

Jesus' half-brother James' writing style is blunt, direct, and practical. I sort of feel for him—can you imagine what it might have been like to grow up with a big brother who always did everything right, more than likely was Mom's favorite, and never once messed up? Boy, that would sure be tough on a guy! Perhaps from experience, in chapter 3 of his epistle, he uses two powerful word pictures to metaphorically describe the power of our speech.

Just as a bit in the mouth of a horse can turn the entire animal, and a small rudder can steer a large ship, James instructs us that, "Likewise the tongue is a small part of the body, but it makes great boasts. Consider what a great forest is set on fire by a small spark. The tongue is also a fire, a world of evil among the parts of the body. It corrupts the whole person, sets the whole course of his life on fire, and is itself set on fire by hell" (verses 5-6). Furthermore, he goes on to tell us that, "All kinds of animals, birds, reptiles and creatures of the sea are being tamed and have been tamed by man, but no one can tame the tongue. It is a restless evil, full of deadly poison. With the tongue we praise our Lord and Father, and with it we curse men, who have been made in God's likeness" (verses 7-9). What, when, where, why, and how we speak is crucial.

So, too, is listening. As has already been noted, deeply listening is a supreme act of love. But as with everything else, our listening skills are not something with which we are born—we learn them. In his book, *Creating an Intimate Marriage*, Dr. Jim Burns offers what he calls "Seven Effective Listening Qualities" which are worthy of our consideration here:

1. A genuine desire to listen to your spouse,
2. A willingness to accept his/her feelings and emotions, whether he/she is right or wrong,
3. A desire to not always need to be right,
4. A nonjudgmental attitude,
5. Eye contact and little fidgeting,
6. Showing appreciation that your spouse is confiding in you, and
7. A willingness not only to listen, but to continue to be supportive (2006, p. 93).

In the listener role, we are to focus on understanding the other person and their internal experience. Practicing these listening qualities will help us better understand our spouse.

- Speaker: Use "I" language; do not use "you" language or inflammatory speech (e.g. exaggerations, accusations, generalizations, etc.). Do not blame, shame, name-call, criticize, belittle, or threaten.
- Listener: Monitor the temptation to become defensive—this is about them. They have the floor; do not interrupt; try to empathize.

Prior to this point we are halfway through the "Soul Sharing," exercise and no one has yet said a word! Everything up to this juncture has been prayer, planning, and preparation (and perhaps perspiration!). This is a profound opportunity for you to allow your marriage partner to "see into" your heart.

Accordingly, speak for yourself. Talk about *your* thoughts, feelings, and concerns clearly and concisely. Try to use "I" statements, using emotional language and word pictures when possible. "I was hurt and upset when you forgot our date," is an "I" statement. "I feel you don't care about me" is not (that is a judgment; feelings are happy, sad, scared, etc.); "I feel unloved when you do _____" is.

It is true that hurt people hurt people.

Again, keep in focus what our motive is here. It is to give our spouse an opportunity to more deeply know and understand us. It is not an opportunity to hurt them back, change them, or make them agree with us. Simply say what you mean and mean what you say. But keep in mind that as God's people we are to be "... speaking the truth in love" (Ephesians 4:15), not blasting the other with the truth. Often, it is out of the overflow

156

of our heart that our mouth speaks (Luke 6:45), so we must be careful to always employ the Golden Rule (Matthew 7:12) when we are dealing with our emotional pain and woundedness. It is true that hurt people hurt people.

When we use "you" language, it almost always makes the other person feel defensive. Think about it—it's impossible to be hugged by someone who is in a self-protective mode! When we make the other person feel defensive it is impossible for them to be open, empathetic, and loving toward us.

When they hear "you always..." or "you never..." your mate's defenses are instantly activated. The subject is no longer about the speaker; it has become about the listener, and the whole point of interpersonal communication is immediately lost. We naturally defend ourselves when we feel attacked in the form of criticism, fault-finding, and blame because these make us feel invalidated. Consequently, we are prone to interrupt and argue, thus destroying an opportunity for intimacy.

- Speaker: Pause and allow the listener to give feedback.
- Listener: Paraphrase in your own words what you heard the speaker say; respectfully ask clarifying questions in order to understand.

If the speaker gets wound up and carried away, it will be helpful if the listener will politely ask them to try to speak in bite-sized chunks so they can adequately digest their message. Here, the listener should briefly repeat back what you heard the speaker say using your own words. Don't merely parrot back the words they *said* to you, try to truly understand what your mate is *meaning.*

This is a fabulous opportunity to display genuineness, respect, and love in your marriage system. When you are unguarded and vulnerable, you can be open and receptive to what your mate wants to share with you. But if you robotically prac-

157

tice these communication principles with technical precision without displaying love, you can end up being, "... only a resounding gong or a clanging cymbal" (1 Corinthians 13:1). If you are defensive, guarded, and self-protective, it's very difficult to come across as warm and real. Try to hear them the way you want to be heard.

It is often helpful to politely ask clarifying questions in order to more fully understand what was said. Remember that these requests for explanation are used only in an effort to understand more fully what you heard. Make every effort to be kind, considerate, and sensitive in these efforts to understand your mate's heart (Romans 12:18, 14:19, Hebrews 12:14).

> **The key for the listener here is to attempt to empathize with your partner.**

The key for the listener here is to attempt to empathize with your partner. Try to identify if there is any way you can relate emotionally to their experience. While keeping it fully about them, is there any way in which you can walk a mile in their moccasins, so to speak? The Parrotts report, "Research has shown that 90% of our struggles in marriage would be resolved if we did nothing more than see that problem from our partner's perspective. Empathy is the heart loving" (2005, p. 123).

The deepest way to connect with your spouse and make them feel cared about is to identify with their thoughts and feelings as if they were your own. This is because, "True communication does not occur until each person understands the *feelings* that underlie the spoken words. People generally feel more understood, cared for, and connected when the communication focuses on their emotions and feelings rather than merely on their words or thoughts" (Smalley, 2004, p. 133).

- Speaker: Clarify and if necessary amplify your message; gently restate and politely reword your meaning.
- Listener: Don't rebut or argue; patiently summarize what you understand the speaker to have said. Don't try to apologize, problem-solve, or change the subject. Ask if they feel understood.

> **Perhaps the hardest part of being a good listener is endeavoring to keep the message exclusively about the speaker.**

This final stage in the process is important in order to refine the message heard and received. Perhaps the hardest part of being a good listener is endeavoring to keep the message exclusively about the speaker. Remember, it's about *them,* and it's *their* issue. Do not offer your opinion or thoughts; do not try to fix it or apologize at this point. If you are personally upset about what they are saying, monitor your own feelings, and deal with them later. Your only job is to pay close attention to what your partner is saying, in order to make them feel understood and validated.

Finally, the listener asks if there is anything else the speaker wants to share regarding the issue they just discussed. It is important that the speaker does not go on to discuss other matters but stays with the specific subject at hand. Remember, the goal is to facilitate closeness and understanding.

At this point, you can switch roles. The person who was the speaker gives the "floor" (literally) to the listener. This transition is best facilitated by saying something like, "Thank you for listening so intently; I really appreciate it. Why don't you share your thoughts and feelings, and I will listen to you?" Now the former listener has an opportunity to share their soul with their spouse about the same topic or any other they may choose.

Conversational Prayer

Much misunderstanding and even confusion exists about prayer. Many have made prayer into a mystical, religious, and/or super-spiritualized ritual. Yet, accurately understood, prayer is simply talking with God. When we talk to God *in front of* our spouse, it can be potentially threatening, scary, or embarrassing. Maybe these are the reasons why research reveals that very few Christian couples actually pray together on any regular or systematic basis.

> **Research reveals that very few Christian couples actually pray together on any regular or systematic basis.**

But when we talk to God *with* our spouse, it can be a revolutionarily intimate, deeply meaningful, and wonderfully enlightening experience. What makes the difference?

Years ago, Linda and I learned of a very simple yet very profound little process called "Conversational Prayer." The "nuts and bolts" of this idea are very practical: both people just have a conversation with God and each other at the same time.

Basically, it involves both partners taking turns talking with God about one subject or issue at a time, pausing, and giving their spouse an opportunity to reflect on and discuss the same topic before moving on to talk about something else. For example, one spouse may pray about Grandpa Elmo's lumbago, and then give their mate an opportunity to reinforce that same prayer, petition, or praise. Next, the second person may introduce a topic, then pause and give their spouse an opportunity to discuss the same topic from their heart and perspective. And so on.

When Linda and I do this, two amazing things tend to take place. First, I learn a lot more about her heart, concerns, and perspective on the things that really matter to her than I do in any other way. But more surprisingly, I also learn a lot about her husband when I hear her perspective about me and concern for me, as I see myself through her eyes. God can really speak to and through each of us in this easy, nonthreatening, and informal process—therefore I recommend it highly, both spiritually and relationally.

Connected communication is defined as *having each spouse express his or her own thoughts, feelings, and desires in a way that the other hears, values, and understands.* It is a powerful and profound way in which we can truly share our souls. But this does not occur naturally or automatically because, "Communication is an art, and like any art form it requires disciplined practice. Initially, the practice may be tedious and unfulfilling. Many people drop out or look for shortcuts, but those who stick with it are rewarded with deep and fulfilling relationships. Like a musician who has mastered his instrument, they are free to make beautiful music—and communication is the music of marriage" (Richard Exley, 2008, p. 84).

Scriptural Search

1. Psalm 19:14
2. Matthew 12:34
3. Ephesians 4:29-5:2
4. James 1:19-20
5. James 3:1-12

Ponderable Points

1. What are the skills necessary in order to effectively send a message? Describe and discuss these.

2. What are the skills necessary in order to effectively listen to a message? Describe and discuss these. What are some of the things which make it so difficult?

3. Think of a word picture someone used that was powerful to you. What made it memorable?

4. What are some things that make you feel defensive? How do your reactions impair effective communication? What can you do differently in order to listen more effectively?

5. How do you feel inside when you are deeply heard? What is it like for you to hear your spouse at a deeply intimate level?

Activation Activities

1. List some things you can do in order to improve your listening skills. Share them with your spouse. Ask for their honest—and loving—feedback.

2. Think of the last time the communication process did not succeed with your mate. What did you not do effectively? Ask for the Holy Spirit's gentle enlightenment to help you see the situation differently.

3. What is something that your spouse does not feel understood about? Consider dedicating yourself to more clearly and deeply understanding and empathizing with them. Practice and apply the principles of *"Soul Sharing"* with them.

Recommended Resources

Love Talk, Les and Leslie Parrott (2004).

Communication: Key to Your Marriage, H. Norman Wright (2000).

More than Marriage!: Ten Keys to Intimacy for a lasting Marriage, David and Teresa Ferguson (2000).

Men are Like Waffles, Women are Like Spaghetti, Bill and Pam Farrel (2001).

Creating an Intimate Marriage, Jim Burns (2006).

CHAPTER SEVEN

Fighting Fair

Be careful when criticizing your mate's faults, because those same deficiencies more than likely prevented them from getting a better spouse!

"If you keep on biting and devouring each other, watch out or you will be destroyed by each other."

—COLOSSIANS 4:6

onflict in marriage is inevitable and unavoidable. There is simply no way on earth that any two people will ever see eye-to-eye about everything (and if you disagree with me about this, that would prove my point!). Show me a married couple who says they never have a disagreement, and I will show you a couple who probably lies about other things too, or perhaps even worse, has such a superficial relationship that they never get close enough to experience friction. All couples experience conflict—but not all couples survive it.

Actually, conflict per se is not really the problem in marriage. As Drs. Cloud and Townsend point out, "...most of the time, conflict is not the problem. The issue is the way that couples disagree and argue" (2005, p. 167). According to the research, it is the ways in which couples perceive and process their differences that will make or break their relationship.

Emerson Eggerichs, author of *Love and Respect,* says, "The difference between successful couples and unsuccessful couples is that the successful ones keep getting up and keep dealing with the issues. Unsuccessful couples want it easy. They want it now. They want their needs to be met. They don't want conflict; they just want everything to be 'happy.' This approach is the epitome of immaturity" (2004, p. 277). As we will later discover, attempting to avoid conflict actually accentuates and amplifies it.

> **Good conflict actually enhances a good love life and can lead to passion and romance.**

So it is not the absence of conflict which makes for a good marriage; it is the presence of constructive conflict resolution. All couples will argue about their differences from time to time. Not only is that okay, the truth is that good conflict actually enhances a good love life and can lead to passion and romance. This is because, "Married couples who learn to work through conflict tend to be closer, more trusting, more intimate, and enjoy a much deeper connection afterwards" (Kendrick and Kendrick, 2008, p. 62). Kissing and making up can be sublime!

After all, we do not get mad at or upset with someone we don't care about. In a healthy marriage, fighting is a significant part of the ongoing dance which defines, connects, distances, and reconnects two separate, distinct, autonomous individuals. Conflict *per se* is not the problem; what matters is how the conflict affects the relationship and how the couple handles the dispute. *It is the way in which the couple fights that in large part determines the health of their relationship.* In this chapter we will examine some of the details, descriptions, and dynamics of effective conflict resolution within marriage.

The fundamental question we need to ask ourselves is, "Are we *compatible* or are we *combatable*?" If your duet has deteriorated into a dual, your marriage might be in trouble. If your relationship has become vindictive, victimizing, and vicious instead of vitalizing, vibrant, and vigorous, then your relationship has definitely become definitively dysfunctional.

> **If your duet has deteriorated into a dual, your marriage might be in trouble.**

Causes of Conflict

James tackles this issue head-on when he asks rhetorically, "What causes fights and quarrels among you? Don't they come from your desires that battle within you? You want something but don't get it. You kill and covet, but you cannot have what you want. You quarrel and fight. You do not have because you do not ask God" (James 4:1-2). The Greek word translated here "desires" comes from the same root word from which we derive the word "hedonism." Connect the dots and fill in the blanks yourself on this one. We are all selfish, arrogant, fallen sinners. We want what we want when we want it because we want it. And it kills us, in lots of different ways.

> **"Would you rather be right, or be loved?"**

Early on in my ministry, I was working with an exceptionally contentious couple that seemed to fight all the time. Nothing I did therapeutically appeared to have a positive impact on them. In desperation, I took this case to my supervisor and expressed to him my astonishment at their depth and degree of chronic, systemic dysfunction. After listening to my description of their hopeless power struggle, he wisely suggested: "Jared, why don't you ask this man, 'Would you rather be right, or be loved?'"

The next session, I did indeed ask the gentleman my supervisor's question. After thoughtful reflection for a moment, he replied, "I'm thinking, I'm thinking!" Just kidding—it did lead the couple to an insightful breakthrough about the universal internal contradiction most of us humans struggle with in relationship: we want to both be right, and be loved. This couple ultimately decided they wanted to be loved more than to just be right.

Specifically applied to marriage then, we must ask ourselves what makes so it difficult to, "Enjoy life with your wife [husband], whom you love..." (Ecclesiastes 9:9). Dr. Tim and Julie Clinton (2000) identify six specific culprits which can cause confusion, contention, chaos, and conflict:

1. Stress (hurried, hyper, hassled, hectic lifestyles),

2. Evil (attacks from the adversary who desperately desires our destruction, 1 Peter 5:8),

3. False expectations (e.g. "marriage will complete me," "my spouse won't ever hurt me," "we will live happily ever after," and "love will keep us together," etc.),

4. Selfishness (the dating and courtship "tropical island of we" becomes the marital "deserted island of me"),

5. Old scripts and painful experiences from our past (which we unconsciously transfer and project onto our spouse; i.e., they reap everything which everyone else sowed into our life before they showed up), and

6. Our unwillingness to invest the time necessary to nurture our mate and our marriage (we live in a microwave-oriented culture which is addicted to shortcuts and speed).

I humbly suggest the above "culprits" would make a healthy and helpful prayer guide for you to use for yourself and your marriage partner, as you insightfully intercede for your relationship.

Identify which of these are particularly challenging for you and/or your spouse, and dedicate yourself to be a help-mate instead of a hurt-mate with respect to these issues. You'll be glad you did, and you'll wonder what took you so long to become part of the solution instead of part of the problem!

Confronting Conflict

Many people naturally want to avoid conflict. They try to ignore it, look the other way, deny it, shrug it off, suppress it, or sweep it under the rug. But that doesn't mean it goes away—it just means that you can eventually sprain your ankle from all the lumps under the carpet!

It is completely understandable that people don't necessarily want to deal with conflict. They want to be perceived as nice, especially if they're Christians. They do not want to be seen as being a quarrelsome, argumentative rabble-rouser. Why upset the apple cart? Or they might just be more laid back and easy going by nature than others.

Burying conflict never makes it go away.

But burying conflict never makes it go away. Not only does that build resentment and walls of protection, it drains you of energy and robs the relationship of vibrancy and vitality. When conflicts are buried, they are buried alive and will eventually resurrect themselves, typically with a vengeance.

Think of it this way. The further you push a beach ball under the surface of the water, the more latent power you give it. When you finally do let go, it bursts to the surface with explosive energy. That's how unresolved conflict works in a marriage system. The more issues we suppress and the farther we push them down, the greater the likelihood that we will experience violent volcanic eruptions at some point in the future.

Nonetheless, many couples would rather sidestep disagreements in a conflict-avoidant marriage. When they find themselves on opposite sides regarding a certain issue, they're likely to just "let it go." Instead of arguing or becoming upset, they just agree to disagree. Conflict-avoidant couples can get by for years by simply ignoring or minimizing their differences. These couples can be stable and content in their basic shared philosophy of marriage. They accentuate the positive and accept the rest. Although they resolve very little, they decide to live and let live in order to keep feeling good about each other. They may even be proud of the fact that they never fight like other couples.

But there are many inherent dangers, which lurk below the façade of this kind of superficial, emotionally distant relationship. To begin with, these partners don't get to know each other as well as couples do who are more open to exploring their individual differences. They're more apt to keep quiet about their dissatisfactions and not voice their unmet needs. Many develop a secret or fantasy life, which they do not share with their spouse. In short, the spouses live parallel lives as strangers. One of the laws of physics is that parallel lines never intersect, but when a couple does cross each other, there is the potential for interaction and growth.

The hazards of a conflict-avoiding marriage are most dramatically evident when couples face crises in life.

The hazards of a conflict-avoiding marriage are most dramatically evident when couples face crises in life, such as serious financial problems, job loss, chronic illness, disability, and/or death in the family. Because they have rarely bent, they often break apart under the pressure and stress. Lacking the resilience which comes by being strengthened from years of exercising flexibility, many marriages of this type collapse and crumble under the weight of such a crisis.

Because these couples have not practiced communicating their feelings of helplessness, grief, sadness, or anger, they lack the experiential know-how to find the friendship, comfort, and solace they need to cope with the crisis. Consequently, they become more emotionally alienated and distant from each other. Lacking intimacy, they live out parallel lives, sharing the same physical space, but not interacting in meaningful ways. Feeling terribly lonely in such dark and difficult times, many are tempted to turn to extramarital relationships for companionship and support.

The Bible says, "As iron sharpens iron, so one man sharpens another" (Proverbs 27:17). I am a member of Frontiersmen Camping Fellowship (FCF), a service auxiliary of Royal Rangers for high achieving older boys and for commanders. It is a pre-1840s historically-themed reenactment guild, celebrating the pioneering spirit of the American frontiersman. We dress in mountain man outfits with furs and buckskins, start our campfire with a flint and steel, and enjoy knife and tomahawk throwing, trap setting, and primitive longbow and black powder rifle shooting competitions. It's a blast (literally).

At the upper levels of advancement in FCF, you are required to develop period authentic skills in a craft or trade of your selection. My friend, Bob Triphahn, is a master blacksmith who expertly makes all kinds of tools, cookware, and primitive implements out of iron by hand. Let me tell you, the way that iron sharpens iron entails some of the most difficult and exhausting work there is. Suffice it to say that a lot of intense heat, relentless pounding, acrid smoke, and flying sparks are involved in the process of forging a useful tool or award-winning implement. It takes a lot of mettle to fashion metal into something that will win a medal (sorry, couldn't resist)!

Marriages which are forged in the fiery trials of life—in which differences have been hammered out on the anvils of conflict— are tempered and steeled, strong and serviceable, to be mightily used in God's Kingdom. Such marriages are stable, resilient, and enduring. Much like a finely crafted iron tool, if properly cared for, it can bless and benefit many for generations to come. Strong and healthy marriages are in large part shaped by the ways in which spouses have perceived and processed conflict.

When couples experience conflict, there are six potential ways to manage it, as can be seen from the following table:

ACTION	YOU	I	WE
We both ignore the problem.	Lose	Lose	Lose
I defer; I give in.	Win	Lose	Lose
You defer; you give in.	Lose	Win	Lose
You demand; you insist on your way.	Win	Lose	Lose
I demand; I insist on my way.	Lose	Win	Lose

We both hon-estly face our problem.	Win	Win	Win

Everyone loses in a power struggle.

A couple of things clearly emerge from this simple illustration. First of all, the only thing that matters is the all-important right-hand column. A marriage is a team, and if either member loses, then they obviously both lose. A mixed doubles tennis player can't win a match while their partner loses. Everyone loses in a power struggle.

Second, the only lose-lose-lose outcome on the whole chart is when we refuse to face our issues. When we normalize our arguments, it will take the fear and power out of them. Couples who become anxious and avoidant about fighting will either have their conflicts go unresolved or will have volatile blowups when they do argue. Facing the truth of our reality is always liberating.

Caustic Conflict

Drs. John and Julie Schwartz Gottman are renowned for their groundbreaking research into the causes of divorce. Their studies revealed that certain kinds of negative interactions are so lethal to a marital relationship that if left unchecked, they will send couples into a downward spiral ending in divorce. The Gottmans identified these destructive methods of dealing with conflict as "the Four Horsemen of the Apocalypse" (1999, 2006). They are as follows:

Criticism

You will always have some complaints about your marriage partner, but there is a world of difference between a complaint and a criticism. A complaint only addresses the specific area in which your spouse failed or with which you were displeased. A criticism is a global attack on your partner's personality or character. Criticism frequently begins with "you always" or "you never," or even worse, with "what's wrong with you?"

Defensiveness

Defensiveness is the reactive counterattack people use to try to maintain their innocence or avoid taking responsibility for a problem or issue. It involves self-justification, excuses, and rationalization and can often take the form of counter-complaining or whining. Defensiveness typically escalates the conflict because it is a subtle form of blaming your partner for the problem; in effect, it says, "the problem isn't *me*, it's *you*."

Contempt

Contempt is criticism bolstered by hostility or disgust. It often involves sarcasm, mocking, shaming, name-calling, sneering, blaming, nagging, and belligerence. Laden with disrespect and dishonor, contempt is completely anti-relational and typically escalates and exacerbates existing conflict. Just imagine how thoroughly demeaning it is to have someone roll their eyes and sigh when you're trying to be open and vulnerable.

Stonewalling

Finally, the negativity created by these first three "horsemen" results in a calloused insensitivity to further injury. Reeling from ongoing barrages of criticism, exhausted by perpetually feeling defensive, and deeply wounded by repetitive experiences of contempt, the person disengages and turns away. Rather than fight, this person resigns emotionally from the relationship, and attempts at conversation with them are consequently like "talking to a stone wall."

Happily married couples exhibit two surprisingly simple

behaviors: they treat each other like good friends, and
they handle their conflicts in gentle, positive ways.

From their over 60 years of combined experience and clinical
research, the Gottmans discovered that happily married couples exhibit two surprisingly simple behaviors: they treat each
other like good friends, and they handle their conflicts in gentle,
positive ways. "The basis for coping effectively with either solv-
able or perpetual conflicts is the same: communicating basic
acceptance of your partner's personality... If either or both of
you feels judged, misunderstood, or rejected by the other, you
will not be able to manage the problems in your marriage"
(1999, p. 149).

From decades of research conducted by many different marriage experts, and through their own extensive study and analysis of marital conflict, Drs. Howard Markman, Scott Stanley, and
Susan Blumberg (2001) found that there are also four general
ways couples commonly destroy their relationships. Likewise,
they found that the presence of these four toxic dynamics is
completely corrosive to couples' closeness and companionship:

Escalation

Escalation is the snowball effect in which each person reacts
with increasing anger and hostility as the argument continues.
Back-and-forth negativity spirals into increasing emotional intensity and erupts into a full-blown, nasty confrontation. As the
fight ramps up and out of control, couples go from wanting to be
heard by the other to wanting to hurt the other. It is here that
mean-spirited reckless remarks hit below the belt.

Invalidation

This happens when one partner subtly or directly puts down
the thoughts, feelings, actions, or words of their mate. Invalidation is different from simply disagreeing with your spouse or dis-

liking something he or she is doing. It is a painful put-down that includes an element of belittling or disregarding what is important to your partner. Invalidation is not only insensitive and destructive; it is an outright assassination of one's character and personhood.

Negative Interpretations

These occur when one spouse consistently believes that the motives of the other are more negative than they really are. It is a judgment that results in the other person feeling guilty until proven innocent. This is a defensive stance in which the other person unconsciously attempts to protect themselves by means of quitting before they get fired, and/or bracing themselves for the worst possible outcome.

Withdrawal and Avoidance

When a spouse feels helpless and hopeless about working through a conflict, they often feel like taking their ball and going home. They pull away for self-protection and shut down emotionally. This may be as obvious as simply getting up and leaving the room or simply nodding to placate their spouse's emotional outrage. According to the research, men are much more likely than women to withdraw from relational conflict. Conflict-avoidant men are also found to be at the highest risk for affairs.

As you can plainly discern from this brief summary of these two bodies of research, in describing how couples mismanage conflict, both are saying essentially the same things; they just use different labels. It seems that if we are to help couples avoid these potential pitfalls and problems, we need to help them learn healthier ways to address and deal with their differences. In a healthy marriage, couples can disagree with dignity, dialogue with diplomacy, and differ with decorum.

> In a healthy marriage, couples can disagree with dignity, dialogue with diplomacy, and differ with decorum.

A family friendly Formula for Fair Fighting

The most important task in helping couples deal effectively with conflict is challenging each partner to take personal responsibility for their part of the dispute. Pure and simple, it takes two to fight.

No matter how upsetting or irritating your marriage partner may be, they are still *your* marriage partner. (You chose them, remember? And hopefully there were no loaded firearms present at the ceremony!) How you choose to respond to them is always and only *your* responsibility. What is profoundly powerful is that when either spouse assumes appropriate responsibility for their involvement in the argument—regardless of whether or not their mate does—the conflict will quickly be de-escalated and defused. We can no more blame others for our actions then we can blame the mirror for our appearance!

This principle is reminiscent of the call to personal maturity found in Chapter 2, regarding each spouse making a free and unconditional covenantal commitment before God to their marriage. In that same spirit, I want to propose that you individually consider a challenge to abide by the following 10 biblically-based guidelines for addressing conflict, whether your spouse does or not.

1. I promise to listen first before speaking. "He who answers before listening—that is his folly and his shame" (Proverbs 18:13).

2. I promise to speak quietly, calmly, and gently. "A gentle answer turns away wrath, but a harsh word stirs up anger" (Proverbs 15:1).

3. I promise to ask the Holy Spirit to help me deal with my own issues first. "Why do you look at the speck of sawdust in your brother's eye and pay no attention to the plank in your own eye?" (Matthew 7:3).

4. I promise to never mention divorce. "I hate divorce says the LORD God of Israel..." Malachi 2:16).

5. I promise to not be verbally destructive. "Do not let any unwholesome talk proceed out of your mouths, but only what is helpful for building others up according to their needs, that it may benefit those who listen" (Ephesians 4:29).

6. I promise to not be emotionally destructive. "Finally, all of you, live in harmony with one another; be sympathetic, love as brothers, be compassionate and humble. Do not repay evil with evil or insult with insult, but with blessing, because to this you were called so that you may inherit a blessing" (1 Peter 3:8-9).

7. I promise to not be physically destructive. "... 'Love your neighbor as yourself.' Love does no harm to its neighbor..." (Romans 13:9-10).

8. I promise to not go to bed angry and allow conflict to go unaddressed. "In your anger do not sin: do not let the sun go down while you are still angry, and do not give the devil a foothold" (Ephesians 4:26-27).

9. I promise to apologize and accept responsibility when I am wrong. "Therefore confess your sins to each other and pray for each other so that you may be healed…" (James 5:16).

10. I promise to freely and fully forgive. "Bear with each other and forgive whatever grievances you may have against one another. Forgive as the Lord forgave you." (Colossians 3:13).

Of all these commitments, I believe the last is farthest from the least. Forgiveness is not only required for eternal life (see Matthew 6:14-15), it is essential for healthy and harmonious marital life. Bonhoeffer wisely advises:

> In a word, live together in the forgiveness of your sins, for without it no human fellowship, least of all marriage, can survive. Don't insist on your rights, don't blame each other, don't judge or condemn each other, don't find fault with each other, but accept each other as you are, and forgive each other every day from the bottom of your hearts… (1997, p. 31).

Full and free forgiveness and forbearance are absolutely necessary and completely non-negotiable.

It has been said that love is not a fight, but that it is worth fighting for. Fighting *for* your marriage means that you build a bridge instead of burning one down. It means that you are spiritually proactive instead of emotionally reactive. It means that you are willingly submissive instead of willfully stubborn. And it means that you are your spouse's advocate instead of their adversary.

> **Fighting *for* your marriage means that you build a bridge instead of burning one down.**

"But," you may ask, "what about those things that my spouse does/doesn't do that really irritate me?" Or, "What about those things they do/don't do which really get on my nerves?" And, "It's just not fair for them to do/not do this!"

Glad you asked. My question to you would be, "Do you have enough faith to believe that those things about your mate which really irritate you and rub you the wrong way are being used by God as 'divine sandpaper?' Do you have enough faith to believe that the Lord is using those irritants to smooth off your rough edges, so that when He looks closely into you, He sees Himself more clearly reflected?"

I can hear some of you saying at this point, "Yeah, I know, I know. But why does He have to use such rough 80 grit sandpaper instead of something smoother like 300 grit?" Ouch.

Speaking of irritants, consider a single speck of sand. If a tiny piece of silica inadvertently gets into a human eye, it can cause irritation, then infection, and if not properly cared for, eventually loss of vision. But if that same little speck of sand were placed inside an oyster, the resulting irritation would activate a unique secretion, which would ultimately create a pearl.

Did the speck of sand cause the blindness? Did the speck of sand cause the pearl? In both cases the answer is no, but even if it were yes, the results would be the same. The sand was merely an agent, which revealed the inner properties of the eye and of the oyster. The response of each is what made the difference. In the same way, when that doggone person who uses your spouse's toothbrush causes you irritation (notice I didn't say "if"), it's up to you to determine whether it becomes an infection which hinders your ability to see clearly, or a treasure of great price, worth, and beauty.

A Creative Course to Cope with Combative and Contrary Couples' Clashes, Collisions, and Combustible Commotion Concerning their Contentious and Controlling Conflict

The deepest, most heartbreaking damage you're ever likely to do to your marriage will occur during the hot and horrible heat of conflict. *That's because this is likely when you are the most proud and the least humble, the most selfish and the least loving, and the most judgmental and the least gracious.* Your anger is at its most intense, your decision-making is at its most irrational, and your words are at their most venomous.

Astoundingly, neurological research has verified that when we are angry, our brain chemistry dramatically changes to the extent that we temporarily lose between 15 and 30 IQ points! When we are upset and tempted to give our spouse a piece of our mind, there is actually less of it to spare than normally. Work "smart." We need all the brains we can get to be married well.

> **Words matter. God called the cosmos out of chaos with a Word.**

As we saw in the last chapter, words matter. Scripture teaches that, "The tongue has the power of life and death, and those who love it will eat its fruit" (Proverbs 18:21). God called the cosmos out of chaos with a Word. Similarly, Drs. Allender and Longman (1995, p. 92) tell us that, "Marriage partners either call order and beauty out of chaos or intensify the chaos" in their relationship by the ways in which they communicate and contend with each other. The same authors conclude, "How we talk to each other reflects the quality of our relationship as well as the depth of our character" (ibid., p. 99). So what will it be—divine order and heavenly beauty or carnal chaos?

181

For those of you who are determined to make a magnificent marriage, I trust it will be the former. In the previous chapter, we explored the communicative principles of how to share our souls with each other, and in this chapter we have examined how each individual in a marriage system can choose to fight fairly. Before we turn to how each of you as a couple can constructively resolve conflict, I want to make three fundamental assumptions regarding conflict in general:

Conflict is Normal: it is a natural, inevitable reality in the fallen world.

Due to our human limitations and our predisposition to sin, it is impossible for us to always relate with others in perfect peace and harmony. We should not feel ashamed, guilty, or embarrassed for experiencing conflict; rather, the existence of conflict is proof positive that we are alive and kicking (but hopefully not each other)! Conflicts can also be symptoms of underlying problems. Many times the problem is not the real problem—things may not be as they appear on the surface.

Conflict is Nightmarish: it is scary and often mismanaged in painful, abusive, and/or destructive ways.

In some respects, conflict is very much like fire. Fire is neither intrinsically good nor bad; it is simply raw energy. Cultural anthropologists tell us that without the discovery of fire, civilization itself could not have been developed. However, the same fire that can warm us can also burn us when it's out of control. Likewise, the raw energy of conflict can deeply heal us or severely harm us, depending on how it is managed and directed.

Conflict is Necessary: it is a divinely ordained, necessary means of producing growth and intimacy.

It has been said that Jesus came to comfort the disturbed and to disturb the comfortable. When you think about His ministry, He did each of these about half of the time. Everywhere Jesus went, He was either resolving or creating conflict. As the Prince of peace, He once said He came not to bring peace but a sword (Matthew 10:34-38). In addition, when you consider the Creator's universe, nothing in it grows by any means other than conflict—from the single cell which must divide itself in order to reproduce, on up. Unresolved conflict interferes with God-ordained growth and transformation.

What follows are the most powerful relationship tools I have ever discovered. But before we discuss them, I want to issue a caution and a couple of instructions. Just as knives and scalpels are sharp metal objects, these tools are "sharp" principles. Whether a blade harms or heals depends upon one's training and motive, and likewise, whether these relationship tools harm or heal also depends upon one's motives.

First, assuming your motives are for healing, please do not feel guilty, intimidated, or inadequate as you read through these rules for engagement and are confronted with how you do not always succeed in adhering to them. Although they are eminently practical, they are also theoretically idealistic. There is only one guy in the entire history of the universe who was capable of fully living up to these all day every day, and keep in mind that He chose to remain single!

Second, please resist the temptation to either sweetly or sarcastically point out to your mate in which of the following areas they could stand some basic improvement. (I realize many of you are just trying to be a blessing to your dear, sweet, darling, precious, beloved honey, but recall the joke at the very beginning of the chapter!) As you quiet yourself and let the Holy Spirit encourage and empower your spouse, perhaps you will then be able to more clearly hear His still, small voice speak to you about where *you* need to change and grow. After reading through the following relationship principles, select two or three of them which are most difficult for you to regularly apply with your mate. Then sit down together and discuss them, using the principles of "Soul Sharing" outlined in Chapter 6.

Coping with Conflict

1. If possible, prepare the setting and plan for constructive confrontation.

Avoid distractions and interruptions, having non-private discussions, being overly tired and stressed, or being emotionally reactive (Proverbs 16:1-3).

2. Take responsibility and initiative to address the issue directly.

Avoid running from the problem, using the "silent treatment," waiting for the other person to make the first move, or allowing problems to accumulate (Matthew 5:23-24).

3. Attack the problem—not the person—and propose viable options or solutions.

Avoid judging and criticizing the other person (and/or their personality, appearance, family of origin, etc.), name-calling, power messages or manipulative actions, or attempting to change or "fix" them (Proverbs 15:1-2).

4. Stay on the subject and focus specifically and concretely on the facts, actions, feelings, and events.

Avoid sweeping generalizations, using the "kitchen sink" attack, bringing up the past, making comparisons to others, or bringing in irrelevant issues (Proverbs 17:14).

5. Take responsibility for your part of the conflict, and be willing to humbly admit when you're wrong.

Avoid being proud, stubborn, and arrogant by immaturely blaming the other person for your feelings or actions; avoid denying your own humanness and blind spots (Philippians 2:3-5).

6. Learn and practice effective communication and active   listening skills, including the use of self-disclosing "I" language.

Avoid making accusatory "you" statements, using exaggerations and extreme language (e.g., "never," "always," "all," "everyone," etc.), or interrupting the other person (Ephesians 4:29).

7. State your needs, wants, hurts, disappointments, and feelings clearly.

Avoid pouting, nagging, complaining, denial, putting words in the other person's mouth, or assuming that the other person can (and does) read your mind (Matthew 12:34-37).

8. Be honest, respectful, honoring, and courteous.

Avoid lying (to protect yourself or someone else), name-calling, sarcasm, or belittling and/or degrading the other person; avoid being abusive, intimidating, forceful, or violent (Proverbs 15:4).

9. Learn to respect, appreciate, and understand each other's needs, feelings, interests, and differences.

Avoid needing to think or feel the same way; avoid denying one another's differences in tastes, upbringing, viewpoints, customs, and coping mechanisms (Romans 14:19-15:4).

10. Be willing to forgive (functionally defined as "giving up our right to hurt back") an offense in order to cultivate

the growth, healing, and well-being of the other person and the relationship.

Avoid becoming resentful, bitter, punitive, alienated, or controlled by vengeful fantasies and actions (Ephesians 4:31-5:2).

11. Strive for mutual understanding, a "win-win" outcome, and the development of an "us-we-ours" view of the situation.

Avoid trying to change the other person, endeavoring to get your way and/or get your point across in order to "win," or maintaining a self-centered "me-my-mine" attitude (Romans 15:7).

12. Agree to disagree, arrange to discuss an unresolved issue later, and/or agree to get outside help from an unbiased, neutral, objective mediator/therapist/arbitrator.

Avoid letting conflict go unresolved, withdrawing, or pulling in biased family members or friends for your support; when arguments escalate too intensely, suggest calling a brief time-out to allow flaring tempers to subside (Proverbs 15:22).

Nothing can impact and affect your marriage as significantly as how well you resolve conflict with each other. Conflict can absolutely make or break a marriage system. In healthy marriages, conflict is accepted, welcomed, and utilized to invite growth and potential healing into the relationship. It is no longer feared as being destructive, but is celebrated as being constructive. Although perhaps never comfortable, conflict can be God's way to help us hear each other more clearly, understand each other more deeply, and come to know each other more intimately.

Scriptural Search

1. Proverbs 15:16-18
2. Proverbs 20:3
3. Proverbs 27:15-16
4. Colossians 3:12-15
5. James 4:1-3

Ponderable Points

1. What is your general attitude toward conflict? Are you afraid of conflict? Do you avoid it?

2. What is the concept or style of conflict you were taught while growing up? Do you now agree with that? Why or why not? What can you learn about what your spouse was taught regarding conflict while growing up?

3. How do you typically experience and express anger? How does your spouse?

4. Try to identify areas in which your relationship has typically had power struggles over the years. Do you notice any similar themes, patterns, or areas of conflict?

5. Try to identify any triggers or sore spots within you which usually start or escalate conflicts with your mate. Consider discussing these with your spouse in order to help you get to know one another more deeply. Ask them if they can give you feedback, ideas, or suggestions on how to approach these issues differently in order to prevent future destructive conflict.

Activation Activities

1. Both you and your spouse compile lists of issues on which you typically experience conflict (don't be surprised if your lists are different!). Then compare your lists and discuss the reasons why you have conflict in these areas. Try to learn more of how different you are from one another.

2. Be willing to prayerfully and humbly ask God to show you what you can do differently and what you need to change regarding your relationship conflicts and conflict patterns. Try to understand what and how you contribute to the issue. Ask God what He wants you to learn about both yourself and your mate through this conflict and how you can become progressively more Christ-like as a result.

3. Using the techniques described in the previous chapter, consider asking your spouse to do "Soul Sharing" with you regarding the conflict issues you are experiencing. Remember to keep in mind the goals of achieving a fuller understanding of your partner's uniqueness, achieving deeper intimacy, and developing greater closeness with one another.

Recommended Resources

Fighting for Your Marriage, Howard Markman, Scott Stanley, and Susan Blumberg (2001).

Fight Your Way to a Better Marriage: How Healthy Conflict Can Take You to Deeper Levels of Intimacy, Greg Smalley (2013).

Intimate Allies, Dan Allender and Tremper Longman III (1995).

Love Busters, Willard Harley (2002).

The Good Fight: How Conflict Can Bring You Closer, Les and Leslie Parrott (2013).

CHAPTER EIGHT

Routine Respon-sibilities

It has been said that a marriage license is just another term for a work permit!

"Whatever your hand finds to do, do it with all your might..."

—ECCLESIASTES 9:10

egardless of how wonderful and romantic your marriage is, at the end of the week someone has to take out the trash. No one can live indefinitely atop the lofty peaks and majestic pinnacles of matrimonial bliss. At some point, most of us have to get up and go to work. It is then that we are confronted with the realities, responsibilities, routines, ruts, and rigors of life together.

Menial chores are not very glamorous or romantic, but dishes must be washed, laundry must be done, floors must be swept, and toilets must be cleaned. The problem with these and other chores is quite simple: they are *chores*! No one in their right mind likes to do chores. Chores are work. Besides, who wants to come home from work, *and do more work*?

The diplomatic division of domestic duties is perhaps one of the most prevalent and persistent source of power struggles, hurts, and conflicts in the average marriage. We all know intuitively that marriage should be a partnership of equals, but often that is not the case. Frequently, one or both partners feel unfairly treated because they are left with what seems to them to be a disproportionate amount of the work, or most of the dirty jobs. Tension mounts, needs go unmet, expectations are unfulfilled, and resentment builds.

Why is who does the housework such a loaded issue?

You may wonder, "Why is who does the housework such a loaded issue?" *Because it is an issue of power.* "Who cleans the toilet can become a teeth-grinding microcosm of the power struggle going on throughout your relationship" (Louden, 1994, p. 105). And as we discovered in the last chapter, no one ever wins a power struggle.

Unless and until these issues are addressed openly and in a mutually satisfying manner, couples are likely to continue to struggle with their relationship on an ongoing basis. These issues are much more complex and far-reaching than the average engaged or newlywed couple may possibly foresee. And if not dealt with to both spouses' satisfaction, the relationship inevitably suffers.

Doing daily domestic duties involves the practical administration of your life together and how you manage the sharing of the responsibilities of your home in a fair and functional manner. Many different issues and dynamics simultaneously contribute to these everyday skirmishes on the home front, which all too often escalate into full-scale battles. Let's look at some of the major factors involved in this almost universal marital problem, and try to figure out healthy ways to call a permanent truce to these civil wars (as well as how to get that garbage taken out!).

Gender Roles

Up until roughly two generations ago, gender roles were typically defined and proscribed along stereotypically sexist lines: most women were nesters and nurturers, and most men functioned as providers and protectors. For thousands of years, these roles and responsibilities were remarkably stable and uniform across the vast majority of cultures. Historically, to compensate for technological innovations and improvements in the ways in which people lived, only minor adjustments were made to these general roles. The division of labor was fairly straightforward: men worked outside the home while women worked inside the home.

In the 1950s and 1960s, a plethora of popular television comedies were created which typified American family life. Perhaps the most iconic example of these, *Leave it to Beaver*, caricaturized the adventures of a stereotypic middle-class Caucasian family, the Cleavers (for you younger folks, Google the show). Ward and June lived happily in a white two-story suburban colonial house, along with their sons Wally and Theodore— curiously but affectionately nicknamed "the Beav"—and their dog. Ward came home late every afternoon from his undefined (but implicitly thought to be important) downtown office job, wearing his impeccable dark suit, starched white shirt and black tie, and carrying his obligatory briefcase.

June was a full-time, stay-at-home mom who always greeted her husband at the door with a beautiful smile, an affectionate kiss, and perfectly coiffed platinum blonde hair, while wearing a lovely dress, heels and hose, and of course, her ubiquitous pearl necklace. The house was always sparkling clean, and fresh-baked warm cookies with cold glasses of milk were always waiting there for the boys and their friends when they came home after school. Wally was the dutiful, somewhat serious, if not boring big brother who always seemed to rescue his carefree, adventurous, yet rather squirrelly younger brother from his frequent and amusing trials and tribulations. The Cleavers constituted the ideal American family.

Well Myrtle, things have changed! Radically changed. Whereas 50 years ago the Cleavers were the overwhelming norm (comprising about 80% of American families), according to the latest United States Census Bureau statistics, that kind of traditional family has become almost extinct. Now less than 7% of American families are composed of an intact first marriage from which all of their children are born, where the man works full-time outside the home and the woman works full-time inside the home. And by the way, I have always been confused by the term "housewife." Who wants to be married to an inanimate object? (Please, ladies—resist that temptation... don't even say, "but you haven't met my husband!")

Whereas some women are wonderfully fulfilled in their role as domestic engineer—and indeed view it as a highly honored calling—many ladies have resented that role and have revolted against the expectation of being chief cook and bottle washer of the home. Not only are more women working outside the home than ever before, they're expecting their husbands to do their fair share (i.e. half) of the housework inside the home. When there is a cultural revolution that redefines and liberates the roles and responsibilities of wives, that can't help but drastically affect husbands. Many contemporary men are confused and insecure about their leadership role in the family.

Consequently, Dr. Judith Balswick observes that, "With most of today's marriage partners holding down two careers, the challenge of establishing ground rules for household chores is often a source of heated conflict" (2001, p. 66). Similarly, Dr. Willard Harley goes on to specify, "With the advent of so many dual career marriages, the division of domestic responsibilities has become a major source of marital conflict. Changes in our cultural values have contributed greatly to the problem, be-cause there is now almost unanimous agreement that both the husband and wife should share these responsibilities, particularly child care. But change in behavior has not kept pace with the changing values" (2001, p. 135). Hence the hassles, harassments, and hurts of hectic, harried households.

According to Harley's research, one of the most important marital needs for a man is to have his wife furnish him with domestic support along with a home filled with peace and quiet. As he explains:

> Men often fantasize about a home life free of stress and worry. After work each day, his wife greets him lovingly at the door and his well-behaved children are also glad to see him [this proves that men have been thoroughly brainwashed, if not spoiled rotten, by June Cleaver's portrayals!]. He enters the comfort of a well-maintained home as his wife urges him to relax before taking part in dinner, the aroma of which he can already smell wafting through the air. Conversation at dinner is joyful and free of conflict. Later the family goes out together for an early evening stroll, and he returns to put the children to bed with no hassle or fuss. Then he and his wife relax and talk together, watch a little television, and go to bed to make love, all at a reasonable hour (2001, p. 134).

Must be nice, huh? Especially if you're a man!

> **One of the most important marital needs for a man is to have his wife furnish him with domestic support along with a home filled with peace and quiet.**

Meanwhile, the reality for many wives in our contemporary society is that they are in essence now expected to work at two full-time jobs: one outside the home and one inside. Obviously, this is completely unfair. While most men seem to grasp how inequitable this discrepancy is on a cognitive level, they have yet to manifest that understanding behaviorally. The indisputable bottom line is this: according to the research, most men aren't helping around the house much more than they did *one hundred years* ago (Harley, 2001)!

> The reality for many wives in our contemporary society is that they are in essence now expected to work at two full-time jobs: one outside the home and one inside. Obviously, this is completely unfair.

Guys... seriously? We must step up to the plate here. Scripture teaches us as men to be servant leaders. God's organizational structure for the family begins, not with the husband, but with Christ: "... the head of every man is Christ, and the head of the woman is man, and the head of Christ is God." (1 Corinthians 11:3). As husbands, we are to love our wives, "... just as Christ loved the church and gave himself up for her..." (Ephesians 5:25). Jesus' love was exemplified by personal sacrifice, an attitude of submission, and actions of service. Far from being regarded as second-class citizens, women are esteemed by God to be equally valuable (Galatians 3:28), interdependent (1 Corinthians 11:11-12), yet different creations, who reflect the glorious image and likeness of divinity (Genesis 1:26-27). We must not allow ourselves to be defined by the culture; as Christ followers we are to redefine the culture (Romans 12:2, 21, 1 John 2:15-17).

Men, let's be loving leaders and serve our wives and families unselfishly—do what she needs whether she does what you need or not. And keep on doing it. Regardless. Now, let's look at some other aspects of this complex issue, all of which also definitely affect how domestic duties are delineated.

Socio-Cultural Dynamics

Historically, American culture has defined the masculine role as the primary breadwinner (by the way, I've always wondered, how do you win bread?) and the feminine role as the primary homemaker (I do know how to make a home—it requires carpentry and construction skills!). Preparation for these tasks usually begins in early childhood. Stereotypically, a girl is given dolls and dishes as toys to prepare her for adult roles as mother and cook for her family. A boy receives trucks and guns as toys in preparation for his future roles as employee and soldier.

With few exceptions, this paternalistic type of family structure has permeated the majority of Western and Eastern civilizations from the ancient past to more recent times. However, many African and Polynesian cultures have been structured in a more femininely dominant manner, and some European societies have attempted to be more egalitarian in nature. Specific ethnic backgrounds may accentuate the role of one or both genders regarding family structure and household responsibilities more strongly than others.

To further complicate things, in wealthier family systems, many of the normal household managerial duties have traditionally been hired out. Today however, there are far fewer live-in housekeepers, cooks, butlers, gardeners, nannies, and other servants than there were just a generation or two ago. Yet more couples now hire others to do their yard work and household and automobile repairs than ever before. Additionally, the average couple eats out far more frequently than did their parents and grandparents before them. The culture at large has changed drastically relative to these and many other ways of caring for the home and the persons who dwell within it.

> **Being sensitive to and taking into consideration these socio-cultural differences is very important in a marriage relationship.**

Being sensitive to and taking into consideration these socio-cultural differences is very important in a marriage relationship. All of these historical practices, social values, cultural influ-

197

ences—and much more—come installed as original equipment inside the person you marry. These all contribute to the multitude of expectations we have about marriage and how it is supposed to work and function, and we bring these expectations (often unconsciously) into the marriage relationship. Furthermore, all families have both spoken and unspoken rules and rituals which regulate the routine and running of their homes. But these are rarely thought of, much less discussed, prior to marriage. We just naturally assume that the way we've been used to things being while growing up is the way things will keep being in our marriage—happily ever after.

How couples understand and deal with keeping these differences in balance is important to the function and operation of their home life. Additionally, a grasp of or a working understanding about these issues can help them to effectively and efficiently manage their resultant power struggles about these differences. Otherwise, both partners are in for confusion, frustration, hurt, and disappointment.

Family of Origin Differences

Not only do you marry a complete stranger; in essence you also marry a foreigner.

In addition to all the foregoing, even if you marry someone from the same social strata and ethnic background, every family system is unique and differs from everyone else's, even within the same subculture. So not only do you marry a complete stranger; in essence you also marry a foreigner. We never really get to know someone until some point well after that extremely expensive, highly stressful, meticulously planned 15 to 20 minutes in most couples' lives known as the wedding ceremony.

What happens when in the Smith family the husband always did X, but in the Jones family, the wife typically did that job? Who knew? Or let's say one of you came from a family where the beds had to be made so tightly that a quarter flipped onto it would bounce foot-high, whereas the other believed in saving time and energy and just learned to close the bedroom door behind them when they left the room.

Many other differences are expressed and emphasized among families even with similar moral, socio-cultural, ethnic, and/or political values. For example, some families spend a lot of time, money, and energy on keeping a lushly landscaped, well watered, and meticulously manicured yard, whereas other families believe that God made goats and cows in order to naturally keep the weeds down. What if a woman grows up in a home where her father religiously made coffee early every morning, and she marries a man whose parents never drank coffee, so that he doesn't even know what a coffee machine is—much less how to operate it? Or what about when she was raised in a family that seldom ate breakfast and never did on Sunday, but she marries a man whose mom traditionally prepared a sumptuous Sunday morning pre-church brunch, consisting of her famous award-winning French toast recipe, freshly baked sugar ham, and a tropical fruit platter? Both members of these marriages are in for a rude awakening.

As you negotiate who does which housework tasks, also remember to take into account whose standards of cleanliness are observed. There is frequently a disparity in a couple's understanding of what constitutes "clean." For some individuals, vacuuming once a month seems adequate. But if they're married to someone who believes vacuuming should be done every other day (and should involve moving all the furniture in the process), there are going to be potential growth opportunities in that relationship! I would advise these couples to keep an open mind, keep being flexible, keep communicating, and keep growing as you discover the differences that you both bring to your marriage relationship. To a "messy," a "neat freak" is either a diabolical tormentor of the devil or a divine inspiration of growth and sanctification, and vice-versa.

> **These kinds of issues are like accidents waiting to happen in a marriage system.**

These kinds of issues are like accidents waiting to happen in a marriage system. Not only are they reminiscent of an irresistible force meeting an immovable object, but both people's expectations can't help but collide. Consequently, both husband and wife are likely to feel devalued, uncared for, and therefore unloved. Although both of you can be reared in families with the same basic values, these individual differences can greatly strain a young marriage. *The challenge for most newlyweds is to relinquish their parents' models for marriage and jointly develop one that is uniquely their own.*

Technological Innovations

In today's modern culture, we take a lot for granted. 150 years ago, if someone got hungry, they would take their gun, clean and load it, and walk out deep into the forest. There they would wait for perhaps several hours, aim for and take their best shot at an animal, track it, and if necessary, finish the kill. Then they would take out their hunting knife and field dress the game. Next, they would drag the carcass back to their cabin. At this point, they were about half done. Bucket in hand, they would walk down to the creek or pond and bring water back up the hill. Then they would sharpen their axe or saw and go cut up a lot of firewood. Finally, about an hour after starting their fire with a piece of flint and steel, they would be eating!

A few hundred years before that, before the invention of firearms, hunting was even more difficult. In those days, people had to use bows and arrows, spears, traps, snares, clubs, and rocks in order to bring home the bacon. Everyone in the history of the world clear back to Adam and Eve had to live that way. And we complain if the supermarket is out of stock on a sale item we want or is located more than a fifteen-minute drive away. Admit it—don't you also become impatient if either the drive-through or the microwave takes more than three minutes?

Contrary to what our teenagers believe, I actually don't remember when firearms were invented, but I do recall when both the drive-through and the microwave were devised. Both save a ton of time and work, as do many other fabulous laborsaving devices. Washing machines, dryers, lawnmowers, indoor plumbing, dishwashers, chainsaws, vacuum cleaners, power tools, small kitchen appliances, and electric curlers have saved zillions of man and woman hours down through the years. And personally, I am thankful for them! Life in general and married life in particular would be a lot harder without these and other wonderful innovations. Still, someone has to push the buttons or turn the knobs to activate the machine.

Outside Involvements

In addition to the foregoing, the multiplication of other important duties in our fast-paced, multifaceted culture contributes to the difficulties many couples experience in attempting to keep their roles in balance. A man may be a husband, father, and wage earner; he may also be a Sunday school teacher, deacon or elder, volunteer fireman, soccer coach, and city councilman (or he may sing a secondary aria in the local opera and enjoy a watercolor class at the community college).

Meanwhile, a woman may be not only be a wife, mother, and wage earner. In addition to any or all of those roles, she may also have other demands upon her time and energy. She may lead the worship team at church, be a member of the PTA executive committee, serve as a youth group sponsor, and chair the local Cancer Society fundraising drive (or drive a monster truck in the regional demolition derby and go base jumping).

With all these responsibilities and many others, it's pretty easy to see why dusting the knickknack shelf may not be the highest priority in the average busy, overcommitted American home. Juggling all of one's roles and responsibilities is indeed quite a challenge, especially since many of these outside involvements may change during the different seasons of one's life. For example, the demands upon one's time as a parent often change greatly from toddlerhood times to the teenage years.

> **The common curse of busyness can affect and infect many marriages.**

The common curse of busyness can affect and infect many marriages. One of the most frequent complaints of the average middle-class American is that they do not have enough time. Yet we are all given 168 hours per week to allocate as we see fit. If an individual has too many tasks on their to-do list and cannot do them all well, obviously something has to be eliminated. This means learning to set boundaries and say no, often to good and important things. Many times spouses feel neglected because their mates seem to have interest, time, and energy for other things and/or persons, but not for them.

This is a particularly subtle and complicated problem for many Christians, especially those involved in ministry. In the average church, someone with a willing spirit and leadership ability will often be asked to do progressively more and more service. Unfortunately, in most churches, about 80% of the work is done by about 20% of the parishioners. But this over-functioning is very stressful and many times leads to being burdened, burned-out, and bitter.

God intends everybody to be involved in ministry to the church in some capacity, so that everyone is blessed and benefited and no one is overworked. People who do more than their fair share of ministry work are not only doing themselves and their families a disservice, they are also inadvertently depriving those standing on the sidelines from getting into the game and gaining valuable experience. And to those who are run down and depleted from chronic over involvement, Jesus declared "Come to me, all you who are weary and burdened, and I will give you rest. Take my yoke upon you and learn from me, for I am gentle and humble in heart, and you will find rest for your souls. For my yoke is easy and my burden is light" (Matthew 11:28-30).

Setting, balancing, and maintaining each person's priorities vis-à-vis the other person's needs and preferences in your marriage may be a lifelong process. People change, needs change, and responsibilities change throughout life. But babies, light bulbs, automobile oil, and furnace filters also need to be changed, and the resulting garbage set by the curb.

Personal Preferences

Some people are just more inherently suited for and interested in certain tasks than other persons. In order for a couple to work smart as well as to work hard, it would be prudent for each of them to understand their own and each other's natural gifts, tastes, and predispositions. For example, it would not be wise to have a "big picture" type of person always do detail-oriented work like dusting or polishing the silver. Furthermore, it would be an equally bad idea for a "messy" to fold and put away the laundry if they are married to a "neat freak." In such cases, both parties would be destined to a life of misery.

Opposites attract. It is simply a law of physics that opposite poles of a magnet naturally gravitate to each other. So too, it is often the case in marriages that people who are totally different from one another experience those personal differences as complementary, if not compelling. In their hilarious book, *Incompatibility: Grounds for a Great Marriage*, Chuck and Barb Snyder put it this way:

> What we want to say over and over again is that it's okay to be different. And because of these differences there are going to be disagreements and conflicts. One of the benefits of this, however, is that when you come from different points of view and still agree on an idea, you just know it has to be good! The longer you are married, the more differences you will find. You don't raise children the same; you don't spend money the same. One person wants all the windows up when they go to bed; the other wants them closed. One wants to go to sleep with music, the other wants complete silence. Even if both want to listen to music, it will probably be classical versus country and western (1988, p. 17).

The irony—and certainly the challenge—in marriage, however, is that *those differences which made you crazy about the other person originally often end up driving you crazy later!* Her organizational skills which he found so admirable now seem abominable. That carefree, easy-going nature he displayed which she at first found to be so alluring and attractive now seems to be awful and atrocious.

> The very same things about your spouse that make them who they uniquely are, and which attracted you in the first place, will more than likely end up eventually annoying you.

This is because every personality characteristic or feature has both strengths and weaknesses. A person with good organizational skills can become compulsive and controlling. A genial, affable personality can also be seen as weak and wishy-washy. In other words, the very same things about your spouse that make them who they uniquely are, and which attracted you in the first place, will more than likely end up eventually annoying you. In all marriages, the quintessential question becomes, "How can we use these distinct differences to work for us rather than against us?"

In children's literature, the familiar story of Mr. and Mrs. Jack Spratt illustrates this point vividly. As the narrative goes, one spouse could eat no fat and the other could eat no lean, but between the two of them, they licked the platter clean! They obviously let their differences and preferences work for them instead of against them. But unfortunately the story doesn't tell us who washed, dried, and put away the platter afterward! Hopefully they did it together.

T.E.A.M.W.O.R.K.

By now you might be saying, "Okay, I see that there are a lot of issues involved in defining and doing routine responsibilities. But I still want to know who takes out the trash, and how is that decided? " Glad you asked. I want to propose the following eight-step, biblically-based process for couples to negotiate a fair division of labor in their home, described by the acronym "T.E.A.M.W.O.R.K."

Togetherness

> **Sharing a load is easier on both people than if either attempted the task alone.**

The words "co-operation" and "collaboration" both have to do with the concept of working together. The old adage "many hands make light work" suggests that sharing a load is easier on both people than if either attempted the task alone. The essence of this concept is encapsulated in Solomon's observation that, "Two are better than one, because they have a good return for their work" (Ecclesiastes 4:9). From the beginning of the creation account, a spouse is referred to in terms of their potential for the mutual benefit of the relationship; they are definitively and functionally a *helpmate.*

Doing chores together can not only take some of the drudgery out of the duty; it can actually be fun, and it has the potential to become a bonding experience for the two of you. (I personally believe that the couple who sweats together sticks together!) If you both work outside the home, you are probably both tired when you hit the door, and you have more to do than either of you can possibly do well alone. Don't make things worse and lose time by fussing over who is or is not doing their share. Commit to help each other as much as possible at home. Doing this will ease both of your loads considerably and will help you feel much better about your spouse and your marriage relationship. Use it as an opportunity to talk about your day. Think of ways to reward yourselves with a fun activity directly after finishing. My wife, Linda, always feels loved when I work alongside her, particularly if the task is an unpleasant one. At the very least, the dirty job gets done faster.

Although many chores cannot be done directly together, one very important thing couples can do together is to compile a comprehensive list of all your household responsibilities, including childcare. This is a practical way to identify what needs to be done, as well as when, why, and by whom. Such a list should include the following:

1. Describe each task or chore—from the most menial to the most complex, and from daily chores like dishes to infrequent tasks like taxes. Include things like earning money, purchasing and preparing food, cleaning house, paying bills, caring for children, maintaining home and automobiles, planning trips/vacations, scheduling appointments, keeping connected with family and friends, caring for pets, etc.;

2. *Denote what must be done in order to accomplish it.* This way you are both on the same page and agree on the criteria for measuring success and/or completion of the task;

3. *Determine when or how often it needs to be done.* Again, misunderstandings and resentments won't accumulate and your expectations are clear and agreed upon;

4. *Decide who is best suited or talented for it.* Remember that no one is good at everything, but everyone is good at some things; and

5. *Delineate a ranking of how important that task is to each spouse on a 1–10 scale.*

Each person should then go through the combined list and claim ownership for the chores they are interested in and good at, so that each person has a fairly even list for which they will assume responsibility. Later, we will address those tasks which neither person claims.

Equality

It is downright deflating, discouraging, defeating, and demoralizing for one spouse to feel like they are stuck with most of the work. When there is not an equitable and mutually shared division of labor in a home, the one doing the disproportionate amount of the work will understandably struggle with the temptation to become resentful (or at least spit in their spouse's soup when they're not looking!).

Like it or not, we live in a culture that is still very sexist when it comes to the world of work. It is unequivocally unfair that with the same training, background, and experience, a woman still earns only about $.77 on the dollar of a man's income at the same job. Unfortunately, this same discriminative disparity in the marketplace also exists in the majority of dual career homes. The research suggests that when both partners work full-time outside the home, it is often the wife who does the vast majority of the housework and childcare.

Practically speaking, "The bottom line about housework is *it isn't who is doing what but how each partner feels about the arrangement*" (Louden, 1994, p. 105). Ideally, a home is where two equally valuable and equally capable adults live. And again, ideally-speaking, when shorter people start arriving in the home, remember that both adults shared equally in their creation. Accordingly, it just stands to reason that responsibilities for the home and children should be shared equitably. Again, both spouses have different strengths and gifts, but equal value and responsibility.

God seems to view labor in His kingdom from this practical perspective of equality. With respect to serving in God's kingdom, the apostle Paul helps us understand:

> What, after all, is Apollos? And what is Paul? Only servants, through whom you came to believe—as the Lord assigned to each his task. I planted the seed, Apollos watered it, but God made it grow. So neither he who plants nor he who waters is anything, but only God, who makes things grow. The man who plants and the man who waters have one purpose, and each will be rewarded according to his own labor (1 Corinthians 3:5-8).

Both are different, yet equally valuable. All the work needs to be done—but in a fairly distributed way.

Attitude

It has been said that attitude is everything. Realizing there are some jobs that no one wants to do, Paul just flat out orders us to "Do everything without complaining or arguing" (Philippians 2:14). Groaning and griping about unpleasant chores doesn't get them done any faster or more easily. It does, however, create a climate of tension and dissension which not only doesn't help anyone, but which can make a proverbial mountain out of a mole hill.

Perhaps you've heard the old expression which says that no matter how you dress it, a pig is still a pig. Some jobs are never going to be ones to which we look forward with eager anticipation. They just have to be done. A certain TV personage tells us to just git 'er done!

One psychologically and spiritually mature way to adjust our attitude about doing menial, mundane, and/or messy chores is to focus on a higher plane such as worship or prayer while cleaning the toilet or cat litter box. The medieval monk, Brother Lawrence, provided a powerful and profound example of how to adjust our attitude toward difficult work. Part of his humble job as a cook for the monastery was to get up well before daylight every day and scrub by hand the cast-iron pots in which their food was cooked over an open flame.

As he did this decidedly "dirty job" every day for many years, he kept a journal of his attitude of gratitude toward God and his internal dialogue with Him late at night by candlelight. Many of these became letters he sent to a dear friend. These compiled writings of a seemingly unimportant, uneducated, unsung underling are now treasured as one of the greatest devotional books of all time, entitled *The Practice of the Presence of God*. One can only wonder—did He whistle while He worked or did He have to take a vow of silence?

Management

> **When it comes to the division of labor at home, it is important
> to not just work hard but to also work smart.**

Many American households do not employ sound manageri-al strategies or techniques. Basic workplace skills such as communication, negotiation, cooperation, compromise, organi-zation, brainstorming, and delegation also work well in the home. When it comes to the division of labor at home, it is im-portant to not just work hard but to also work smart. For exam-ple, it stands to reason that the spouse who possesses the best arithmetic skills should probably be in charge of the checkbook or Quicken/QuickBooks account.

In Matthew 25:14-30, Jesus told an intriguing story of con-trasting management styles. Three people were given varying amounts of money to invest by their employer, who gave them complete autonomy as to how they would do it. Two of them invested wisely and were highly commended with praise and promotions. The third was paralyzed by fear of taking a risk, and so did nothing; he consequently ended up losing not only the principal but his job.

Think of your marriage as a small business. If the partners share an equal investment, have the same vision and goals, communicate those clearly and effectively, respect and appre-ciate one another's differing strengths and weaknesses, and resolve disputes or differences in a mutually equitable way, then that business will prosper. God's high value of these household management properties is seen as a basic qualifica-tion for leadership in the church. Specifically, Paul instructs Timothy that, "A deacon must be the husband of but one wife and must *manage* his children and his household well" (1 Timo-thy 3:12) [emphasis added].

Willingness:

Let's face it. Neither one of you will ever want to do the dirty work. And that's okay. The night before His crucifixion, Jesus was open to negotiating any other available option, because He did not *want* to go to the cross for me and you. But the good news is *He did it anyway.*

The reason Jesus sacrificed His life for us was because of His willingness to demonstrate unconditional love for us. In a similar, yet considerably less drastic way, what if you decided to do something that is important to your spouse—even though you would ordinarily not want to do it—just because you love your mate and know they really strongly dislike doing it? As Harley observes:

> In marriage you do things for each other because you care about each other's feelings... if cooking dinner or ironing shirts or picking up socks triggers the feeling of love in your spouse, why not do these things? It is not only an act of care, but is an act of supreme wisdom. By doing for each other what you appreciate most, you will have what few marriages have, the feeling of love throughout your entire lives (2001, p. 139-140).

So whether it's pulling weeds or scrubbing toilets, Solomon commands us, "Whatever your hand finds to do, do it with all your might..." (Ecclesiastes 9:10). Just keep an open mind and willing heart in the process. And practice the Golden rule (Matthew 7:12). Be considerate and don't ever leave a mess for your spouse to have to confront.

Outsource

I'm a lousy plumber. The truth is that I have never taken the time to learn how to do plumbing adequately. A plumber friend of mine says that plumbers only have to know two things: that sewage always runs downhill and that payday is on Friday. But in my experience at home, it's always been quite a bit more complicated than that, and I generally end up paying a plumber (and not always on Friday!) to solve our "gravitational" problems.

Don't always assume you can't afford to hire someone.

It's certainly true that everybody can do some things, but nobody can do everything. On the lists you made above, identify the tasks that neither of you wants and/or is able to do. Consider hiring someone else to do that job. Don't always assume you can't afford to hire someone. It may make economic sense to work more at what you are good at in order to be able to pay someone to do work you are not good at. It may be that outsourcing a job would actually be cost-effective in the long run. A weekly babysitter is far less expensive than a divorce attorney!

Remember that there are many ways to get things done. Brainstorm and think creatively outside the box. Life is short and then we die! Hiring someone else to do a burdensome or unpleasant task can give you an opportunity to enjoy more time together and reduce your stress levels.

Relinquish

Another important factor in reducing both stress and power struggles in your marriage is to be open to looking at what you can give up or let go of. Sometimes people "major on the minors," becoming preoccupied with things that simply don't matter that much. Does it really make relational sense to spend excessive amounts of time and energy on things that are relatively unimportant to your spouse? If you're so exhausted from perfectly polishing the floors that you are unable to spend meaningful time with your mate, then what good is it?

Jesus confronted this issue—an excessive preoccupation with housework being considered more important than relationship priorities—head-on. In Luke 10:38-42 we read:

As Jesus and his disciples were on their way, he came to a village where a woman named Martha opened her home to him. She had a sister called Mary, who sat at the Lord's feet listening to what he said. But Martha was distracted by all the preparations that had to be made. She came to him and asked, 'Lord, don't you care that my sister has left me to do the work by myself? Tell her to help me!' 'Martha, Martha,' the Lord answered, 'you are worried and upset about many things, but only one thing is needed. Mary has chosen what is better, and it will not be taken away from her.'

She was unwilling to let go of her obligatory duties and enter into relationship, but she was jealous and resentful of her sister who did. Jesus tried to teach her that people are more important than things. We all need to learn that.

> **Most Americans have way more than they need. Consider simplifying your life. Do you really need to buy that new toy?**

Speaking of things, most Americans have way more than they need. Consider simplifying your life. Do you really need to buy that a new toy? It will probably be obsolete in six months, anyway, due to ongoing technological innovations. Give stuff away. Clean out your basement, closets, and attic, and have a garage sale. That's what Jesus told the rich young ruler to do (Mark 10:17-23). If your possessions own you instead of you owning them, perhaps you should consider experiencing the freedom of letting them go.

Kids

Finally, children need to have the character-building experience of having a good work ethic instilled within them. They not only need to know that work is a gift from God (Ecclesiastes 2:24, 3:12-13, 22), but that many blessings and benefits are provided through it. As Solomon wisely states, "All hard work brings a profit, but mere talk leads only to poverty" (Proverbs 14:23). Dozens of scriptures warn against the dangers of being lazy, idle, or sluggardly. In fact, Paul warns us that "...if a man will not work, he shall not eat" (2 Thessalonians 3:10).

Of course, the best way to teach children the value and virtue of work is by example. When they see their parents doing household chores, they will naturally want to imitate those behaviors. Even very young children can be taught to help Mom and Dad. Honest, hard work builds self-esteem, character, a sense of independence, purpose, meaning, accomplishment, and fulfillment, as well as muscle. As with all things, of course, there needs to be moderation and consideration for age-appropriateness. After all, most states do have child labor laws.

> **The best way to teach children the value and virtue of work is by example.**

The keys in delegating domestic duties to children are to not do it harshly (Colossians 3:21), and if possible, to make it fun. Making chores into a creative and/or competitive game can be both motivating and memorable. A great way to tackle an unpleasant chore is to see how quickly one can do it. Set a timer and award a small prize or privilege if it's done within the allotted time. Multitask—fold the laundry together while watching TV and wearing your underwear on your head. Mop the floor by covering your feet with moist rags and doing the twist to an upbeat, lively song. Life can be whatever we make it.

Another reason your children need to be taught how to work well is so that your future sons-in-law and daughters-in-law won't hate you! All boys need to know how to iron a shirt and sew on a button, cook a complete, well-balanced meal, and clean the bathroom. Girls need to know how to change a flat tire, start and safely operate a lawnmower, and properly use a paintbrush. They will enter into adulthood with self-confidence, and your grandchildren will live in a much happier home.

I hope that when you and your marriage partner approach housework with this concept of T.E.A.M.W.O.R.K., it will have a positive impact on your relationship, and neither of you will feel taken advantage of or used. Humble household helpfulness happens in happy, healthy, harmonious, holy, hospitable homes!

Scriptural Study

1. Romans 12:3-8
2. Galatians 3:28
3. Ephesians 5:21
4. Philippians 2:1-5, 14
5. 2 Thessalonians 3:6-14

Ponderable Points

1. Make a list of which parents did which chores in your home as you grew up.

2. Make a list of which parents did which chores in your spouse's home as they grew up.

3. Compare and discuss these respective lists with your mate. What similarities and differences do you see in the two families' approach to the division of labor?

4. Think of a favorite memory from childhood that involved doing some chore or housework. What was it like, and what made it a pleasant memory for you?

5. As you were compiling the lists at the beginning of the T.E.A.M.W.O.R.K. exercise, what were you feeling inside? Share that with your mate and find out what that experience was like for them, too.

Activation Activities

1. Do you believe that your spouse expects too much from you? Do they understand all the roles and responsibilities you try to balance in a day's work? How do you feel about this?

2. Think about which chore(s) you dislike doing the most. Does your spouse know this? If not, consider communicating your feelings about that to them. Then consider and discuss possible options for change. This can include compromising or alternating, trading your unpleasant task for one your spouse finds equally distasteful, outsourcing, etc.

3. Prayerfully consider how you can make your marriage partner's workload easier. Then without telling them, dedicate yourself to that.

Recommended Resources

Incompatibility: Grounds for a Great Marriage, Chuck and Barb
   Snyder (1998).

Starting Your Marriage Right, Dennis and Barbara Rainey (2000).

Love for a Lifetime, James Dobson (1987).

Marriage: Love and Logic, Foster and Hermie Cline (2005).

Extraordinary Marriage, Rodney and Selma Wilson (2004).

CHAPTER NINE

Money Matters

*Money can buy you everything except happiness, and
take you everywhere except heaven!*

*"Do not be overawed when a man grows rich, when the
splendor of his house increases; for he will take nothing
with him when he dies, his splendor will not descend with
him... A man who has riches without understanding is like
the beasts that perish."*

—PSALM 49:16-17, 20

*I*n all my years of clinical experience, I have never once
seen a married couple have a fight about money.

Money is simply an economic commodity, consisting
of shiny pieces of metal or small pieces of paper with pictures of
dead presidents and inventors printed on them in green and
black ink. If you gave a dollar bill to an Aborigine or primitive
tribesman, he might smell it or taste it, and then he would probably shrug his shoulders and drop it on the desert or jungle floor
as he wandered away. This is because that little piece of paper
would have no meaning or intrinsic value to him.

What couples fight about are the *meanings* and *values* they
ascribe to money. Research consistently singles out money

matters as the number one trigger for everything from the occasional marital skirmish to all-out wars. Many experts accordingly declare money problems to be the number one cause of divorce in America. However, while couples are ostensibly arguing over what to do with the income tax refund (and by the way, it is always a bad fiscal idea to get a refund—why give the IRS an interest-free loan? Exercise the self-discipline to save on your own, and adjust your withholdings so that you come out even with the government every April 15th), or even whether to save or spend at all, what they are really clashing about is much more than mere dollars and cents.

Money is, and always has been, a symbol. It represents many different things to people, depending on their individual personality, socio-cultural status, family background, and upbringing. Money can signify power, happiness, status, freedom, comfort, hope, prestige, security, love, survival, trust, self-esteem, and control—among many other things. Typically, when couples fight, "Any conflict they have over finances is probably not over money itself, but over what money *means* to them" (Conway and Conway, 2000, p. 239).

Most couples who frequently fight over financial frictions never really communicate in a healthy way about money simply as the commodity of exchange which it is. They rarely discuss in a calm and businesslike way how each person feels about money. What's a necessity and what's a luxury? Should we save or spend? How, when, and by whom should the bills be paid? What are our long-term financial goals? What if one of you was raised in a family that emphasized saving money for a rainy day, and your mate grew up in a family that enjoyed living for the day with no thought of tomorrow?

The different customs and backgrounds in which each spouse was raised will affect many areas of the couple's approach to and philosophy about finances.

In fact, the different customs and backgrounds in which each spouse was raised will affect many areas of the couple's approach to and philosophy about finances. Families often have considerable differences with regard to things like charitable giving, types and lengths of vacations, lifestyle choices, investment strategies, buying versus renting, insurance options, and retirement planning. In order to avoid predictable and often painful conflict, both marriage partners should try to become aware of and sensitive to the other's accustomed tastes and preferences about money and how it's used.

Mary Hunt summarizes the issue this way:

> Money exposes the differences in our personalities, the ways we were brought up, our money beliefs, and goals. The way we think about money and what we do with it reflects what we believe about it. But money issues are buried so deeply in our emotions, it is often difficult to know what we believe or where our money attitudes came from. And if you don't know a lot about yourself, it's likely you know even less about your spouse (2003, p. 44).

Many times money is used as a weapon in other marital battlegrounds.

Many times money is used as a weapon in other marital battlegrounds. Money can be employed as a means of instilling guilt, manipulating behavior, expressing anger, or acting out power struggles. For example, a shopaholic wife may run up excessive charges on her credit card because it's the only way she can retaliate against a workaholic, domineering, or neglectful husband. A husband may balk at supporting his wife's children from a former marriage because he feels resentful, used, and furious that her ex-husband is reneging on his obligations.

Along with understanding the manifest meanings in many marital money misunderstandings, it is essential to recognize how these symbolic representations play themselves out against a shifting backdrop of social and economic change. Today, more than two-thirds of all wives work outside the home full-time, many times earning as much as, if not more than, their husbands. Thus, the assumptions and expectations about who is entitled to wield financial power no longer remain as traditionally divided along gender lines as they were just a generation ago. If couples don't agree on the division and accountability of financial decision-making, conflicts are inevitable and often insurmountable.

What's more, assumptions and expectations about money may change dramatically over the lifetime of the marriage, due to a variety of both internal and external circumstances. A wife, for instance, may work full-time for a few years, stay at home when the children are small, and later return to the workforce to resume her career. Divorce, remarriage, and caregiving obligations to step-children and elderly parents may also create new and potentially volatile financial battlegrounds. Lower interest rates for their nest egg may mean that a couple facing retirement age has disappointing, if not drastic decisions to make regarding the lifestyle about which they once dreamed. Each of these new challenges or situations demands sensitivity, flexibility, and understanding on the part of the couple in order to accommodate those changes.

Additionally, after several generations of unprecedented economic growth, our country's recent economic downturn has dealt a swift and painful blow to families, sometimes creating seismic shifts in relationships. Couples with two incomes frequently find that although they are working harder than ever, their purchasing power has functionally become less and less. Recent college graduates are confronted with record high jobless rates and are saddled with enormous debt from student loans. Young dot-commers who had independently achieved financial success now find they are forced to boomerang back to their parents' home. Corporate layoffs, plummeting stock prices, record bankruptcies, rampant inflation, uncertain global markets, unstable currencies, mortgage foreclosures, and sky-rocketing unemployment rates can cause severe anxiety and worry for couples everywhere.

Finally, it is imperative to realize that many money management misgivings are a symptom of deeper and underlying emotional and/or psychological issues in the lives of one or both partners. A husband who is insecure about his masculinity may feel threatened if he permits his wife to handle money. A wife with low self-esteem may secretly return her husband's extravagant gifts for her because she feels unworthy of them, unaware that in so doing she hurts her husband's feelings.

Furthermore, one spouse may secretly try to hide an addiction to gambling or shopping—behavior they engage in to try to soothe their stressed nerves, make them happy, or even get them high. Many compulsive spenders are subconsciously trying to compensate for an internal sense of emptiness and impoverishment by perpetually buying more things—things which can never fill that inner void or satisfy that longing of the soul. Obviously, all of these dynamics and issues are much deeper and more complicated than a casual surface disagreement over fiscal philosophy. And all of them can create a firestorm of conflict.

In this chapter, I will attempt to equip you with some helpful diplomatic strategies to negotiate a cease-fire in your marital money wars. *The truth is if we don't master our money, our money will master us!* The bottom line is, "How you handle your marriage in the context of finances—and how you handle your finances in the context of marriage—will go a long way toward determining whether or not you will have a life worth living" (Dayton, 2009, p. 12). Let's now direct our attention to understanding some of the conditions and dynamics necessary for economic disarmament and for calling a truce.

Monetary Management

Our methods of money management mirror and magnify our marital mindset! If we consistently live beyond our means by creating a standard of living we cannot realistically meet, we may be unwittingly creating for ourselves a mountain of stress and a huge pile of debt that may be insurmountable. To very roughly paraphrase Jesus, what does it profit us to gain the whole enchilada, yet work ourselves into an early grave in the process (Matthew 16:26)? No one on their deathbed ever laments that they didn't spend more time at the office, store, or factory.

In a similar way, Solomon cautions, "Do not wear yourself out to get rich; have the wisdom to show restraint. Cast but a glance at riches, and they are gone, for they will surely sprout wings and fly off to the sky like an eagle" (Proverbs 23: 4-5).

Many times less is more: "Better a little with the fear of the LORD than great wealth with turmoil. Better a meal of vegetables where there is love than a fattened calf with hatred" (Proverbs 15:16-17). And again, "As goods increase, so do those who consume them. And what benefit are they to the owner except to feast his eyes on them? The sleep of a laborer is sweet, whether he eats little or much, but the abundance of a rich man permits him no sleep" (Ecclesiastes 5:11-12). Down deep, we all know we can't take it with us (Job 1:21, Psalm 49:16-20, Ecclesiastes 5:15, 1 Timothy 6:7). I vividly recall hearing Dr. Tony Evans remark at a Promise Keepers conference a few years ago: "I ain't never seen a hearse pulling a U-Haul!"

Obviously, if we spend more than we make, we're not going to prosper.

Obviously, if we spend more than we make, we're not going to prosper. (Unlike the U.S. government, we can't just print more money when we experience a deficit due to incompetent and/or irresponsible management). One year, around tax season, I saw a cartoon, which was satirically commenting on a new tax reform proposal. Touting a new, simplified short form, the first line said, "How much do you make?" The second line said, "Send it all in!"

Though not quite that bad, I recall seeing the shocked and sad expressions on our sons' faces when they read the withholding statements attached to their first paychecks. Although they knew taxes would be deducted from their wages, their net income and buying power was significantly less than they had anticipated. Everyone wants to get rich quick. But if we exercise the self-discipline to consistently spend less than we earn over a long period of time, we will be financially secure and successful (Proverbs 12:11, 13:11, 1 Timothy 6:9).

What follows is a simple and sensible framework to manage your money so that it doesn't manage you. I am certainly no financial guru or investment wizard. But in consulting with and learning from many who are, and from my own personal and professional experience, I would like to suggest that you consider following these nine biblically-based "ABCs" to financial freedom: *A*ccounting, *B*udgeting, *C*ommunicating, *D*eciding, *E*qualizing, *F*inancing, *G*iving, *H*alting, and *I*nvesting.

Accounting

Intuitively, we know that if we fail to plan, we plan to fail. Virtually no one would think of starting a new business without first sitting down and devising a comprehensive business plan, including a complete financial statement. Yet few engaged couples specifically, systematically, and strategically plan their financial future. Somehow that just doesn't seem very romantic. But it is very realistic.

> **The best way to address money problems is before they occur.**

As with most things, the best way to address money problems is before they occur. Prevention is always easier than cure. Jesus clearly illustrated this point when He asked, "Suppose one of you wants to build a tower. Will he not first sit down and estimate the cost to see if he has enough money to complete it? For if he lays the foundation and is not able to finish it, everyone who sees it will ridicule him, saying, 'This fellow began to build and was not able to finish'" (Luke 14:28-30). We must count the cost ahead of time if we are to succeed in our financial life.

Even if a couple had unlimited financial resources, a plan for spending and investing them would still be essential. The vast majority of us are not burdened with that particular problem, so developing a plan for fiscal management is all the more necessary and prudent. Before any financial plan can be created, a couple must first know what they own and what they owe. Hence, every couple would do well to sit down together and spell out a joint financial statement as a necessary first step in managing their marital monies. Any bank or lending institution has forms available for this purpose. Assets and income are listed on one side, and liabilities and expenditures on the other. From this beginning point, you will learn what you own and what owns you.

Budgeting

Next, take the time to sit down together with all of your bills and bank and financial statements, along with your software program, or pencil, paper, and calculator. List everything you spend each day for a month, so you can see where every penny actually goes. Most of us are aware of the big or fixed expenses, but it's usually the smaller ones that slowly, steadily, surreptitiously, subtly, and surely sabotage success. Frequent stops at "convenience stores" or "Fourbucks" can badly bust the budget.

Formulating (and adhering to) a budget is essential to achieving financial stability.

Certified financial planners all agree that formulating (and adhering to) a budget is essential to achieving financial stability. But many couples have yet to take this instrumental step toward financial freedom. Once a couple accounts for what they have, then they can allocate their resources where and as they choose. Thus, "A budget is nothing more than a plan for spending money. It doesn't limit expenditures, it defines them" (Burkett, 2001, p. 46). Remember, *when you manage your assets properly, you don't ask where the money went—you tell it where to go.*

A budget is a manifestation of proactively assuming responsibility for one's life and prosperity.

When we live according to the freedoms made possible by a budgetary plan, we begin to grasp the fact that, "The plans of the diligent lead to profit as surely as haste leads to poverty" (Proverbs 21:5). People who don't have a budget typically live under perpetual anxiety, stress, fear, and worry. A budget is a great example of exercising—and facilitating—mature self-control. A budget is a manifestation of proactively assuming responsibility for one's life and prosperity, rather than immaturely reacting to external circumstances and situations.

The hardest part of making a budget is actually deciding to sit down and do it. The nuts and bolts of establishing a budget are remarkably straightforward. Just put down your income, and then list your expenses (obviously persons who are self-employed or have fluctuating income levels need to budget according to a worst case income or commission scenario). After writing down your fixed costs (e.g. tithing, taxes, mortgage or rent, childcare expenses, insurance, diapers, etc.), then include costs that are more flexible and/or variable (e.g. utilities, food, clothing, gift giving, dry cleaning, automobile expenses, holiday expenditures, new or updated home décor, etc.). Next, think about discretionary expenditures like impulse purchases (i.e. most things bought at convenience stores, nearly all items bought near a cash register or checkout line, costs of personal addictions like junk food, smoking, getting a fix on a sugar and/or caffeine addiction, etc.). Finally, itemize things like savings and investments, entertainment, "toys," vacations, and so on.

The purpose of making and sticking to a budget is not to be constricting, but freeing. Whether you keep a bookkeeping journal to itemize expenditures as they are made, or use an "envelope system" where the money for each expense category is allocated to its designated envelope after payday, it is important to keep track of where your money goes. What a budget affords you as a couple is knowledge, and knowledge is power. *Financial freedom has much less to do with how much you make than it does with how much—and how—you spend.*

Communicating

For some strange reason, talking about money or one's income is an absolute taboo in many sectors of our society. Yet ironically, there is perhaps no other area of marriage where communication is more essential. Couples need to know which of them is a risk taker and why, what each other's dreams and fears are about, and what their financial goals, values, and priorities are. This person is your lifelong business partner! Most couples fail to recognize that running a marriage is like running a small business. If the partners don't talk about all aspects of their commercial enterprise, there is no way it can even succeed, much less prosper.

Not only do you need to thoroughly discuss these things with each other, it's also wise to consider employing the services of a financial expert, particularly in areas such as taxes, insurances, and investments. As Solomon said, "Plans fail for lack of counsel, but with many advisers they succeed" (Proverbs 15:22). Also, read books like those listed at the end of this chapter, and go to financial seminars to educate yourself about complex money matters. Don't just work hard—work smart. It's good to reach out for help.

As was suggested previously, we need to learn to talk smart about money. Converse with your spouse in a calm and businesslike way at a time when money isn't the issue and neither of you is stressed or upset. When are you most relaxed? Consider taking a leisurely walk or go out for an ice cream cone (or better yet, take the walk after getting the ice cream!), and listen to each other's feelings about issues surrounding money.

Share with your spouse how you feel about their overspending (or their difficulty letting go of a nickel) and how that impacts you, being particularly sensitive to not make them feel defensive or judged. Share what you admire about your mate's attitudes ("I really wish I could enjoy myself more spontaneously like you do. I'm always fretting that I'll be a bag lady when I'm 70"). But also don't be afraid to bring to their attention specific things which make you feel uncomfortable ("I know we're both working hard, but eating out every night seems extravagant to me, and I'm not sure we can afford it"). Using the communication skills from chapters 6 and 7, including "Soul Sharing," work through your differences and misunderstandings because,

"Whoever gives heed to instruction prospers, and blessed is he who trusts in the LORD. The wise in heart are called discerning, and pleasant words promote instruction" (Proverbs 16:20-21).

Deciding

After thoroughly discussing money matters with each other, jointly decide the practicalities of how you choose to live out your financial plan. Determine who is best suited to pay the bills and keep the books. Decide what to do about your lifestyle choices, expenditures, and indebtedness. Put into action the plans you discussed for your financial future.

> **Most couples get into financial predicaments because of a passive, reactionary stance toward life.**

Most couples get into financial predicaments because of a passive, reactionary stance toward life. They don't appropriately account for their resources, develop a budgetary plan for their use, or communicate with each other about how they manage those resources. They choose to not resist impulse buying. Consequently, most Americans wallow in unnecessary credit debt that they never intended to owe, and they have lots of stress and conflict with their partner as a result.

Establishing and maintaining control of your finances requires a decided commitment to the practice of consistent self-discipline. Sometimes making decisions can be hard, unpopular, or painful. We may need to humbly admit to our greed of wanting it all, or honestly confess our desire to live above our means in order to look good to others and/or artificially boost our self-esteem. Recall Jesus' warning (Luke 12:15) about the subtlety of greed—it can grab us by the throat without our even knowing it. But don't let greed deceive you; Paul denounces it as idolatry (Colossians 3:5).

We may need to bite a proverbial bullet! In Luke 16:1-15, Jesus tells a story about an underperforming CFO who was commended for rapidly increasing his boss' cash flow by his bold, shrewd, and decisive actions. We may need to stop buying personal indulgences, sell some cherished possessions, get a second job, or act in other decisive ways for the good of our marriage. Don't be afraid to think outside the box in nontraditional or unconventional ways for the sake of your marriage if your cash flow is too tight or your indebtedness is too high. Frugality, belt tightening, and joint sacrifice can be good for both partners and for your relationship.

Equalizing

I always cringe inwardly when I hear a married person use the words "me, my, and mine" (or for you grammarians, first person singular possessive pronouns) to talk about "their" money, income, house, or other possessions. Among other things, marriage is a mutual equity partnership of two people who are different in nature and roles, but equivalent in value and worth. Most states' marriage laws consider all property which married persons have to be owned jointly. Plus, you can't take any of it with you, and it will all burn eventually anyway.

> In a mature marriage, both independent adult individuals must choose to unconditionally relinquish their egocentric "me/my/mine" attitudes and jointly create an interdependent "us/we/ours" mentality.

But to me those things aren't even the issue. In a mature marriage, both independent adult individuals must choose to unconditionally relinquish their egocentric "me/my/mine" attitudes and jointly create an interdependent "us/we/ours" mentality. Both spouses were created to be each other's helpmate and become one flesh (Genesis 2:24, Ephesians 5:31). If couples truly love one another more than their stuff, they will have far fewer turf battles and power struggles.

In many American homes, controversies and resentments frequently arise over who pays for what, how financial resources should be fairly distributed, whether there should be separate or joint bank accounts, etc. Again, fights over these topics are never the real issue. If disputes like these regularly rear their ugly heads in your marriage, consider looking beneath the surface to root issues like lack of trust, unresolved power dynamics, unhealed childhood wounds, self-esteem concerns, hurts left over from other marital problems, and/or a variety of other individual and relational concerns.

Financing

Debt is bondage. The biggest trap most couples fall prey to today is consumer debt. The entire American economic system is based upon the widespread utilization of and reliance upon credit. How you choose to deal with the world of finance and debt determines not only your credit score, but to a significant degree, the health and well-being of your life and marital relationship, as well.

> Advertisers have carefully and craftily perfected the art of seductively increasing our desires, while insidiously decreasing our satisfaction.

Advertisers have carefully and craftily perfected the art of seductively increasing our desires, while insidiously decreasing our satisfaction. We have been diabolically duped into thinking in terms of financially-friendly monthly payments instead of total price. The long-term upshot of this manipulative brainwashing has caused us to think, "Can we afford the (*convenient!*) payment?" rather than, "Do we have enough cash to buy it?" Everything seems so simple: "Buy now (often with nothing down), pay later." And later. And later. And later...

The Bible calls this curse of indebtedness slavery because, "The rich rule over the poor, and the borrower is servant to the lender" (Proverbs 22:7). And notice these stern warnings: "He who puts up security for another will surely suffer, but whoever refuses to strike hands in pledge is safe" (Proverbs 11:15), and "Do not be a man who strikes hands in pledge or puts up security for debts; if you lack the means to pay, your very bed will be snatched from under you" (Proverbs 22:26-27). Repo men have always had great job security!

> **Credit is not something to be feared and avoided; it is something to be understood and used correctly.**

That being said, credit is not something to be feared and avoided; it is something to be understood and used correctly. If you buy something on sale with your credit card and only make the minimum payment, the item is no longer a bargain—you end up paying for it several times over because of the exorbitant interest rate your credit card company charges you. Most couples in this country buy big-ticket items such as furniture, vehicles, and houses on an installment plan, rather than delaying their gratification until they have saved enough to be able to actually afford it. Except for tax-deductible home mortgages (which are at significantly lower interest rates), this kind of indebtedness traps and enslaves millions of Americans.

Linda and I actually *make* several hundred dollars every year from our credit cards. We get a certain percentage back off of everything we charge, so we charge everything we possibly can. But here's the key: we only charge what we need, and we pay off the balance *in full* and *on time* every month. If you don't have a high level of sales resistance and self-discipline, then I would recommend that you perform "plastic surgery" (i.e. cut up your credit cards and throw them away) and learn to live on a cash basis.

Giving

We already established that everything we have comes from and belongs to God, that what we are is God's gift to us, and that what we become is our gift to God. Therefore asking how much we should give to God is not the right question. As mature Christians, we need to learn to ask instead, *"How much of God's money do I keep for myself?"* Radical, huh?

Everyone who has ever been disillusioned or turned off by churches and preachers (particularly certain televangelists) knows that all they want is your money. Much confusion, consternation, controversy, and conflict has always surrounded giving to God. But God doesn't want—or need—your money. What He wants is you!

Polls and surveys consistently show that about 30-35% of self-described born-again, church-going, evangelical Christians tithe. Many people who don't give to God attribute it to a lack of faith—they don't believe they can live on 90% or less of their income (actually, taken together, the tithes and other gifts that are commanded in the Old Testament total 23%—not 10%!). The cold truth is that it's not a lack of faith; it is actually disobedience to God's command—which He views as robbery (Malachi 3:8)—the consequence of which is a curse (Malachi 3:9).

> **A stingy, miserly, hoarding mentality and attitude is something we all come by naturally.**

A stingy, miserly, hoarding mentality and attitude is something we all come by naturally. As I recall, all four of our sons automatically closed their fingers around whatever was placed into their (formerly) tiny little hands as an infant. And I know from whence they inherited that selfish and egocentric tendency!

But if we understand God accurately, we will know how loving and generous God truly is and how much He wants to richly bless us. Note well the manifold blessings and benefits which follow from His command to:

> 'Bring the whole tithe into the storehouse, that there may be food in my house. Test me in this,' says the LORD Almighty, 'and see if I will not throw open the floodgates of heaven and pour out so much blessing that you will not have room enough for it. I will prevent pests from devouring your crops, and the vines in your fields will not cast their fruit,' says the LORD Almighty. 'Then all the nations will call you blessed, for yours will be a delightful land,' says the LORD Almighty (Malachi 3:10-12).

God wants to give us far more than we can ever give Him, because He loves us far more than we do and far more than we can possibly imagine!

The rewards of generous giving are phenomenal. Just look at these incredibly abundant promises of how God's bounteous blessings and benefits are bestowed upon those who do not worship the false god of greed: "Good will come to him who is generous and lends freely, who conducts his affairs with justice" (Psalm 112:5), "A generous man will prosper; he who refreshes others will himself be refreshed" (Proverbs 11:25), "A generous man will himself be blessed, for he shares his food with the poor" (Proverbs 22:9), "Give, and it will be given to you. A good measure, pressed down, shaken together and running over, will be poured into your lap. For with the measure you use, it will be measured to you" (Luke 6:38), and finally, "Remember this: whoever sows sparingly will also reap sparingly, and whoever sows generously will also reap generously" (2 Corinthians 9:6).

The New Testament does not establish a legalistic, definitive amount or percentage that Christians are to give to God's service. What Scripture does teach is much deeper than the specified dollar (or drachma or denari) amount of our weekly or monthly tithe and offering check. As always, God addresses our heart, our motivation, and our attitude more than our behavior.

We are first to give ourselves devotedly to the Lord (2 Corinthians 8:5) and treasure His work (Luke 12:32-34). Then we are to give before we can afford to (2 Corinthians 8:2), beyond our ability (2 Corinthians 8:3), in complete earnestness (2 Corinthians 8:7), with a willing heart (2 Corinthians 8:12), and without grudging (2 Corinthians 9:5). God only wants happy dollars because, "Each man should give what he has decided in his heart to give, not reluctantly or under compulsion, for God loves a cheerful giver" (2 Corinthians 9:7). Consequently, God will make all grace abound to you (2 Corinthians 9:8), meet all of your needs, and give you prosperity (Proverbs 28:27, 2 Corinthians 9:10), which will result in thanksgiving and gratitude to God (2 Corinthians 9:11).

Halting

A friend of mine, Rev. Kevin Shorey, is fond of quoting Albert Einstein's wise old saying, "If you keep doing what you've been doing, then you'll keep getting what you've been getting." The enormous difficulty of changing our behavior is belied by the old Henny Youngman joke: "Doctor, Doctor, it hurts when I do this!" "Well, then don't do that!"

> **It certainly is much easier to get into debt than to get out of it.**

It certainly is much easier to get into debt than to get out of it. But although it is difficult to get out of debt, it isn't really complicated. *What it requires is determination, willingness, self-discipline, cooperation, and sacrifice.* Both of you have to decide to quit doing what you've been doing—if you really want to reduce your stress levels, increase your credit score, and not have your evenings interrupted by debt collectors making threatening phone calls.

After you have accounted, budgeted, communicated, decided, equalized, financed, and given as a couple, you can start to call a halt to your indebtedness. The next thing to do is to activate what is called the "Debt Snowball" (Ramsey, 2007). This is the fastest, simplest way to rescue yourself from the trap of credit debt.

But this kind of snowball will require an attitude shift. Being in debt is humbling and embarrassing.

> But godliness with contentment is great gain. For we brought nothing into the world, and we can take nothing out of it. But if we have food and clothing, we will be content with that. People who want to get rich fall into temptation and a trap and into many foolish and harmful desires that plunge men into ruin and destruction. For the love of money is a root of all kinds of evil. Some people, eager for money, have wandered from the faith and pierced themselves with many griefs. But you, man of God, flee from all this, and pursue righteousness, godliness, faith, love, endurance and gentleness (1 Timothy 6:6-11).

This is why, and how, we must change.

The Debt Snowball works like this. First, curtail all unnecessary spending to stop the bleeding of the red ink. Then make a list all of your debts in order from least to greatest. Pay everything you can toward the debt with the smallest balance, while maintaining minimum payments on all the others. Then after that debt is retired, rejoice, celebrate (inexpensively!) and put all of the money you were paying on that bill onto the second smallest, and so on. Don't worry about interest rates unless two debts have similar payoffs; if they do, then obviously pay off the one with the higher rate first.

Consider other ways of generating extra cash flow to pay off your indebtedness. You may want to get a part-time job, sell some assets (have a garage sale, get rid of some unnecessary luxuries or "toys," replace an expensive vehicle with an older and/or more economical model, etc.), consider refinancing and consolidating your debt to get a lower interest rate (if possible within a tax-deductible second mortgage on your home), start a Health Savings Account for all your healthcare expenses (which shelters them from tax liability), and review your income tax withholdings so that you receive more of your money now in lieu of an income tax refund later. Tough times call for tough measures. Halt what you did to become indebted, and start to live financially free.

Investing

An old saying asks: "Do you work for your money, or does your money work for you?" Although nothing is certain except death and taxes, it is wise to not only prepare for a rainy day but also to plan for the future (Proverbs 21:5, 20). Remember to pay yourself, because "… he who gathers money little by little makes it grow" (Proverbs 13:11).

Experts agree that after you eliminate high-interest and short-term debt, you need to keep at least $1000 in an interest-bearing emergency fund, so that you can replace an appliance that goes out, pay for an unexpected car repair, or handle other unforeseen events in life without plunging yourself back into the depths of despairing debt. Next, an amount equal to three to six months' living expenses should be saved in a money market fund or fixed-term savings account to hedge against an unantic-ipated job loss, pregnancy, extended health crisis, or other ma-jor financially threatening life circumstance.

After that, a couple can start saving for major purchases. By the way, generally speaking, credit unions, followed in order by savings and loans, banks, and then finance companies, respectively, will pay you higher interest rates on savings and will charge you less on loans. Always shop around for the best bargain and safest risk. College funds (including Education Savings Accounts and 529 plans) and retirement plans (including traditional and Roth IRAs and employer matching savings) should be implemented at this point. Finally, you are ready to pay your house off early and speculate in potentially higher risk, diversified investments in order to meet long-term goals and accumulate wealth in order to give it to others.

Estate planning is much more than who gets Aunt Mabel's cedar chest.

Precisely because death and taxes are inevitable, it is imperative that every couple, regardless of the size and scope of their financial portfolio, make provision for how their estate will be distributed upon their passing. Estate planning is similar to other types of financial planning in that it requires thought, discussion, cooperation, and diligence. Estate planning is much more than who gets Aunt Mabel's cedar chest. In addition to equitably allocating your resources, a comprehensive estate plan can save your loved ones much grief and expense regarding how you want your healthcare directed, your funeral conducted, and your loved ones cared for.

Estate plans can be fairly expensive to set up, but many Christian ministries and Christian colleges and universities will customize a trust and/or will for you without charge if you promise to leave a tithe to their ministry or institution upon your passing. Without estate planning, taxes, attorney fees, probate costs, unplanned funeral expenses, and so on will siphon off a huge percentage of your estate.

Title and place all of your personal property into a trust, put all your financial holdings into Transfer on Death accounts, and designate who will have legal authority to put your estate plan into action. This will alleviate much stress, and you will have peace of mind knowing that everything you have will go where and to whom you want, because, "A good man leaves an inheritance for his children's children..." (Proverbs 13:22). You cannot choose whether or not you will leave a legacy. But you can choose what kind of a legacy you will leave!

Scriptural Search

1. Proverbs 23:4-5
2. Ecclesiastes 5:10-12
3. Matthew 6:19-21
4. Luke 12:15
5. 1 Timothy 6:6-10

Ponderable Points

1. What were your parents' attitudes toward and practice regarding money? Consequently, what did you learn about the meaning, power, significance, and value of money?

2. Who made your financial decisions before you were married? Who paid your bills?

3. How did you acquire money as a child and teenager (job, allowance, gifts, etc.)?

4. To what degree is money a topic of discussion or misunderstanding, or a source of tension and friction in your marriage? Can the two of you discuss money issues calmly, rationally, and in a businesslike manner? If not, why?

5. Is your marriage more of a "Miserly Mortimer" and "Frivolous Francine," a "Thrifty Thelma" and "Tightwad Tyrone," a "Spendthrift Sylvester" and "Shopaholic Suzette," or some combination thereof? Is there anything about your lifestyle that may be in conflict with godly values and/or may place a heavy strain on your family budget? What is your current standard of living? Do you both feel happy with it? Do you have enough money to meet it? If not, what changes do you need to make to balance your budget?

Activation Activities:

1. Ask your spouse about their answers to the above questions. Listen for their emotional experiences they had regarding money while growing up (e.g. fear, guilt, anxiety, worry, shame, responsibility, enjoyment, hope, security, love, and/or satisfaction) in order to more deeply understand them in the area of mastering monetary management. How did money make them feel? Try to empathize and understand, not judge or criticize.

2. Attempt to compassionately understand what makes your spouse's possibly conflicting stance towards money so different from yours. What feelings or issues for both of you get channeled into disagreements or misunderstandings about money in your relationship? Identify what is most valuable to you in terms of your priorities and preferences (i.e. would you rather save money for a vacation or spend money for new furniture?).

3. Consider doing an in-depth biblical study of money management and financial freedom. Invite your spouse to join a video class or enroll in a small group study using curriculum such as that offered by Crown Ministries, Christian Financial Concepts, or Financial Peace University.

Recommended Resources:

The Challenge of the Disciplined Life: Reflections on Money, Sex and Power, Richard Foster (1985).

Money Matters, Larry Burkett (2001).

Taming the Money Monster: Five Steps to Conquering Debt, Ron Blue (2000).

The Total Money Makeover: A Proven Plan for Financial Fitness, Dave Ramsey (2007).

Money and Marriage God's Way, Howard Dayton (2009).

CHAPTER TEN

Together Time

One man to another: My wife and I have discovered the key to a successful marriage. Every week we go to this quiet, little out-of-the-way restaurant for a nice, romantic candlelight dinner and dancing. Second man: It sounds wonderful! First man: It is—she goes on Tuesdays and I go on Thursdays!

"Finally, all of you, live in harmony with one another; be sympathetic, love as brothers, be compassionate and humble."

—1 PETER 3:8

*I*t is true that the couple who prays together stays together. But it is equally true that the couple who *plays* together also stays together! For a marriage to remain strong, secure, and stable, couples must find ways to keep injecting fun times and invigorating experiences into it. "Together time" is essential for a healthy and vibrant marriage.

Let's take a brief, nostalgic trip down memory lane. Think back to when you first met your spouse. What are some of your most pleasurable and cherished memories with each other? What made you want to spend mutually meaningful and personally prioritized time with them? What made those times so special? Chances are it was because you both had a lot of fun and shared a lot of laughter doing playful, silly, carefree, and zany things with each other.

Many long hours were spent together doing mutually enjoyable activities. Times for being together were usually carefully or even meticulously planned, eagerly anticipated, longingly fantasized about, and carried out in the utmost detail. Other times, you were probably able to just spontaneously have fun in whimsical, childlike ways that you would have never anticipated, because the other person just naturally brought that innocent inner child in you out to play.

Both of you probably thought to yourselves, "Wow, if dating and courtship is this fun and wonderful, just imagine how awesome it will be to spend the rest of my life with this person!" You looked longingly and lovingly into each other's eyes while time seemed to somehow both stand still and fly by. You spent every moment you could together. You wanted to be together forever... so you got married.

> **Marriage can eventually become much more work than play.**

Unfortunately, over the years things usually change. Life happens and reality sets in. With the responsibilities of jobs, kids, church, school, community service, and the umpteen other things in which you and your spouse may have become involved, sadly there is often little time or energy left over for each other. The demands and cares of life often ironically drain the marriage relationship of the very energy, excitement, and enthusiasm which originally brought the couple together. Marriage can eventually become much more work than play.

When couples reach this disappointing, depressing, and deteriorating point in their marriage, romance can become routine, passion can become predictable, and monogamy can become monotony. Jim and Sally Conway poignantly encapsulate the dynamics of this all-too-common marital degeneration process. They warn, "If you and your mate aren't taking time for fun and leisure, you likely have a boring marriage with overtones of danger. Boredom is the slow, insistent destruction of a marriage; it works similarly to the way arthritis inexorably debilitates the body. Movement is gradually restricted. Pain increases, and the simplest tasks may become impossible undertakings" (2000, p. 155). Ouch. No engaged couple expects to end up like this. And none should!

To illustrate this point more deeply, let's continue with the physical analogy. A world-class Olympic or professional athlete invests and exerts an incredible amount of time, effort, dedication, and energy into getting in top-notch shape, in order to perform at their peak or optimum levels of performance. But do you know what happens to our muscle tone and cardiovascular system if we sit around and do nothing for just a few weeks? Years' worth of hard work, determination, sweat, and possibly tears are slowly but surely lost. Unexercised muscle tissue all too quickly turns to flab. What used to win trophies now merely atrophies.

> The most passionately hot, starry-eyed, deliriously happy couple can gradually grow bored and apathetic if they fail to
> find ways to keep playing and recreating with each other.

This same universal law of physics (called entropy) also applies to marriage relationships. The most passionately hot, starry-eyed, deliriously happy couple can gradually grow bored and apathetic if they fail to find ways to keep playing and recreating with each other. They may live together but never be stimulated by one another. They may eat together, sleep to-

245

gether, watch TV together, attend church together, have kids together, go to movies together, or entertain friends together, but have no fun with or interest in each other. She no longer laughs at his jokes that she used to think were so hilarious. He no longer breaks the speed limit to get home from work each night to be captivated by her flirtatious, dazzling smile. They have lost that spark, that certain something, that elusive and illusory lightning in a bottle that they both once enjoyed.

Again in the Conways' words,

> Living in a boring marriage is just like being prisoners unable to escape from a prison camp. They have given up hope. They watch each other slowly age and gray, knowing they will die in this trapped existence. The more boring the marriage, the greater the vacuum. Sooner or later something will rush in and fill that vacuum. That something—or someone—may cause the marriage to break. A boring marriage is like putting on extra weight. It happens gradually, but at some point you say, 'Hey, I'm fat!' A dull marriage may exist quietly for years, but at some point, one of the partners will finally say, 'our marriage stinks' (ibid. p. 156).

To borrow a line from the classic poem, *Casey at the Bat,* it can get to the place where, "There is no joy in Mudville" tonight. Or any other night, for that matter.

The Power and Purpose of Play

That wonderful wizard of word-smithing, Theodore Geisel, more affectionately known as Dr. Seuss, was all about playing and having fun in life. In his *magnum opus* (most famous work), *The Cat in the Hat*, an outrageously comedic feline spends an entire day doing everything he can to get two rather dull, unimaginative children to loosen up and let their hair down. Exhausted and perhaps a bit exasperated that his most hilarious antics and uproarious escapades fail to elicit any laughter from these two boring, uptight kids, the Cat famously concludes, "It's fun to have fun, but you have to know how!"

Play is the work of children.

It is been said that play is the work of children. This apparent paradox makes more sense when we understand that it is through the magic, marvel, and mystery of play that healthy children process and discharge stress. Children can naturally spend hour upon hour—without even noticing or being constrained by the time expended—doing a wide variety of creative and fantastic activities without inhibition or reservation. Children are free to run, climb, dance, romp, jump, and dive as they adopt mythical personas; singing, yelling, and chattering their way through imaginary worlds of their own unique creation.

Can you harken back in your mind's eye to those days of long, long ago when you could play like that with an innocent child-like quality? If not, then perhaps you will identify with the wise words of Tim Hansel in his tellingly titled book, *When I Relax, I Feel Guilty*. He asks: "Is it possible that your days are hurrying by so fast that you don't fully taste them anymore? Are play and rest foreign words in your living vocabulary? When was the last time you flew a kite, went for a bike ride, or made something with your hands? When was the last time you caught yourself enjoying life so deeply that you couldn't quite get the smile off your face? Chances are, it's been too long" (1979, p. 11-12). And if—because you grew up with harsh, punitive, and/or guilt-inducing parents—you were never allowed to be an innocent, carefree child, then being able to play well becomes all the more difficult and complicated. But it is absolutely necessary.

Research clearly demonstrates that successful couples have learned the secret of prioritizing and including fun,

247

leisure, and humor in their marriage relationship.

Research clearly demonstrates that successful couples have learned the secret of prioritizing and including fun, leisure, and humor in their marriage relationship (Conway and Conway, 2000; Exley, 2008; Markman et al, 2001). These couples don't think play is a waste of time or has to be expensive. Furthermore, they don't put play off for some distant day in the future. Nor do they carry around the burden of punitive, puritanical guilt, which drives them to be about all work and no play.

For these couples, the common factor in intimate play of all kinds is its ability to stabilize a relationship, maintain connectivity, reduce conflict, and facilitate feelings of closeness and attachment. The capacity for playfulness includes fun, but it is considerably more than the partners' ability to amuse themselves and one another. Private nicknames, shared jokes, gentle teasing, fantasy, spontaneity, emotional safety, and make-believe all contribute to a couple's ability to relax and play. They simply enjoy each other and being around each other, especially in fun, "happifying" ways.

In their fun new book, *Little Book of Great Dates* (2013), which emphasizes the importance of marital dating, Dr. Greg and Erin Smalley cite research proving that couples who spend weekly quality time together are 3.5 times more likely to report being "very happy" in their marriage than those who don't. These couples also reported a 300 percent increase in their communication and sexual satisfaction. Holy matrimony, Agnes, what are we waiting for!?

Benefits and Blessing of Re-creating

Specifically, the big, sophisticated adult word we have developed for play is "recreation." But I believe we typically mispronounce and misunderstand what that word is truly designed to mean: RE-creation. *When you play, it is good for you physi-*

cally, emotionally, mentally, relationally, and spiritually. As you rest, reboot, and recharge, you become literally and figuratively re-created, renewed, restored, and regenerated. Let's now briefly examine some of the ways in which play, or re-creation, is good for us and for our marriage.

> The toxic effects of stress are reversed as you re-create. Your immune system is revitalized. Your entire body is refreshed and renewed.

1. Physically

At the physiological level, the benefits of play and fun leisure activities are enormous. Chemically-speaking, powerful natural pain killers, disease fighters (even that very word, DIS-ease, implies we become ill when we are stressed and not relaxed!), and energy boosters called endorphins are released into the bloodstream. The toxic effects of stress are reversed as you re-create. Your immune system is revitalized. Your entire body is refreshed and renewed in many different ways.

At the cellular level, white blood cell production is significantly elevated when someone relaxes, laughs, and has fun. Several thousand years ago, Solomon documented these many bodily benefits and blessings of play, fun, and laughter when he observed that, "A heart at peace gives life to the body" (Proverbs 14:30), that, "A cheerful look brings joy to the heart, and good news gives health to the bones" (Proverbs 15:30), and that, "A cheerful heart is good medicine..." (Proverbs 17:22). Leisure activities produce a heart at peace, cheerful looks, and a cheerful heart which help us to live happier, healthier, longer, more fulfilling lives.

As with most things, although leisure and recreational activities are very important, they need to be kept in balance along with other key aspects of life. Inadequate sleep, lack of regular exercise, and/or an improper diet will most assuredly diminish the quality and quantity of everything else you do in life because your health will be negatively impacted. On the other hand, a healthy, mature, and meaningful life can never be all or only about fun and games. Obviously we must keep play, leisure, and recreation in balance accordingly.

When we feel good on the outside it's much easier to feel good on the inside, and vice-versa.

2. Emotionally

When we feel good on the outside it's much easier to feel good on the inside, and vice-versa. When we are regularly and religiously re-creating, it prevents us from getting into the pitfalls of predictability, the ruts of routine, the blues of boredom, and the doldrums of drudgery. As Solomon observed, "A happy heart makes the face cheerful, but heartache crushes the spirit" (Proverbs 15:13). Playing and having fun will generally boost anyone's spirits and mood.

We live in a frequently stressful and depressing world in what has been called "the age of anxiety." But it's hard to become stressed and depressed—much less stay stressed and depressed—when we prioritize and emphasize the importance of meaningful play in our lives and marriage relationship. We just have to exercise the choice to allow our inner child to go out and have fun with our playmate.

Dozens of scriptures refer to the manifold blessings and benefits of being in a relaxed state of peace. When we experience the condition of peacefulness, it results in our being happy, healthy, and harmonious (Proverbs 14:30). Periodically getting away from the demands and pressures of work, kids, and a myriad of electronic devices helps us to unwind and relax. By reducing our anxiety and stress levels, we can emerge re-energized and reinvigorated to conquer the next challenge or obstacle in our marriage relationship and/or in life in general.

3. Mentally

Regular recreation also enables us to focus and concentrate more effectively. The Bible declares, "You will keep in perfect peace him whose mind is steadfast, because he trusts in you" (Isaiah 26:3). It's hard to steadfastly think clearly and rationally when we are under a continual load of stress and pressure.

> **Rest and recreation will defrag and decontaminate your cognitive operating system.**

If they are honest with themselves, most people today will admit that their brain is frequently on overload or in overdrive from the persistent pressures and problems of life. But by temporarily getting our mind off our current circumstances and being able to relax, our ability to think clearly and creatively—to effectively problem-solve and figure out solutions to perplexing predicaments—is significantly enhanced. Rest and recreation will defrag and decontaminate your cognitive operating system.

Fun cannot be forced, but it can be fostered. Sit down with your spouse and make a list of fun things you would like to do together. Your list can include simple things such as going to a carnival, attending a seasonal local festival, exploring a nature trail, driving out into the country on a starry night to watch for falling stars, playing cards, going for a bike ride, heading to the park or beach and throwing a Frisbee around, and major things like elaborately planning your ultimate dream vacation. What you do to have fun is not nearly as important as making the decision to do it. Deciding to have playful fun is much more of a mindset than a maneuver.

4. Relationally

I know it sounds gross, but I believe *the couple that sweats together sticks together*! Play and exercise will not only keep your body in shape, they will keep your marriage in shape. Whether it's working out at the gym, playing coed volleyball or softball, raking leaves into a big pile and gleefully jumping into them, riding bicycles, jogging, gardening, or taking long, leisurely walks together, couples that regularly engage in fun activities together can't help but feel close and connected.

A state of relaxed togetherness results when you and your spouse are playful with each other.

A state of relaxed togetherness results when you and your spouse are playful with each other. Typically it was fun, relaxing times and activities that created your emotional attachment to the relationship in the first place. When we are relaxed, we are usually emotionally open and nondefensive. This naturally causes us to feel safe enough to become honest and transparent, which leads to in-depth communication and self-disclosure. These conditions are a surefire prescription for couples to enhance their feelings of being in love.

An additional benefit of regularly prioritizing meaningful time together is that it enhances each partner's self-esteem. Both people know that they are valuable to the other, and this keeps them from feeling neglected by or unimportant to their spouse. *Spending meaningful time together makes both people know they matter to the other.*

When you make plans to establish ongoing, quality couple time, both people gradually begin to desire and look forward to spending more time together having fun and re-creating. They find ways to arrange their schedules to meet for lunch. They protect their days off and spend them together. They try to eat dinner together every evening. They look forward to developing mutual interests and taking up hobbies they both can enjoy. As result, the marriage is strengthened, solidified, and sustained.

5. *Spiritually*

Jesus Himself understood the necessity of keeping all of life's important needs in balance. Though He was fully and completely dedicated to fulfilling His mission (John 10:10), there were times when the stress and demands of His ministry were so great that He and His friends had to get away for some R and R and go hiking, boating, and fishing (Mark 6:30-32). He took time to specifically hang around with, value, and enjoy the innocent wonder of little kids (Matthew 18:1-6). And He regularly took time to get away and "re-create" by Himself in solitary places to pray when the people, problems, and pressures of ministry became more than He could handle in His own human capacities (Luke 5:16).

Numerous studies over the years have verified the many physical and psychological benefits of prayer, meditation, praise, and worship. Throughout the Psalms, David frequently marvels at the majesty and magnificence of God, when he considers the wonders of nature or contemplates the vastness of the heavens. In a similar way, we can feel closer and more connected to God when we take a leisurely stroll throughout His beautiful universe and consider His glorious and mighty works (Psalm 19:1-6 89:6-11, 148:1-13).

How long has it been since you had fun with God? Seriously! Maybe this notion seems far-fetched to your theology, or perhaps even downright heretical. But I believe the Almighty Creator had a blast designing the universe, which He customized for us—His creatures—to thoroughly enjoy. From making the big nose on the aardvark to the awesome kaleidoscopic variety of tropical fish to painting the stripes on the zebra, God's absolute delight in His handiwork is unmistakable (Romans 1:20). From the macroscopic expanse of far-off galaxies to the microscopic complexity of subatomic particles, the many varieties of creative critters and the multiplied vastness of the collective cosmos fabulously display God's playfulness, provision, and power.

> **I believe our loving Heavenly Father is absolutely thrilled when we have fun—and He gets a kick out of it when His children are delighted.**

I believe our loving Heavenly Father is absolutely thrilled when we have fun—and He gets a kick out of it when His children are delighted. Especially when we are delighted in and with Him! Throughout the Psalms, David uses the expression of "delight" to describe the joy and pleasure he derives from worship, meditation on God's word, and personal relationship with Him (Psalm 1:2, 35:9, 43:4, 111:2, 112:1, 119:16, 119:24, 119:35, 119:47, 119:70, 119:92, 119:143, 119:174).

Was God so totally exhausted and completely wrung out from His creative work that He had to rest on the seventh day so He could summon enough strength to get right back to it the next week and do it all over again? I seriously doubt it. I believe God was setting a precedent and a pattern for us—demonstrating that it is okay to lazily lounge, leisurely laugh, and lackadaisically lollygag after we have worked well. After all, "...anyone who enters God's rest also rests from his own work, just as God did from his" (Hebrews 4:10). God is not a harsh, hard-driving task master. He just wants us to hang out with Him at least one day a week because He delights in us and wants us to delight in Him.

Consider scheduling a personal retreat to get alone with God and specifically listen to, deeply relax with, and enjoy Him (Psalm 46:10). You might just find Him to be thoroughly delighted and overjoyed with your decision. The Bible says God orchestrates all of heaven to rejoice when one sinner decides to enter into relationship with Him, and He's planning to throw a huge party for all of us who do so when we finally get to meet

Him face to face (Revelation 19:6-9). Heaven is going to be incredibly *fun*!

Dare to Deliberately Date: Planned Play with a Purpose

Unfortunately, for some couples, there is a sense in which monogamy and monotony have come to mean the same thing. This is because both can become stale, repetitious, predictable, and boring. These are couples who no longer date each other like they used to. They do not take the time, effort, and energy needed to plan meaningful play times together. To make and maintain a magnificent marriage requires that a couple invest time, effort, and energy to do so.

> To make and maintain a magnificent marriage requires that a couple invest time, effort, and energy to do so.

As the Arps said, "Show us a marriage that is faltering, and we will show you a marriage where the fun is gone. And where the fun is gone, there's a mighty good chance there is no 'date their mate' with that couple" (in Stoop and Stoop, 2002, p. 153). According to one large study, the average married couple only goes out on a date with their spouse once every two months (Markman, et al, 2001). That is simply not nearly enough to maintain, much less nurture, a healthy marriage relationship.

I want to state right out of the gate that it's great to date your mate before it's too late to relate. (Wait—don't groan and bemoan your fate! I'm just having fun; that's the whole point of this chapter!) A date is an intentionally planned time to be together with your spouse in a fun and relaxing way. A successful date is a time to reminisce and rekindle those times of mirth and merriment as you have fun and frolic together.

Again, let's hear from the Arps, who said:

We believe that having a healthy, growing marriage relationship requires friendship, fun, and romance. And there's
no better way to encourage all of these things than having
dates! Great dates are more than going to see a movie
and tuning out the world for a while. Great dates involve
communicating with one another, reviving the spark that initially ignited your fire, and developing mutual interests and
goals that are not focused on your careers or your children.
Great dates can revitalize your relationship (1997, p. 12).

So if dating is so fantastic, fun, and fabulous, why doesn't the
average couple do it more often? I suspect most couples have
three basic reasons why they don't date on a regular, weekly
basis.

**Most couples complain that their life is simply too busy to
engage in regular, relaxing re-creation with their mate.**

1. Busyness:

First of all, most couples complain that their life is simply too
busy to engage in regular, relaxing re-creation with their mate.
Yet before marriage, most people typically put the rest of their
lives on hold for the sake of investing in and building their new
romantic relationship. Countless long hours were spent being
together and dreaming of being together forever. But once a
couple "closes the deal," they naturally shift their energies toward constructing their careers, homes, and families. Consequently, their marriage often gets neglected, the romance cools,
one or both people feel taken for granted, both spouses' needs
go unmet, and ultimately, the couple begins to gradually drift
apart.

We all have 168 hours allocated to us every week. And for
many couples, it's hard to have fun together without intentionally setting aside time in order to actually make it happen. It may
not seem very fun or spontaneous to pull out your personal
electronic devices or take the family calendar down from the

refrigerator to coordinate schedules, but for most couples, time together needs to be deliberately arranged, or it simply doesn't happen. Most people find it easier to religiously schedule dates on an ongoing, recurrent basis.

One of my professors in graduate school lived out an impressive and inspiring example of this very important relationship principle. At the time I took a class from him, he had—for the previous *37 YEARS*—never once missed dating his wife on Friday nights. As a busy, successful, and well-known clinical professional, author, and speaker, he received many opportunities to conduct weekend seminars, conferences, and retreats. His standard response to these invitations was that he would say yes on two conditions: first, that they buy two plane tickets, and second, that he would be glad to speak on Friday afternoon or Saturday—but that he would be free from any obligations on Friday evening. Sometimes the organization or conference agreed to those conditions, and sometimes they did not, but later on, I had the opportunity to meet his wife. Suffice it to say that she had smiley wrinkles! She knew she was deeply cherished and highly prioritized by her famous husband.

Think back to the automobile illustration at the beginning of the book. After going to all of the hard work and investment involved in acquiring our marriage partner at the beginning of our relationship, if we don't ever "fill up the gas tank," we can't expect that wonderful, fancy new "vehicle" to take us very far. *Dating is like filling each other's fuel tank—it needs to be done on a regular, weekly basis.*

Furthermore, a vehicle's oil and filter need to be changed every few thousand miles. In a similar way, all marriages need a weekend getaway every few months to keep the relational engine running clean and strong. And annual vacations are analogous to tune-ups and other regularly scheduled maintenance that a vehicle requires. But often, once the "new car smell" gradually evaporates, owners just do not have the same sense of urgency to care for their vehicle like they used to, particularly if hasn't been running smoothly lately.

2. Cost:

A second common objection to regular, weekly dating is that couples believe they can't afford it. However, I believe we simply can't afford not to. It's much cheaper to properly maintain a vehicle than to overhaul it when it breaks down. As always, prevention is easier—and much less expensive—than cure. Fun doesn't have to be elaborate or expensive.

Call me cheap (and admittedly I really do love a good "deal"), but I believe there is actually an inverse correlation between the amount of money spent on a date and the amount of relational benefit it provides. The traditional "dinner and a movie" date actually offers very little opportunity for intimacy or exclusivity. Having strangers sit within a few feet of you during your meal naturally keeps your conversation superficial and non-private. Then, sitting side-by-side jointly viewing the entertainment in front of you maintains the law of physics, which states that two parallel lines never intersect. Conversely, a walk in the park and a picnic is not only much less expensive; it can be a terrific opportunity to maintain your marriage because of the intimacy it potentiates. Watching a glorious sunset over a serene lake or beautiful beach from a grassy hillside or a lofty mountaintop can be wonderfully romantic.

> The traditional "dinner and a movie" date actually offers very little opportunity for intimacy or exclusivity.

In Jim and Sally Conway's words, "Saying that you can't have any fun because it costs too much money is a copout for being too lazy to think creatively" (2000, p. 165). Sit down together and think about the most enjoyable and fun things you've ever done or would like to do—without considering the cost. Use brainstorming techniques to make a list of all types of possible activities you can think of, no matter how foolish or outrageous they may seem. There are many free or low-cost activities available in most communities, from exhibits to lectures to tours to shows to sightseeing opportunities. I encourage couples to "play tourist" in their own hometown. People are often amazed at the irony that they have never seen or experienced the very things, which visitors come to their community to do.

Explore your area through the eyes of a visitor. Go for a walk, hike, or bike ride. Visit a museum, art fair, or music festival. Take a day trip into the surrounding countryside and see historical sites, browse through flea markets and antique stores, and enjoy unwinding at nearby regional or state parks. Check out your local visitors' bureau or Chamber of Commerce website or the weekend section of your local newspaper for things like free concerts, farmers markets, high school or college theatrical productions, conservation department classes, and other community events.

Be adventurous. Don't be afraid to try new things or things you haven't done in a while. Start a new hobby together. Do something neither of you has ever done before. Who knows, she could have fun at a tractor pull, and he might enjoy the opera. Just think about how much serious fun you can have together!

> Paradoxically, children are both a natural outgrowth of and an inherent barrier to marital intimacy

3. Childcare:

It is perhaps one of life's greatest ironies that the ultimate consequence of a husband and wife being thoroughly intimate

259

with one another results in perhaps the greatest obstacles there are to maintaining that very intimacy. They're called children! Paradoxically, children are both a natural outgrowth of and an inherent barrier to marital intimacy.

The Bible says that children are a reward from the LORD (Psalm 127:3-5), but from a worst-case marital relationship scenario, at times they can seem a lot more like a curse from the devil. The presence of children will rarely strengthen a marriage; research shows they are more likely to undermine and weaken it. The difference is quite literally in how we manage the details and dynamics as a couple.

By virtue of merely breathing, the existence of children makes it challenging for a married couple to easily and naturally be alone together. But obviously, no children are ever responsible for their existence––their parents are. And because children are a miraculous, priceless gift from God, they need to be nurtured and treasured as such, and should therefore never be neglected or abused. Children are both innocent and defenseless, and they need to be cared for with the utmost concern and protected with the most stringent standards of safety and security.

So, for many couples, childcare challenges are a prime reason for not regularly dating and re-creating with each other. When children are very small and demanding of parental attention, it can be very difficult to summon the time, energy, and desire to keep playfully loving and focusing on one another in order to keep the marital friendship and passion fires burning. When your energy is drained, the dirty diaper pail is overflowing, and your nerves are shot from hearing fussing, whining and crying all day, it can be very difficult to think about playfully dating your mate. However, that's generally the time when you need to do it the most!

This calls for creativity, flexibility, and outside-the box-problem solving. Use your baby's nap times to spend time together, or perhaps take a nap then yourself, so you can put the kids to bed early that evening and plan to enjoy fun alone times at home with your spouse. Grab an hour or two together during your kids' practices, rehearsals, and/or club events before you have to go back to pick them up. For school-aged children, attempt to arrange your schedules so that you can take a long lunch hour to spend fun time together while the school is providing free child care. See if you can hire a babysitter to take your kids to the playground on Saturday morning for a couple of hours. Plan to have special getaway times together during your children's summer camps or extended visits to their grandparents' house.

The entire issue of babysitting or childcare can be very complicated and problematic for many couples. If you don't have healthy, loving grandparents or other extended family members nearby with whom you can confidently leave your children, or if you do not have the funds to pay a reliable and responsible teenager (whom you can trust not to have their friends over and host a huge party at your house while you're not there), I would suggest forming a child care co-op.

The way this works is actually quite simple. Find one or two other couples with whom you have common values, beliefs, and parenting standards, and offer to trade child care with them once a week. For example, on Monday night, you and the Joneses leave your kids at the Smith's house. On Thursday night, the Joneses and the Smiths leave their children at your house. Then on Saturday, the Joneses host the Smith's children and yours while you go out on a date. The date nights can either be fixed or set up on a rotating basis.

This way you will have the peace of mind that your children are going to be safely cared for in an acceptable environment, so that you and your spouse can go out and relax and have fun without fear or worry. An added built-in bonus is that your children are exposed to a couple of other healthy families and have opportunities to develop close and enduring friendships with two other sets of children. Plus, no money need exchange hands (see, I told you I was thrifty!), and three marriages are strengthened in the process.

The two most predictable times of greatest stress on a marriage relationship are when you have toddlers and teens. Your children will eventually grow up and leave home. As important as it is to nurture them, it is even more important to nurture your marriage. Your relationship needs to be strong, so that your children will eventually have a healthy place to leave their kids when *they* go out on their dates with their spouses!

Make sure to plan for fun. Flirt with each other. Read a joke book or watch a silly comedy. Prioritize "together time" to both intentionally and spontaneously laugh and play with each other. You will both be glad you did. *Remember: life is short and then we die.* Relax and re-create your relationship.

Scriptural Search

1. Proverbs 14:30
2. Proverbs 15:13, 30
3. Proverbs 17:22
4. Mark 6:30-32
5. Luke 5:16

Ponderable Points

1. Think back to fun, silly, and playful times you had with your spouse early in your relationship. What made those times special? How might you re-create those or similar experiences?

2. Examine yourself objectively. Are you fun to be around? Does your spouse look forward to being with you in a relaxing way? Have you become boring, predictable, and unexciting to your mate? How often do you laugh? Are you playful, flirtatious, and spontaneously affectionate?

3. Does it take money in order to relax and have fun? Why or why not?

4. Do you and/or your mate feel neglected or taken for granted?

5. Share with each other some memories of the most fun experiences you've ever had in your life.

Activation Activities

1. Fun cannot be coerced, but it can be cultivated, and if we fail to plan, we plan to fail. How long has it been since you and your mate have had a fun, relaxing date? A weekend getaway? How many dates have you had in the past 90 days? Strongly consider scheduling a regular, weekly date night.

2. List and discuss the challenges that stand in the way of having fun in your relationship (e.g. time and fatigue pressures, stress, unresolved conflict, lack of privacy, etc.). Communicate

with your spouse what you would like to do about these obstacles, and together develop a plan of action to address them. Make yourselves accountable to each other as to when you will begin.

3. Do you schedule regular "together time" away from work and household demands in order to prioritize and invest in your marriage relationship? Do you regularly and intentionally date your mate? Brainstorm and discuss with your spouse the kinds of dates you would find fun, interesting, relaxing, and enjoyable, and put them on the calendar. Remember to have fun during this exercise—allow all wacky/crazy/outrageous ideas, regardless of how comical, unrealistic, or impractical they may seem. Be creative! Make a list of fun, mutually enjoyable, relaxing things you'd like to do together. List simple things like walk in the park or a picnic, as well as elaborate events such as an ultimate dream vacation or second honeymoon.

Recommended Resources

The Healthy Marriage Handbook, Louise Ferrebee (ed.) (2001).
10 Great Dates to Energize Your Marriage, David and Claudia Arp (1997).
Little Book of Great Dates: 52 Creative Ways to Make Your Marriage Fun, Greg and Erin Smalley (2013).
The Ultimate Marriage Builder, David and Claudia Arp (1994).
52 Fantastic Dates for You and Your Mate, David and Claudia Arp (1993).

CHAPTER ELEVEN

Attractive Appear-ance

Wife: Honey does this dress make me look fat?
Husband: Sweetheart, I don't know how to tell you this,
but it's not the dress!

"...The LORD does not look at the things man looks at.
Man looks at the outward appearance, but the LORD
looks at the heart."

—1 SAMUEL 16:7

We live in a culture that is absolutely obsessed with physical appearance. The degree to which a person's physical characteristics are considered to be desirable or aesthetically pleasing is often a huge initial and ongoing factor in how and why someone is attracted to another person. This "chemistry" between two people is actually a significant and literal bonding agent in first cementing a relationship, and is also very important to ongoing feelings of attachment and attraction.

As it turns out, there is a lot of pretty cool scientific stuff involved in that certain and often-elusive "chemistry" of the proverbial first magical look between star-crossed lovers from across a crowded room. As a matter of fact, according to neurological research, it only takes the brain about one second to register powerful—and often permanent—images of physical and sexual attraction! Whereas love is not born at first sight, attraction normally is. By the way, it has been said that "love at first sight" is often cured by a second look!

In this chapter, we will address several fascinating aspects of this whole physical appearance/attraction phenomenon, beginning with various physiological-biochemical issues involved in the process. Next, we will explore several key socio-cultural dynamics and standards which typically regulate the laws of attraction. Third, we will discuss important but intangible elements of attraction, such as how one's attitudes and actions interact with the other factors involved in attraction. Fourth, aspects of aging, maturation, and health and/or medical issues related to physical appearance will be considered. Fifth, we will consider crucial self-care factors, which affect one's attractiveness and attractability. And finally, we will examine various scriptural issues relating physical appearance and attraction.

Physiological Factors

According to Dr. Barton Goldsmith, the phenomenon of being in love produces some of the most powerful drugs on earth (2009). Furthermore, this all happens inside our own brains without us ever even taking a pill! It turns out that chemistry actually does play a very significant and substantial role in the science of attraction and the experience of feeling in love.

When we first gazed in awe and wonder at that attractive person across that crowded room, as our eyes locked in on each other, our pupils dilated. As our heart went pitter patter, our pulse quickened. This caused our metabolism to escalate, which in turn caused the embarrassing consequences of dry mouth and sweaty palms. Brain scan studies show that when one falls in love (or more accurately, when one is attracted to and infatuated with someone else), areas in the brain with a high concentration of receptors for dopamine are activated. Dopamine is a powerful neurochemical which is highly correlated with motivation, feelings of euphoria, and functional dynamics of addiction. Dopamine is the same chemical which gets triggered by certain stimulant drugs or medications.

Thus, there is a scientifically-based reality to the "high" one experiences from feeling in love. Correspondingly, when one goes through a break-up with a loved one, this chemical supply is cut off and the individual goes through a very real sense of chemical withdrawal. It turns out we actually *can* get hooked on a feeling. No wonder breaking up is so hard to do! It's super painful and really stinks.

Speaking of scent, certain body chemicals called pheromones are God's natural love potions. When women are ovulating, they secrete powerful chemicals known as copulins—a scent which genetically attracts men. When a man gets a whiff of this natural feminine aroma, his testosterone levels automatically raise. Consequently, he, in turn, secretes androsterone, an odor which tends to naturalistically repel women who aren't ovulating but attracts those who are!

The olfactory impact of most pheromones is greatly diminished, however, as a result of daily, regular hygienic practices such as bathing or showering. Isn't this wonderfully romantic? Maybe the old blunt and crude pick-up lines like, "This is bigger than both of us, baby," or "There's no use fighting it, gorgeous; we just can't help ourselves," really are true! (Remember to keep all this straight and in balance the next time you buy cologne, perfume, or shaving lotion for your spouse. It may actually mask or suppress that "animal" within them!)

Truly, there is a lot to the fact that a couple who is attracted to one another has a unique or certain chemistry

between them.

While all this smelly stuff is going on within the attraction process, the brain is hard at work secreting various other chemicals in addition to dopamine and pheromones. When sex appeal is registered, the brain first of all generates oxytocin, a very powerful "glue" chemical, which naturally bonds feelings of romantic attachment. As this process unfolds, several more neurochemicals are released, including testosterone, serotonin, and vasopressin, all of which augment and facilitate feelings of physical attraction. Truly, there is a lot to the fact that a couple who is attracted to one another has a unique or certain chemistry between them.

Speaking of physical attraction per se, scientific research has consistently validated certain cultural stereotypes regarding which physical attributes seem to most strongly activate those complex chemicals of physical attraction. Generally speaking, women are instinctively drawn to males who are taller than them, have broad shoulders, and possess a deeper-toned voice, a relatively narrow waist (rock-hard abs are a definite plus), a V-shaped torso (along with a pleasing posterior), and a high degree of facial symmetry.

Men, on average, are naturally attracted to women who are shorter than them, have a youthful appearance, possess a high degree of facial symmetry, and have full breasts, large dilated pupils, full lips, and a low waist-to-hip ratio. Additional factors such as body scent, posture, general healthfulness, and various neurochemicals also play important roles in the whole business of male-female attraction.

Socio-Cultural Factors

The costs of looking attractive run to well over 100 billion dollars per year (the cosmetics industry's huge and lucrative profits greatly exceed the annual gross national product of many coun-

ATTRACTIVE APPEARANCE

tries), and are exceeded only by the costs of not being considered one of the "beautiful people." It is been said that beauty is in the eye of the beholder, but it is usually more greatly emphasized in the eyelashes, eyebrows, lips, cheeks, skin tone, and shape of the beholden! I used to feel really sorry for ladies who in our society are expected to put ground-up pig innards and bat poop on their faces—and then I realized that when we gentlemen kiss our wives, we ingest that stuff! Now I feel sorry for both women and men!

Culturally, emphasis on men's physical attractiveness has historically been disproportionally lower than that for women. Recently however, the cosmetics industry has been churning out progressively more products and services aimed toward helping men become more attractive, especially regarding the so-called "metrosexual" man. Who knows? A generation or two down the road we may well see more of an equalization of these issues between the genders.

But as of now, Patti Endrei declares, "Looks are very important to men!...God has wired men in such a way that their sex drive is connected to their eyes. Let's face it, men are aroused visually whether we like it or not...men care about appearance at least twice as much as we do and quite frankly, appearances do matter to me and to most women" (2006, p. 209). She wisely concludes: "The male gender's fixation with our appearance may seem shallow to us but it is the way they are wired from birth to the grave. To rewire a home is a very big ordeal and a very costly process. Instead of attempting to rewire your husband, why not get with the flow and put some electricity in your marriage by looking your very best for him" (ibid.).

Due to incredibly intense social pressures, "Women spend a lot of time, energy, and money trying to look as pretty as they can" (Smith, 2012, p. 48). This cultural emphasis upon external beauty and physical attraction is disproportionately aimed toward females and starts at a very young age. From Barbie dolls (talk about an impossibly unrealistic and totally unachievable body type!) to air-brushed/enhanced, photo-shopped magazine cover and centerfold images, girls and women are expected to appear in highly stereotyped and heavily sexualized ways.

This obsessive preoccupation with beautiful appearance continues throughout a woman's lifespan, yet, "... as she gets older, she'll start doubting that she could still be attractive to the opposite sex" (ibid.). No matter how beautiful or attractive someone is (or is considered to be), time and gravity will inevitably and inexorably alter one's appearance. And one's self-esteem—if not their identity—correspondingly suffers.

But as any parent of a preteen or teen-aged girl knows, it is incredibly challenging to go to the mall and buy her clothes that are stylish without being inappropriate and/or provocative. In her eye-opening book, *Sexy Girls: How Hot is Too Hot?*, youth ministry expert Hayley DiMarco sympathizes with this dilemma by telling girls:

> You might not claim to be sexy. You might not want to be sexy but if you're a normal, red-blooded girl, then I bet you want to be attractive to the opposite sex. You want the attention of guys, and you do certain things to get it. You wear that cute baby doll top. You pick jeans that make you look just so. You know exactly what to wear to accentuate your good parts. It's natural, you know, to want to attract the opposite sex. The trouble is that sometimes we don't really realize what we are doing to the opposite sex in this dance for attention (2006, p. 9).

To further compound and complicate this highly individualized and subjective issue of physical attraction, societal standards vary and change over time and from one culture to another. In medieval times, for example, females were not considered to be attractive unless they were quite pleasingly plump or even downright corpulent by contemporary standards. But in the 1960s the phenomenon of the young, waif-like model, "Twiggy," revolutionized standards of feminine beauty and attractiveness by encouraging girls to be very thin, to deemphasize larger body types, and to focus on secondary sexual characteristics.

> **Millions of people (mostly females) have become obsessed with unrealistic standards of physical desirability.**

Consequently, millions of people (mostly females) have become obsessed with unrealistic standards of physical desirability, resulting in a host of body image issues and serious eating disorders. Tragically, over the years I have worked with many young women whose body images are so distorted that even when they are absolutely emaciated, they feel and/or believe themselves to be fat. Anorexia and bulimia are not only manifestations of severe psychological and relationship problems; they often pose serious health risks and warrant immediate psychotherapeutic and medical care.

Attitudinal Factors

A blunt and rather crass old saying alleges that, "Beauty may be only skin deep, but ugly goes clear to the bone!" Solomon explained this same principle somewhat more elegantly: "Like a gold ring in a pig's snout [and by the way, swine were considered to be unclean animals to Orthodox Jews] is a beautiful woman who shows no discretion" (Proverbs 11:22).

> **No matter how it is said, what's on the inside is definitely more important than what is on the outside.**

No matter how it is said, what's on the inside is definitely more important than what is on the outside. Furthermore, whatever is on the inside is eventually going to come to the surface and be perceived by those on the outside. A lady's drop-dead gorgeous physical features and characteristics can be completely negated and outweighed by a surly, sour, and sullen disposition. A gentleman who is a handsome hunk yet is grouchy, grumpy, and gripey will similarly not be a chick magnet.

When it comes to ongoing and enduring physical attraction, our actions and attitudes toward our loved one trump everything else. Another old and wonderful saying states, "Beauty is as beauty does." There is much power in the demonstration and administration of senseless acts of beauty and random acts of kindness to our mate. Loving attitudes and kind actions are always things of great beauty.

In most unhappy marriages, flirting has become a lost art.

Chief among these are behaviors which couples typically do while dating: *smiling* and *flirting!* Not only does it require much less effort and fewer muscles to smile than to frown, it's much more attracting to others. And flirting, well, it's sad to say that unfortunately in many marriages couples cannot recall the last time their spouse flirted with them. In dating and courtship, smiling and flirting behaviors are foundational to the development of a mutually attracting relationship. But in most unhappy marriages, flirting has become a lost art, buried somewhere between the ruts, rigors, and routines of a life consumed with diapers, debt, and duty.

As with many things in life, attitude is everything. *If we want to actively attract our spouse, then we need to act attractively.* Recall the inimitable words of the ancient Greek poet Ovid: "If you would be loved, be lovable." When someone smiles at us, we feel accepted. When someone flirts with us, we feel awesome. And so much the more when that someone is our spouse!

Maturational Factors

As was observed earlier, no matter how beautiful or handsome someone may be, time and gravity will eventually affect everyone's appearance. Most often, middle-aged men will at some point contract "furniture disease." (That's where one's chest falls into one's drawers!) As a result, his former six-pack abs will expand to become a full case. And, to be fair, most middle-aged women will eventually tend to add a few minutes to their hourglass figures!

When one of our sons was being honored for his achievements in Royal Rangers several years ago, one of my friends was acting as the master of ceremonies. After calling our son to proceed to the front of the auditorium, my friend said of him: "Look at this guy walking up here; he is such a handsome young man! He got all his good looks from his dad, because his mom still has hers!" How true.

A few years ago my (gorgeous) wife, Linda, was expressing some frustration over the aging process and what she perceived to be the disparity of its relative effects on men and women. She exclaimed, "Life is just so unfair—why is it that when men age they tend to look *dis*tinguished, but when women age they tend to look *ex*tinguished?!" Classic, huh? But tragi-comical for her, and research suggests likewise for lots of other women, as well.

> "Life is just so unfair—why is it that when men age they tend to look *dis*tinguished, but when women age they tend to look *ex*tinguished?!"

Linda's original but poignant statement illustrates the research findings that two-thirds of women in our culture report being affected sexually by their body image due to their negative perceptions of aging (Hart, Weber, and Taylor, 1998). These researchers report that as a result of aging, women typically say, "We feel disappointed in our body and this negative body image depletes our sexual desire. We don't want anyone, least of all our partners, to see our downwardly mobile bodies. Most women suffer from unrealistic expectations about how their bodies must look and must continue to look" (ibid., p. 76-77).

Busy yet sedentary lifestyles and physical changes accompanying pregnancy and childbirth—much less disfigurations stemming from a mastectomy, a colostomy, various disabilities, significant health issues, a severe or paralyzing injury, surgical scars or an amputation—can significantly affect how a woman perceives herself and/or is perceived by her husband. But although changes resulting from time, gravity, and/or other life events are inevitable, that doesn't necessarily mean that looking *extinguished* is inevitable. Let's now consider key aspects of healthy and healthful self-care.

Self-Care Factors

As people mature, their bodies naturally become less agile, athletic, and appealing. Childbirth, stress, teenagers, fast food, and a lack of regular meaningful exercise often gradually and insidiously culminate in the Battle of the Bulge. Consequently, now one out of every three American adults is obese. Fitness and firmness can be regained and maintained through proper and self-disciplined diet, rest, and exercise, but it takes work. Consistent, concerted, and consecrated work.

Getting in shape and staying in shape are crucial to one's physical, mental, emotional, and relational health. Vim, vigor, and vitality are all extremely significant to one's health, well-being, and attractiveness. But in the busyness and bane of boring living, couples often take essential features of their health and appearance for granted. And like any investment, the yield from our dividends is directly correlated with the frequency and amount of our deposits.

Vim, vigor, and vitality are all extremely significant to one's health, well-being, and attractiveness.

A walk in the park, especially power walking, can revitalize, re-energize, and reunite out-of-shape bodies, as well as out-of-sorts couples. When someone doesn't care about their own body or physical health, it's often very difficult for their spouse to feel romantically—much less physically—attracted to them in a consistently ongoing way. Such lack of appropriate self-care often stems from and yet ironically exacerbates and perpetuates low self-esteem.

The truth is that when a person takes themselves for granted, it often makes their spouse feel taken for granted, as well.

The truth is that when a person takes themselves for granted, it often makes their spouse feel taken for granted, as well. Another area where this principle is frequently manifested is in the area of personal hygiene. Many spouses are hesitant to voice their concerns about their spouse's bad breath and/or body odor. They are reluctant to hurt their mate's feelings or make them feel rejected, so they do not communicate their preference or desire. Or perhaps they're tired and frustrated because they have communicated what they want, but have felt ignored.

These natural inattentions to one's own state of attractiveness nonetheless may unintentionally signal to their spouse that they are selfish, inconsiderate, and unloving. In turn, it is almost impossible to feel attracted to someone when you are physically repulsed by their lack of effort to be attractive and appealing to you. Sometimes it's amazing what a little soap, water, and good-smelling stuff can do for a marital relationship!

Scriptural Factors

Historically there has been a considerable amount of controversy and debate within the church over the issue of physical appearance, particularly within more conservative or legalistic circles. Lengths of hair, as well as style and mode of dress, jewelry, and makeup have all been hotly and even passionately argued about over the years.

I remember the post-hippie era back in the early 1970s when the "Jesus movement" began to filter into and impact the stereotypic middle-class church. Many of these nontraditional yet zealous newborn Christ-followers apparently didn't get the memo that denim blue jeans (of all things!) were not on the approved uniform list for acceptable church attire. Some sanctimonious, self-righteous saints who had been "in the way" for 20, 30, or 40 years were absolutely aghast that these heathens obviously had the audacity to come to church appearing so worldly and carnal.

As was his custom, our wise pastor, Rev. Bill Newby, cut through all the superficiality of externality to get to the heart of the matter in a balanced and healthy way. In reference to this whole brouhaha over style of dress and appearance, he dryly declared, "God looks on the inside. But since I have to look on the outside, I just appreciate whatever you can do!"

He nailed it. First Samuel 16:7 tells us, ". . . The LORD does not look at the things man looks at. Man looks at the outward appearance, but the LORD looks at the heart." In the gospel of John (7:24) Jesus tells his audience, "Stop judging by mere appearances. . . " Likewise, the apostle Paul reminds us that, ". . . God does not judge by external appearance. . . " (Ephesians 2:6). Scripture seems to be clear and consistent on this issue.

But some may retort, "Doesn't the Bible clearly state that women are not to focus on physical beauty, fixing their hair, wearing gold jewelry, and having fine clothes? Should we not address that?" In response to this definitely delicate and divisive dilemma, Chuck Swindoll offers this powerful perspective:

> Let's focus in on the main thrust of this passage [I Peter 3:3-6]. Peter's point is clear. You are warned against going overboard, patching up the externals if your internals are pitifully lacking. Don't place all your emphasis on the outside - but, on the other hand, this doesn't mean there shouldn't be something on the outside worth looking at. Listen, this passage isn't bad-mouthing cosmetics or taking shots at keeping yourself physically attractive, ladies. It's just encouraging you to keep it in balance. Not externally only, remember. Some wives need all the help they can get! Like the old saying, 'If the house needs painting, paint it.' Good advice for wives, too. It's a shame that some have not learned the importance of keeping themselves attractive. All day long their husbands encounter fantastic women who are well-dressed and appealing, and what do they see when they walk in the kitchen at 5:30 PM? The totaled woman. What's the difference? The importance of appearance. A man doesn't stay interested in anyone who smells like she just got dipped in Lysol. Or runs around the house looking like an unmade bed all day. For sure, you need to be pure within—but don't stop when you get to the outside. There's no reason in the world a Christian woman can't look attractive just as often as possible. Whatever it takes, do it! Your appearance is a significant "brick" that helps rebuild a marriage (1980, p. 46).

Thus, as with most controversial concerns, the Bible offers a balanced and reasonable understanding of this issue. It's not that the outside isn't important; it's just that the inside is more important. And our culture strongly tempts us to substitute external appeal for internal (and unfading) beauty.

In fact, what our culture teaches us is directly opposite to a biblical understanding of physical attraction. In his book, *Love,*

Sex and Lasting Relationships (2003), Pastor Chip Ingram de-picts what he calls the "Hollywood Formula" for relationships as being based on an upside-down pyramid which represents the sequence we take in seeking a relationship with the opposite sex: level or phase 1 is the *physical*, phase 2 is the *emotional*, phase 3 is the *social*, phase 4 is the *psychological,* and phase 5 is the *spiritual*. This foundation of physical attraction is obvious-ly narrow, unstable, and precarious—yet that is precisely how Hollywood has taught us to build relationships for several gen-erations. Boy meets girl, boy takes girl to backseat, boy asks girl her name.

What our culture teaches us is directly opposite to a biblical understanding of physical attraction.

Ingram argues that this model is inherently flawed and un-workable, and he suggests a revolutionary method for finding, developing, and sustaining lasting relationships. Rather than an inverted pyramid, he believes establishing a spiritual com-ponent first is the only foundation broad enough and strong enough to sustain the rest of a healthy relationship. So what Ingram calls God's prescription for healthy relationships looks like a right side-up pyramid with the base or phase 1 being *spir-itual*, phase 2 being *psychological*, phase 3 being *social*, phase 4 being *emotional,* and phase 5 being *physical.*

Although attractive external appearance is not a point of pri-mary emphasis in the Bible, it is nonetheless frequently ob-served and noted in a positive way. Feminine beauty is referred to dozens and dozens of times in Scripture regarding many different women. And Joseph (Genesis 39:6), David (1 Samuel 16:7), Absalom (2 Samuel 14:25), Adonijah (1 Kings 1:6), and Daniel, Shadrach, Meshach, and Abednego (Daniel 1:4) are all specifically referred to and praised as being hand-some in appearance.

Furthermore, in the poetically provocative book, Song of Songs, King Solomon notes that the woman mentions eight different aspects of her lover's appearance. She was attracted to his hair, eyes, mouth, lips, hands, legs, cheeks, and head. Meanwhile, he was attracted to 16 different features of his lover's appearance, including her eyes, teeth, lips, mouth, temples, neck, tongue, hair, feet, hips, hands, navel, belly, nose, head, and breasts. God wondrously created our human bodies to be alluring, pleasing, and fulfilling to one another.

Interestingly, in referring to Jesus, the prophet Isaiah foretold that, "He had no beauty or majesty to attract us to him, nothing in his appearance that we should desire him" (53:2). Obviously God did not intend for people to follow His Son simply because of His appealing human qualities or attractive physical characteristics. Actually, quite the opposite. As a result of His horrible torture and cruel abuse, Isaiah also observed that, " . . . there were many who were appalled at him—his appearance was so disfigured beyond that of any man and his form marred beyond human likeness..." (52:14).

However, in His glorified state, the King of Kings and Lord of Lords will be exalted in inexpressible majesty and indescribable beauty (Psalm 27:4, Zechariah 6:13). Certainly then we will be able to fully and accurately grasp and personally experience all of the beauty and glory of the Almighty Creator of the universe.

Scriptural Search

1. 1 Samuel 16:7
2. Proverbs 31:30
3. Song of Songs 4:1, 4:7, 5:9, 7:6
4. 1 Corinthians 3:16-17
5. 1 Peter 3:3-6

Ponderable Points

1. Have you ever understood your body to be the temple of God's Spirit or presence (1 Corinthians 3:16-17)? What are the implications of that concept to you? Based on this realization, what do you need to do differently as you think about the current state of your health and condition of your physical body?

2. Have you ever thought yourself to be physically attractive and/or appealing? Why or why not? Who was it that told you that you were or were not physically attractive?

3. Consider giving your spouse some honest yet sensitive feedback regarding your opinion of their physical appearance. Try to not be critical and be willing to offer some tenderly loving and helpful suggestions as to what would be more appealing to you in terms of their appearance, dress and/or style. What do you want to share with them about this?

4. Consider asking your spouse to reciprocate the previous question; i.e., ask them what they would like to be different about your appearance and/or what you might do in order to make yourself more appealing to them.

5. What kind of nonphysical things (e.g., smiles, flirtatiousness, attitude adjustments, etc.) might make you a more attractive and appealing spouse?

Activation Activities:

1. Make a list of your mate's attributes, attitudes, and actions which you consider attractive and appealing.

2. Which aspects or elements of inward beauty do you believe God wants you to develop and refine?

3. Read through the Song of Songs with your spouse (it's only about four or five pages long). What do you notice about this couple's attraction to one another? What bodily or physical characteristics are discussed or emphasized? What did they notice about one another's appearance and what did they tell their spouse about that?

Recommended Resources

Secrets of Eve: Understanding the Mystery of Female Sexuality, Archibald Hart, Catherine Hart Weber, Debra Taylor (1998).

Love, Sex and Lasting Relationships, Chip Ingram (2003).

Hope, Help and Healing for Eating Disorders, Gregory Jantz (2010).

Sexy Girls: How Hot is Too Hot?, Hayley DiMarco (2006).
Glue, Paul and Patti Endrei (2006).

CHAPTER TWELVE

Sensational Sex

*You know you're getting old when your spouse asks you
to come upstairs and make whoopee, but you only have
the strength to do one or the other! (Hey, I don't know
about you, but if it were me, I'd simply ask my spouse to
come downstairs—just sayin'!)*

*"Let him kiss me with the kisses of his mouth—for your
love is more delightful than wine. Pleasing is the fragrance
of your perfumes... Take me away with you—let us hurry!
Let the King bring me into his chambers."*

—SONG OF SONGS 1:2-4

A hh—at last, the chapter for which many of you have
been waiting, although I suspect some of you may
have already peeked ahead! Experiencing the excitement of erotic ecstasies and the exquisite enjoyments em-
bedded within marital love is certainly one of the most wonderful blessings in all of God's creation.

Unfortunately, this is also the chapter that many others of
you have been dreading. To persons who have been wounded,
exploited, victimized, and/or assaulted in the most intimate and
vulnerable areas of their humanity, sex can also be one of the

cruelest curses in all of creation. While nothing can be more heavenly glorious in the entire realm of the marital relationship, it is also true that nothing can be more horribly grotesque. Our sexual relationship can be our ultimate dream or our worst nightmare.

Thus, somewhat reminiscent of Charles Dickens' famous opening line in *A Tale of Two Cities*, sex in marriage can truly be "the best of times and the worst of times," depending upon our perspective and/or experience. Sex can result in the heights of passion and/or the depths of painfulness. To borrow another line from classic literature, it can literally be agony or ecstasy.

In their book *Intimate Allies*, Drs. Dan Allender and Tremper Longman explain it this way:

> Sex changes the heart. It brings forth either a chorus of praise, wonder, and joy or a song of sorrow and harm. Sex is not incidental to marriage. While sex was never meant to be the heart of intimacy, it is the music of marriage. And when marriage partners experience disharmony in other areas of their lives, the cacophony will inevitably crowd out the sweet trills of sexual passion. A husband and wife either participate in the mystery of sexual union as a taste of intimacy with God, or they see it as nothing more than a momentary pleasure. And for some people the pleasure is so webbed with fear, disgust, or anger that it has lost even its sensual delight. Sex draws the heart toward either greater intimacy or a deeper sense of abuse and harm (1995, p. 211-212).

The aim and intent of this chapter is obviously to attempt to draw your hearts toward that melodious chorus of intimacy, as well as to offer healing for any abuse or harm you may have experienced in your sexuality. To that end, we will begin by first examining the societal/cultural/historical framework within which most of us learned about human sexuality. Next, we will address many of the difficulties and dysfunctions caused by these learning processes. Third, we will briefly explore a biblical paradigm conceptualizing the sexual relationship in marriage in order to better understand how God views the whole business. Finally, the acronym "S-E-X-Y" will be introduced as a way to help you compose a sensational sexual symphony with your dear, sweet, wonderful, darling, precious lover.

Socio-Cultural Context

Queen Victoria was truly a remarkable lady. She inherited the British crown in 1837 and ruled until 1901—longer than any female monarch in history. She married her first cousin, Prince Albert, and their nine children all married into royal or noble families across the European continent. Under her reign, the British Empire experienced unprecedented growth and expansion characterized by extensive scientific, industrial, military, political, and cultural change. The power she wielded and the influence she exerted over most of the world was phenomenal.

The part of this iconic, elegant lady's legacy that was perhaps least endearing—yet most enduring—was her identification with prudish, strict standards of personal morality. Specifically, since she supposedly saw sexuality as sinful, shameful, and salacious, it was subsequently subjected to being suppressed, shunned, and shrouded in silence. This royally repressive attitude led generations of people to believe that coitus was merely for the perfunctory purpose of procreation.

Our culture has been progressively degenerating into more extreme, explicit, and egregious depictions of all forms of sexuality.

This moralistic mentality prevailed until the proverbial pendulum swung radically to the other extreme in the turbulent 1960s. Cumulative, cataclysmic cultural clashes concluded with so-called "free" love (which we now realize has cost us more than ever could have been anticipated). Open nudity and boundary-less depictions of sex in movies, magazines, and mass media led to mainstream acceptance and widespread promotion of the "sexual revolution." Since then, our culture has been progressively degenerating into more extreme, explicit, and egregious depictions of all forms of sexuality.

Consequently, we have witnessed an unprecedented seismic shift in societal standards. Morality of all forms has drastically declined. Rates of infidelity and divorce have steadily soared. Sexually-transmitted diseases run rampant. (The number of known STDs is now 39 and counting. According to a 2013 report by the federal Centers for Disease Control and Prevention, as of 2008, more than *110 million Americans had an STD*—many of which are incurable—costing over 16 billion dollars annually in direct medical care!) Pre-marital sex has become commonplace, friends are now expected to provide "benefits," cohabitation is the norm in many sectors of the culture, and in 2012, 48% of all births in America were to unmarried women. Permissive, hedonistic sexual attitudes, values, and behaviors have been extraordinarily expensive to us as a society.

However, the increased awareness of and growing emphasis on sexuality did provide some redemptive benefits to the Christian community. In 1976, Christian theologian and philosopher Dr. Lewis Smedes authored a groundbreaking understanding of biblical sexuality entitled *Sex for Christians,* which was healthfully liberating and delivered "good news" for many believers. At about the same time, Dr. Ed and Gaye Wheat pioneered a best-selling "how-to" manual and instruction guide from a biblical framework, refreshingly yet boldly entitled *Intended for Pleasure.* These landmark works helped bring a sound balance to our culture's slide down the moral slippery slope, and have paved the way since then for dozens of excellent instruction manuals and much wise counsel on the subject of sexuality for married Christians.

Difficulties and Dysfunctions

It has been wisely noted that the devil does everything he can to get couples to have sex *before* marriage, and everything he can to keep them from having sex *after* marriage! This painful and ironic truth often manifests itself in such a way that what should be a couple's playground many times deteriorates into their battleground. What the Creator designed to be the sweetest union of the sexes often degenerates into the bitterest war between the sexes. *Husbands and wives, this should not (and need not) be!*

Whereas nothing in the whole realm of marriage has more potential for creaturely comforts than the process and pleasures of lovemaking, it is also true that nothing has more potential for catastrophic complications. When you consider that most couples typically experience functional problems like premature ejaculation, dyspareunia (painful intercourse), delayed orgasmic response, erectile dysfunction, and vaginismus (painful muscle spasms) at some point in their marriage, and when you then factor in common challenges involving things like birth control issues, infertility struggles, menstrual and/or hormonal irregularities, lack of privacy after children come along, medication side effects, challenges of normal aging processes, and physical disabilities/diseases/injuries and the like, it's pretty miraculous that couples have much sex at all!

Despite all the foregoing challenges and concerns, sex therapy per se is actually relatively simple and straightforward. Mechanical or functional sexual issues are usually fairly rapidly and successfully addressed. Utilization of procedures such as the squeeze technique, the quiet vagina, sensate focusing, various relaxation and self-awareness exercises, and strengthening of the pubococcygeal musculature can be quite helpful in reducing and/or resolving many of the common functional or physiological sexual difficulties in marriage.

(For help in specifically troubleshooting the previously mentioned issues and challenges, please refer to Dr. Doug Rosenau's *Celebration of Sex* or Dr. Cliff and Joyce Penner's *The Gift of Sex*. These excellent resources will give you wise and useful guidance that is biblically based and clinically sound. If you cannot obtain solid and helpful solutions to your difficulties from these, then I would suggest that you seek professional assistance.)

Otherwise, as Dr. Emerson Eggerichs wisely observed, "If there ever were an issue that really isn't the issue, it is sex" (2004, p. 250). In Jim and Sally Conway's opinion, "Surprisingly, the biggest sexual problems are not usually physical or mechanical but are the result of our thought processes, the stress we are under, or the quality of our relationship with our mate" (2000, p. 145). In essence, *most people are entirely ignorant about the location of their primary sex organ—it is between their ears!* Thus, what we believe about ourselves, our mate, and sexuality in general has an enormous effect on the quality and nature of our most intimate human relationship.

In addition, there is a huge assortment of other obstacles that frequently interfere with a couple's sexual satisfaction. Childhood sexual trauma, pornography, infidelity, previous sexual relationships, emotional immaturity, self-centered attitudes and actions, external stress, sexually assaultive experiences, unresolved conflict, and unforgiveness will all disrupt—if not destroy—a couple's consensual conjugal coupling. It is usually a combination of these kinds of individual and relationship system dynamics which rear their ugly heads in the bedroom, and it is with these challenges that we generally need the most assistance. Let's address a few of these major issues briefly.

Infringement of Innocence

Perhaps the most diabolic evil in our society is the fact that about one in three girls and one in four to five boys will be sexually abused before age eighteen. And until around the mid 1980s, our culture was in almost complete and collective denial about this despicable scourge. During sexual traumatization, as wrong and horrible as what happens on the outside of a survivor is, I believe that what occurs on the inside of them is even worse. Their will—the part of their humanity that is most like the image and likeness of the Almighty Creator—is violated. They were created in innocence. But they typically internalize the perpetrator's guilt and responsibility, therefore unwittingly carrying that slimy shame and heartbreaking horror into their marriages. And that causes big problems.

Accordingly, I call childhood sexual trauma "the raping of the soul." No innocent child (yes, I know that's redundant, but survivors are typically manipulated by the perpetrator to believe the abuse is their fault, so I always emphasize the child's lack of culpability) asks to be abused. Regardless of how cute, adorable, and precocious they may be, no innocent child is ever capable of seducing an adult. No innocent child has the capacity to be responsible for sexualizing their own behavior or anyone else's. No innocent child is so sexually irresistible that the perpetrator just "can't help" himself (or herself). No innocent child is at fault for having their sexuality prematurely and inappropriately activated. No innocent child is responsible for having their body "betray" them by being inappropriately aroused and stimulated.

I call childhood sexual trauma "the raping of the soul."

(For deep and personal healing work in these sensitive areas, I would recommend individual, then marital therapy, along with the excellent book and companion workbook by Dr. Dan Allender, *The Wounded Heart*).

> **We all marry into our spouse's previous traumatic experiences—whether knowingly or unknowingly.**

We all marry into our spouse's previous traumatic experiences—whether knowingly or unknowingly. My favorite professor in graduate school once said, "If you really want to get to know someone deeply, find out what they feel strongly about." Obviously, we need to find out what our spouse feels strongly about, in order to know them deeply. God has some really strong feelings, which help us get to know Him deeply, too.

The Bible lists eight things that God—who is Love personified (1 John 4:8)—hates or detests: divorce (Malachi 2:16), haughty eyes, a lying tongue, hands that shed innocent blood, a heart that devises wicked schemes, feet that are quick to rush into evil, a false witness who pours out lies, and a man who stirs up dissention among brothers (Prov. 6:16-19). Think for a moment about how many of these are involved in this grievous, wicked contamination of innocence. And Jesus was likewise intensely irate about the idea of someone deliberately causing an innocent child to be tripped up (Matthew 18:6; Mark 9:42; Luke 17:2). You might ask why the Lord is so incensed about these areas of diabolic deception and destruction, but I would ask, why aren't we *all* incensed?

> **You might ask why the Lord is so incensed about these areas of diabolic deception and destruction, but I would ask,**
> **why aren't we *all* incensed?**

One of the deepest and greatest truisms pertaining to the marital relationship is that we get to reap everything that every-

one else sowed into our spouse's life before we showed up. Ideally, couples grasp that in premarital counseling—especially as it applies in reference to their same gender about to be in-law. But there are obviously three basic problems with this reality: #1—it isn't fair; #2—it's not fair; and #3—it ain't fair! No spouse should have to reap what a sexual abuser did to the little child inside their mate, and have to pay the consequences of that trauma.

God is ultimately and utterly a Redeemer.

But let's keep in mind that God is ultimately and utterly a Redeemer. That is, He delights in transforming us and producing blessings out of our brokenness. It's perfectly understandable—if you marry a survivor of sexual abuse—for you to feel cheated, ripped off, or baited and switched. But you were not sold a false bill of goods. Many survivors unconsciously repress those traumatic memories (from which they instinctively dissociated in order to psychologically survive) for decades. Ironically, many survivors are unable to address these issues until they feel secure enough in their spouse's love to be able to have the strength to face what they perceive to be their shameful pain and weakness (see 2 Corinthians 12:9-10). They don't mean to be emotionally and sexually shamed and scarred. What they bring into their marriage relationship is in no way deliberate or intentional—even though it may feel like it is. (For further assistance, please refer to *When Victims Marry* by Jan and Don Frank).

Now, here is what is really redemptive and revolutionary about God's grand and glorious design for marriage. *What is even more "unfair" than reaping what you didn't sow is the fact that you can help heal what you didn't hurt, and fix what you didn't break—and when you do, it is an exciting, holy, and miraculous example of God's grace and transforming power!* And your mate's resultant response to your love, patience, and understanding can create a bond of unprecedented safety, security, and satisfaction for both of you. When couples cultivate this kind of deep trust, emotional vulnerability, and interpersonal intimacy, something absolutely profound takes place: they can help heal—or hurt—each other more fully than anyone else on the planet.

To persons who have been deeply battered and broken in their sexuality, I will often recommend with a straight face that it would be best for them to never, ever have sex again! After their spouse recovers from a sudden and unexpected heart attack, I will strongly suggest that they learn to make love a lot! You see, animals can have sex, and strangers can have sex, *but they cannot make love.*

> **We can never be controlled when we are intentionally creating/making love with our spouse.**

For most survivors, sex is all bad: their will was violated, they are filled with shame and confusion, and they hate themselves because they were manipulated to believe it was entirely their fault. I point out that they didn't get to vote on any of what happened when they were shorter—or if they were assaulted as adults. But when they freely and actively choose to share their love with their chosen life partner as an individuated adult, they no longer have to feel controlled or fear being re-victimized. To avoid the possibility of having a reactively-based flashback, I empower them to be proactive and take charge of how, when, and in what ways they make love—with the one partner they freely chose to be committed to for life. We can never be controlled when we are intentionally creating/making love with our spouse. Simply stated, no one can *take* from us what we *give* to them! For many survivors, it's time to take back what the enemy stole from them and live life in the fullness of the prosperity Jesus intended for them (John 10:10).

Perils of Pornography

It has been popularly promulgated that pornography is a "victimless crime." But nothing could be further from the truth. In terms of sheer numbers, this enormous industry generates unprecedented profits (in 2011 alone, the porn business generated $12-14 billion in profits in the United States—which is more than all the combined revenues of professional baseball, football, and basketball franchises combined; revenue estimates worldwide were nearly $100 billion!), infecting and affecting people across the planet like nothing else. Pornography's degree of impact is profound, the number of victims it affects (both directly and indirectly) is astounding, and the damage it inflicts is both widespread and devastating.

> **The untold costs of misused and exploitative sex are incalculable.**

Every study ever conducted on the effects of pornography has demonstrated its strong correlation with violent crimes of all kinds, including sexual assault, sex trafficking, and the sexual abuse of children. The long-term effects of pornography usage—including sexual addiction, marital dysfunctions, negative self-esteem, deviant perversions, and paraphilias (obsessions with perverted sexual practices)—are even more pervasive and invasive. The untold costs of misused and exploitative sex are incalculable.

Basically, "The sexual revolution of the 1960s and '70s radically altered the sexual landscape of our nation, so that today sex before marriage and viewing pornography are the culturally accepted norm...only by seeing sex as a god we worship are we able to make sense of the porno plague" (Driscoll and Driscoll, 2012, p.112). *Sex was not meant to be our god, but our gift from God.* Yet due to the sexual saturation which bombards us in our society, "We in the twenty-first century contend with sexual temptations that no previous culture has ever had to face" (McCluskey, 2004, p. 26).

Pornography in all forms represents a self-centered, idealized, and highly unrealistic perversion and distortion of relationship.

Pornography in all forms represents a self-centered, idealized, and highly unrealistic perversion and distortion of relationship. Whether it is a sexy nymphomaniac ("Veronica"—in all her airbrushed or Photoshopped eroticized perfection) or a romantic stud ("Philippe"—whose strong, virile typology is the stuff of romance novels, soap operas, and chick flicks), the fantasies generated by various unrealistic and pornographic distortions are a counterfeit of God's design and purpose for our sexuality. The Greek word *porneia* occurs 25 times in the New Testament in reference to sexual sin of all kinds. I would strongly encourage you to get a good Greek-to-English concordance and conduct a word study to see exactly how God feels about this topic.

As with all forms of sin, the Church is unfortunately not immune to this one, either. According to an overwhelming amount of research data, in any given month, the vast majority of Christian men and nearly half of Christian women report using pornography. And this epidemic has a trckle-down effect onto our children: the largest consumer group of hard-core pornography in the United States is 12 to 17 year olds.

So what's really wrong with pornography? Basically everything:

Mentally, powerful neurochemicals are released into the pleasure centers of the brain, with effects similar to those of cocaine and other powerful mind-altering drugs. This can create an internal chemical addiction subject to the principle of habituation, which means that it takes progressively more intensive stimuli to produce the same effect (e.g. moving from "soft" to harder forms of pornographic perversion in order to derive the same high).

Socially, it causes one to view members of the opposite sex in a dehumanizing, objectifying manner. Miss Whichever Month is not merely a collection of certain anatomical parts—she is a real person. She is someone's daughter, sister, niece, cousin, and granddaughter who has tragically prostituted herself. And by the way, regardless of how beautiful and attractive she is, next month there will be someone else to ogle. Pornography never absolutely satisfies, it addictively seduces.

Psychologically, the fantasies generated by pornography are not only patently egocentric; they set up unrealistic expectations of sexual behavior which no one can possibly achieve, leading to inevitable disappointment and dissatisfaction in actual relationship.

Relationally, users of pornography gradually pull away from their spouse because they are unlovingly having sex with themselves via a fantasized, dehumanized, object. Besides, no real, live, warm-blooded person can live up to those distorted, idealized expectations generated by obsessive and egocentric fantasies in which everything is sexy, sensual, and seductive—and exclusively about self-gratification—all the time.

Emotionally, an individual who turns to pornography is usually inappropriately attempting to medicate deep levels of pain which then remain hidden, buried, and inaccessible to healing.

Spiritually, pornography constitutes the worship of a body without a soul. This lustful form of idolatry involves worshiping the creation instead of the Creator, and as was discussed earlier in the book, Jesus equated lust with adultery. Harmless? Hardly. The pornographic perversion of personal pleasure prostitutes, pollutes, and poisons people.

(For further help with pornography and sexual addiction issues please refer to *False Intimacy* by Dr. Harry Schaumburg and *Healing the Wounds of Sexual Addiction* by Dr. Mark Laaser).

Awfulness of Affairs

Speaking of adultery, those statistics are epidemic too. Current studies indicate that about half of all marriages will be impacted by at least one of the spouses cheating on their mate. How can this be?

All adultery is based on unrealistic, yet very appealing fantasy.

Well, all adultery is likewise based on unrealistic, yet very appealing fantasy. True, it is an artificial relationship where both parties know the other person doesn't honor the sacred covenant of marriage, so it's impossible for there to ever be a healthy foundation of trust, security, or respect for the other's character and integrity. But the sense of secrecy, collusion, and novelty all artificially heighten the emotional intensity— which far overshadows the boring humdrum of the predictable routines, ruts, and rigors of marriage. Plus, with this "forbidden fruit," there are no sick kids in the middle of the night, mortgage stresses, or in-law hassles with which to contend. *Adultery is always a self-destructive attempt to escape real life and genuine intimacy.*

Dr. Willard Harley points out that when spouses do not meet each other's (very different and often contradictive) needs, they are vulnerable to temptation. He explains, "In marriages that fail to meet those needs...married people consistently choose the same pattern to satisfy their unmet needs: the extramarital affair. People wander into affairs with astonishing regularity, in spite of whatever strong moral or religious convictions they may hold" (2001, p. 20). He goes on to warn, "If changes do not take place within the marriage to care for that need, the individual will face the powerful temptation to fill it outside of marriage" (ibid.). Dr. Kevin Leman boils it down this way: "People find in an affair what's lacking in their marriage...satisfied partners don't wander" (1999, p. 155).

Please understand—not having our basic marital needs met or our love tank filled is never an *excuse* to commit adultery; it's an *explanation.* Nor is adultery ever an excuse to divorce. Jesus pointed out to the self-righteous religious hypocrites who tried to entrap him that Moses only allowed the divorce exception for marital unfaithfulness as an addendum to the law, due to people's *hard-heartedness* (Matthew 19:3-9). God's will is that we always forgive—like He does (see Ephesians 4:32-5:2).

(The fact that we must always *forgive* doesn't mean that we should always *reconcile.* Some situations call for a time of separation for legal, physical safety, financial, or other reasons. For additional assistance with these issues, see *Love Must Be Tough* by Dr. James Dobson.).

If you want a biblically based plan and precedent on how to respond to your spouse's heartbreaking betrayal of you and outrageous violation of their marriage covenant, come with me to the obscure little Old Testament book of Hosea (you'll find it right between Hezekiah and First Whale!). This poignant story of how the prophet redeems and reconciles with his perpetually promiscuous wife is an allegory of how God forgives the repetitive sinfulness and waywardness of His people. Including me and you. And you're absolutely right. It's not in any way fair or easy or just—it's called good news.

To me, healing the excruciatingly painful brokenness of a marriage covenant is somewhat analogous to the treatment process involved in healing a broken bone. Sometimes adultery is like the compound stress fracture of a basketball player's ankle. After many years of accumulative pounding on the hardwood, there comes a torque or tweak which shatters the bone. Or it may be a singular, blunt trauma that cracks or compound fractures the bone. In either case, the pain is nauseating and often overwhelming.

Most offended spouses are tempted to initially react to this horrible pain in one of two ways: they try to ignore it and slap an ace bandage around it and keep limping along (denial), or they immediately and reactively amputate the limb (divorce). Both reactions are totally understandable, but neither one works. What does work is to stabilize the broken bone, set it, and place the fractured limb in a cast to protect it from further injury during the healing process.

Sometimes the pain involved in setting the bone can hurt more than did the original break. Over the years, I have sat with hundreds of couples who were in excruciating agony over the brokenness of infidelity. The most difficult—as well as the most important—thing to do in restoring the marriage relationship is to rebuild the broken trust. Often this is a very difficult, laborious, complicated, and time-consuming process. The purpose of a relationship "cast" is to temporarily suspend the normal reliance and pressures placed upon the marital bond.

The most difficult—as well as the most important—thing to do in restoring the marriage relationship is to rebuild the broken trust.

Just like a hard plaster cast, the "cast" in the reconciliation process can become uncomfortable, inconvenient, and embarrassing. A cast itches, becomes dirty, is heavy, smells, and makes normal hygiene challenging. Consequently, it is tempting for some people to want to remove the cast prematurely as soon as the throbbing pain stops. On the other hand (or foot!), because the safety and structure of the cast protects the vulnerable limb from re-injury, some people are tempted to leave it on indefinitely.

Each of these extremes poses potential problems both orthopedically and relationally. If a cast is removed prematurely, the partially healed bone may re-fracture under stressful circumstances, requiring major surgery involving pins and/or plates. Alternatively, when a cast is left on too long, the muscles will atrophy, thereby permanently weakening the limb. In marital therapy, generally one spouse wants to try to resume "walking" normally before the other one does, which requires a compromise on each party's part.

What physiologists tell us about how the microscopic re-bonding process progresses in a properly set bone is nothing short of miraculous. The calcification surrounding the broken area ultimately becomes stronger than the surrounding bone tissue—thereby making the bone stronger than it ever could have been had the break not occurred! That is redemptive! The same can be true when vows have been broken. When couples give and receive grace, compassion, and forgiveness in a deeply meaningful way, their relationship can become stronger than it ever was before.

> When couples give and receive grace, compassion, and forgiveness in a deeply meaningful way, their relationship can become stronger than it ever was before.

Although God is a Redeemer, two additional aspects of the analogy remain. Whenever anyone looks intently into the history of the marriage, much like an x-ray, even after the break is healed, there will always be evidence of the injury. And secondly, whenever there is a change in the atmospheric pressure, the couple will usually experience a dull ache.

(For further assistance in healing marital adultery issues, please refer to *Torn Asunder* by Dave Carder or *Broken Promises* by Dr. Henry Virkler).

Biblical Paradigm

Sex was, and is, God's idea. In fact, "Sex doesn't make sense unless we understand that it is holy. We can't unlock the secrets of sex and enjoy its greatest benefits unless we approach it as a holy act. Only then will couples truly experience the beauty and joy of great sex the way God intended" (Gardner, 2002, p. 2). The truth is that, "For many people, certainly, sex is the most powerful and moving experience that life has to offer, and more overwhelmingly holy than anything that happens in church" (Mason, 1985, p. 148). Said another way, "Sex is the closest that many ever come to a spiritual experience" (Peck, 1993, p. 220).

Unfortunately, historically the Church has pretty much dropped the ball when it comes to teaching an accurate biblical view of sexuality. Basically, the message of the contemporary church has been something like: "Sex is bad, dirty, sinful, and shameful—so save it for marriage with the one you love!" So much for good news, huh?

But from God's perspective, those magical, mystical, marvelous moments of "one-fleshness" are not only His definite desire for ultimate human intimacy; they are to symbolically parallel Christ's relationship to His bride, the Church. Accordingly, "Most married Christians know that sexual intimacy can produce moments of sheer transcendence—brief, sunset-like glimpses of eternity. On the underside of ecstasy we catch the shadow of a profound spiritual truth" (Thomas, 2000, p. 200). Therefore we can see that, "A husband and wife either participate in the mystery of sexual union as a taste of intimacy with God, or they see it as nothing more than a momentary pleasure" (Allender and Longman, 1995, p. 212).

> **Properly understood from God's perspective, the sexual union of a married couple is designed to figuratively represent and replicate heaven on earth!**

Cloud and Townsend conclude, "From the Creator's view, sex is the ultimate expression of knowing someone" (2005, p. 225). The Hebrew word used to describe sexual relations (*yadah*) means literally "to know and be known" in the deepest, most personal, and intimate kind of emotional vulnerability, without shame or fear. Properly understood from God's perspective, the sexual union of a married couple is designed to figuratively represent and replicate heaven on earth!

Carefully contemplate these words of Tim Gardner:

> By losing sight of sex as a holy act, we're depriving ourselves of the richness and the satisfaction that God designed it to provide... The essence of sexual intimacy can never be enjoyed, nor can true and lasting sexual fulfillment occur, until a wife and a husband grasp the truth that the number one purpose of sex is neither procreation nor recre-

ation, but unification. And I don't mean just the unification that is inherent in physical oneness, but also the relational unity that is celebrated, created, and re-created throughout a couple's married life. This unification is a celebration of the soul-deep bond that is present when a couple knows and experiences the certainty that they are together, permanently, for a divine purpose. They know their expression of love is meant to represent the loving relationship of Jesus and his church (2002, p. 48).

Why do we ever settle for less? Perhaps it is because Christians have unfortunately allowed the world and its values to infiltrate and infect the Church instead of the other way around. Throughout the Old Testament, nearly all pagan religions idolatrized sex in variously inappropriate ways. Then in New Testament times, the hedonistic ancient Greek philosophy of Gnosticism taught that all tangible, material reality is inherently evil. Although several New Testament epistles were written to specifically combat this heresy, many early church fathers seemed to struggle mightily with this issue in their personal, and especially in their sexual, lives. Some early church leaders infamously castrated themselves in order to attempt to maintain a pure and pious life, free from the horrors of sexual temptation. Augustine's denouncement of sexual intercourse as being the evil mechanism through which original sin is perpetuated shaped much of theological thinking all the way through the Middle Ages.

We simply cannot be "one-flesh" with eleventy-three different people!

Today we live in a world that normalizes and even glorifies casual and recreational sex. We're convinced that we should "try before we buy," so we encourage premarital promiscuity and cohabitation. But here's the problem: we simply cannot be "one-flesh" with eleventy-three different people! Whenever we enter into a sexual relationship with someone, we in effect have sex with everyone with whom our partner has ever—willingly or unwillingly—had sex.

Consequently, many people live fragmented, fractured, and frustrated lives. For our peace, pleasure, and protection, God has one simple standard for sex: purity before marriage and fidelity after marriage. But unfortunately, "When we remove sex from the context of marriage—even more, when we remove sex from the realm of the holy—we have unplugged the hard drive from the human relationship" (Gardner, 2002, p. 21).

Pastor Chip Ingram summarizes this issue of God's perspective on sexual holiness powerfully:

> Interestingly enough, the ancients had one thing right—there is a connection between sex and worship. But they made a huge mistake when they applied the truth. They worshiped sex instead of God who gave it. Instead of recognizing sex as one of the wonderful things about creation that point to the Creator, they made part of the creation into an idol to be worshiped by misusing the gift. Our culture has made the same mistake. At the heart of sexual immorality lies an attitude of worship, but it's worship of a terribly wrong kind. In sexual immorality we worship ourselves at the expense of others. Ultimately, sexual immorality is worship of my needs, my rights, my lust, and me. It's not love (2003, p. 134).

God's pronounced plan and purpose in creation was completely good. Accordingly, I find it absolutely amazing that the Holy One creatively crafted the clitoris for no other purpose than to receive and register sensual sexual sensations! Make no mistake. Because God loves you more than you do, He wants what's best for you more than you possibly can, and He wants to give you good gifts more than you can possibly want to receive them (Matthew 7:11).

Therefore, it should not surprise us that "Christ-like values and character traits are the bedrock of a great sex life..."

(Rosenau, 2002, p. xix), nor that "Great sex is not reserved for the tight-body types who master all the latest kinky sex positions. Instead it is the domain of persons who really know themselves, their spouse, and their God" (Roberts and Roberts, 2010, p. 168). Christian couples should be the sexiest and most sexually fulfilled people on the planet. Anything less falls far short of God's will, intention, and design!

Next, I want to introduce the model "S-E-X-Y" as a paradigm for your marriage, in order to help you and your spouse develop a sensational sexual relationship.

Serve

> **Great sex comes from being a great lover, and great lovers are not born—they are made.**

Great sex comes from being a great lover, and great lovers are not born—they are made. Men, if I could promise to deliver to you (with an iron-clad money back guarantee) the most sizzling, sensational, and scintillating aphrodisiac for your wife in the entire world, what would you pay? $79.95 plus shipping and handling? $799.95? How about $7999.95?

Now that I have your attention, it'll cost you a whole lot more than this simple, cable TV-like sounding offer. The most sure-fire, effective aphrodisiac in the universe for your dear, sweet, precious, lovely, adorable, darling wife is definitely priceless, but it isn't some sort of deep, dark secret. Here it is: *learn to serve her.* That's right, serve her.

The greatest leader in the history of the world humbled Himself and washed the feet of His students (John 13:1-17)—including the one who would sell Him down the river for a few bucks in just a couple of hours. By the way, washing feet in that culture was vastly different than in ours. Streets were unpaved, animals walked on them—and did other stuff on them, and there were no sewers—connect the dots. He did not come to be served, but to serve (Matthew 20:20-28). Intensively study the leadership principles Jesus manifested from Philippians 2:1-11, and think of how you can apply them in your role as a husband. It will radically revolutionize your heart, your attitudes, and your actions toward your wife.

For most women, the best way their husband can serve them is to practice the communication skills from Chapter 6. Listen to your wife with complete, undivided, and rapt attention. For most women, *verbal* intercourse is far more significant and essential to her as a woman than that other kind, and it actually unlocks her heart to be receptive to the other kind.

> For most women, *verbal* intercourse is far more significant and essential to her as a woman than that other kind.

Change a poopy diaper without being asked. Do the dishes. Pray with her. Ask her what she would like you to pray about with her; that's most of what is required in order to be a spiritual leader—take the initiative and be like Nike: just do it! Take out the trash—without being nagged; you live there too! Give her a neck and/or foot massage—with no strings or expectations attached. These are the kinds of things that will more than likely make you a great lover to her. Love is an action (not just the kinds of actions you're thinking about!), and it is not only our *career* to serve our wife (yep, it's to be our #1 lifelong vocation, right after serving the Lord); it is also our *calling* and our *command*. The Greek word used for love in the New Testament marital context is "*agape*," which means to do what is best for the other person to the point of self-sacrifice.

But you might say, "Hold it right there, partner. Isn't the husband supposed to be the head of the home?" Glad you asked. Yes sir, you are. And with that privilege comes the responsibility to be called "Chief Foot Washer" at your house. Even if you are the CEO of a Fortune 500 corporation where everyone else at work bows down before you and carries out your orders, you have the awesome opportunity and wonderful privilege to be a servant to the woman at home whom you promised you would love unconditionally for the rest of your life.

As we discussed in Chapter 10, great lovers also practice great courtship skills—and that's not just on the basketball, tennis, or racquetball court! Ask her out—regularly—including arranging for childcare. And be kind. Love is patient, love is kind...

I vividly remember reading the results of the famous 1975 *Redbook* magazine survey where 100,000 American women were asked about their sexual preferences, behaviors, and practices. When I read what the vast majority of women considered to be the sexiest thing about a man and what turned them on the most, I was completely flabbergasted. I mean, you could have knocked me over with a feather! More than the #2 and #3 answers combined, the overwhelming #1 response was... "*kindness!*" Wow, John Wayne, Clint Eastwood, Mr. T, and Rambo sure didn't teach me that. But being nice to your wife isn't anything new. Peter tells us to be considerate of and respectful to our wives; otherwise, God doesn't seem to pay much attention to us (1 Peter 3:7-8)! All right, men. I'll get off your case for a while.

Ladies, I hate to break it to you this way, but if you have been taught that the way to a man's heart is through his stomach... well, you have just been flat out lied to. It's actually somewhat lower. If that seems crass or crude, then please forgive me. It's true to a point; yet it actually goes much deeper even than that. And please don't get me wrong—we also love good cooking!

Nothing makes a man feel more fully vibrant, vital, and

virile than to be the recipient of his wife's attention, affection, and acceptance.

Generally speaking, men in our society have been taught to sexualize their emotions. Growing up, "big boys" are told they can't cry—and according to life insurance actuarial tables we die 5-7 years younger than our wives on average because we stuff our emotions. Therefore many adult males are emotionally illiterate; that is, they don't know how to read their feelings, except for sexual ones. Subsequently, nothing makes a man feel more fully vibrant, vital, and virile than to be the recipient of his wife's attention, affection, and acceptance.

When you think about the whole love-making enterprise from a functional or mechanical perspective, both literally and figuratively the husband is welcomed by his wife in the warmest and most wonderful way he can possibly imagine. So what does this have to do with learning to serve your husband? Absolutely everything.

At this point, some of you may be thinking this is just some kind of communist or sexist male plot. But ladies, *please understand me*—there is a reason why the classic pickup line in the bar is, "My wife doesn't understand me." What does he want you to understand? That the reason he persists in passionately pursuing you is because he wants the most fabulous person on the planet (no, not "Veronica"—you!) to desire him and *make him feel accepted.* Now before you think I'm suggesting you just exist to massage his big ego, and/or all he wants you for is to be his personal plaything, the truth is that God bestowed upon you an incredible privilege and an amazing amount of power in relationship to your husband.

For men, it's really not all about sex—emotionally, it's all about feeling accepted! The truth is that men don't really want sex per se; what they really want is *sexual fulfillment.*

307

Recall that men are taught to sexualize their emotionality. For men, it's really not all about sex—emotionally, it's all about feeling accepted! The truth is that men don't really want sex per se; what they really want is sexual fulfillment. And nothing is *more fulfilling to a healthy mature man than to have the privilege to sexually fulfill his wife and to be sexually desired by her.* Believe me, a sweet smile, a flirtatious wink, a provocative look, a sensual hug, a playful attitude, a lingering touch, or an alluring kiss will make that man of yours (to borrow King David's word picture) want to run through a troop, leap over a wall, vice-versa, or both! This is because you have unlimited and unprecedented access to intimately serve that innermost part of his heart in a way that no one else on the planet ever can.

Over the years, I have worked in psychotherapy with several women who were or who used to be prostitutes. All of them said that if their customers' wives would have only understood their husband's emotional need for acceptance, they would have been out of business. In fact several of these women reported that some men didn't even want to have sex; they just paid to be listened to without criticism or judgment!

The same is true regarding pornography. Wives, one very tangible—and invaluable—way in which you can serve as your husband's helpmate is to understand this key dynamic about his sexual temptation. For men, pornography is all about two things: (#1) he always gets accepted, as long as (#2) he has the money—because all pornography is based on prostitution. When you think about it, whenever a man opens up the magazine, calls the 900 number, walks into the strip bar, accesses the Internet site, pops in the DVD, or flips on the pay-per-view or cable TV channel, he gets (artificially) accepted—as long he has the money.

So am I implying that it's your fault if your husband sinfully succumbs to sexual temptation? Absolutely not. I am fully convinced that the line before the throne on Judgment Day will be single file. We all are responsible before God for our individual choices and behaviors. It's just that you have an incredible amount of power to be his helper in a deeper and more profound way than anyone else.

Shaunti Feldhahn concludes that, "... a chronic lack of affirmation is one reason so many men slip into pornography addiction" (2004, p. 70). In coaching wives about how to meet this deep emotional need for acceptance, she explains:

> First, know that you're responding to a tender heart hiding behind all that testosterone. If at all possible, respond to his advances with your full emotional involvement, knowing that you're touching his heart. But if responding physically seems out of the question, let your words be heart words— reassuring, affirming, adoring. Do everything in your power—using words and actions your husband understands— to keep those pangs of personal rejection from striking the man you love. Leave him in no doubt that you love to love him. And remember, if you do respond physically but do it just to 'meet his needs' without getting engaged, you're not actually meeting his needs (ibid, p. 103).

> **More than any other human relationship, marriage inexorably confronts us with our base, lazy, selfish, and sinful nature.**

More than any other human relationship, marriage inexorably confronts us with our base, lazy, selfish, and sinful nature. Serving seems like senseless and slavish silliness. Yet, "The beauty of marriage is that it confronts our selfishness and demands our service 24 hours a day. When we're most tired, most worn down, and feeling more sorry for ourselves than we ever have before, we have the opportunity to confront our feelings of self-pity by getting up and serving our mate" (Thomas, 2000, p. 186).

Educate

Earlier in the book we mentioned that a healthy marriage is basically a lifelong, mutual educational process wherein we dedicate ourselves to become the world's expert on knowing and understanding our mate, while we teach them to do the same thing for us. Good spouses are both effective teachers and excellent students of themselves and of one another.

> One of the great ironies of marriage is that we work very hard initially to find someone totally different from us, and then we spend the rest of our life trying to change them to become just like us!

In this section we will briefly touch on some of the many marvelous and maddening differences, which exist between the genders. One of the great ironies of marriage is that we work very hard initially to find someone totally different from us, and then we spend the rest of our life trying to change them to become just like us! But instead of fighting these differences, we need to understand and accept them. It is precisely because the basic operating systems of males and females are unique and complementary that wild and wonderful whoopee is possible!

The stereotypic generalizations say that boys give girls love to get sex and girls give boys sex to get love, so men never get enough sex and women never get enough love. Yet the truth is that most men are not maniacs and most women are not frigid. And according to research, in 20% of American marriages the husband's libido is lower than the wife's.

But some gender stereotypes almost always hold true. For example, men are much more visually oriented and aroused than most women. Time and fatigue pressures are the number one and number two killers of sexual desire in women. Men are more like microwaves whereas women are more like crockpots. Women have significantly more potential for experiencing sexual pleasure, but it is more complicated to achieve. And so on.

Dr. Kevin Leman humorously illustrates these built-in differences very vividly in terms of what wives need to enjoy sex versus what husbands need to enjoy sex. Wives need:

1. To feel loved, prized, and valued.
2. To be listened to and respected.
3. A romantic atmosphere.
4. Privacy.
5. To be understood and cuddled.

Alternatively, husbands need:

1. To feel needed (being wanted by his woman is the number one emotional turn-on for a man).
2. A place (2009, p. 64).

Do you want to know why most marriages lose their spark?

To serve one another well, what couples must do is specifically tutor their spouse about how they want to have their needs met and purposefully study how they can meet their mate's needs. Do you want to know why most marriages lose their spark? It is because many couples suffer from amnesia. They have forgotten to do *and keep on doing* what worked to create that original romantic aura that convinced them that they couldn't live without each other.

> **Romance places special value on the relationship because both people feel prioritized, deeply cared about, and unconditionally accepted.**

This is because, "Romance is a special quality that keeps the relationship constantly renewed, energized, and strong. It ensures that the relationship does not become boring, stale, and predictable. Romance has little to do with sexuality per se, but a lot to do with love and caring. Romance is love with spice. Romance adds flavor to a relationship" (Cline & Cline, 2005, p. 163). Romance involves playfulness and a childlike quality of being able to let go and have fun in a spontaneous and carefree way. It involves lighthearted humor, creativity, and kindhearted tenderness. Romance places special value on the relationship because both people feel prioritized, deeply cared about, and unconditionally accepted. Consequently, romance creates an atmosphere of seductiveness, an attitude of sexiness, and an ambience of sensuality.

So how do we learn about each other's core differences, needs, hurts, love languages, histories, fears, values, dreams, preferences, and desires? We must continuously get to know and learn about each other progressively more intimately. Dennis and Barbara Rainey (2000) provide us with valuable tools for doing this. Their research revealed that women's top five romantic needs are:

1. To be spiritually ministered to by her man.
2. To feel safe and secure with her husband.
3. To share intimate conversation.
4. To receive a tender touch and hear gentle words.
5. To be pursued and set apart by her man.

And men most need:

1. A wife who communicates respect for him as a man.
2. A wife who wants and entices him sexually.
3. A wife who communicates she enjoys sexual love with him.
4. A wife who is adventuresome, fun, and impulsive sexually.
5. A wife who lets him know he has satisfied her.

I would suggest that you as a couple dedicate yourselves formally to this lifelong mutual educational process. Keep on learning—there is no reason to flunk out! Study for and prepare an interesting and informative lecture series, some pop quizzes, a few lab tests, various homework assignments, and a comprehensive final exam over the above material to help your mate learn valuable lessons about how to meet and fulfill your unique, personal romantic needs. And ask them to do the same. Who says learning can't be fun!?

eXcel

(Yeah, yeah, I know "excel" begins with an "e" instead of an "x." I guess I'm just not creative enough to do much with xylophone, xenon, or Xerox!) As a life-long, die-hard Kansas City Chiefs fan (which proves I am a man of great faith!), it is very painful for me to begrudgingly give kudos to their hated nemesis, the arch rival Oakland Raiders. But the Raiders' long-time president had a fantastic motto for their organization: *"Commitment to Excellence."* In a much more high and holy way, the Bible exhorts us to *excel* in gifts that edify or build up one another (1 Corinthians 14:12). How can you dedicate yourself to excel sexually as a husband or wife?

How can you dedicate yourself to excel sexually as a husband or wife?

To begin with, what if you dedicated yourselves sexually to achieving overarching oneness more than orgiastic orgasms? (And by the way, the former usually leads to the latter!) The truth is "... many Christians never experience all of the blessings that God has waiting for them in the land of marriage because they are afraid to enter in. They fail to do the things that will let them experience and enjoy of the fruits of the Promised Land of marriage...Very few people enter into a sexual relationship or experience it the way God intended it to be. We fall short of that glorious experience" (Gardner, 2002, p. 63).

Look, everyone knows life is busy. For most married couples, work, kids, laundry, bills, church, soccer practice, cooking, yard work, piano lessons, business trips, dental appointments, and the like consume the majority of our 168 hours every week. But if our marriage is boring and our love life is in a rut, we have probably reaped what we have (or more accurately, have not) sown. Linda Dillow and Lorraine Pintus offer us this encouragement: "We agree that it's difficult to keep the passion burning, but not impossible. Sex isn't an event. It's an environment. We must make passion a priority and then set an atmosphere where passion can reign" (1999, p. 222). Wow, can you imagine an atmosphere where passion can reign?

> We must make deliberate, intentional choices and take definite actions to cultivate and maintain an atmosphere where passion can royally rule and reign in our marriages.

The fact is that we don't 'fall in passion' any more than we 'fall in love.' We must make deliberate, intentional choices and take definite actions to cultivate and maintain an atmosphere where passion can royally rule and reign in our marriages. But let's look at that literal environment or atmosphere more closely.

Particularly for women, the physical setting for lovemaking is crucial. Yet how many American master bedrooms are places where dirty laundry is sorted, where junk mail and magazines pile up, and where clutter gets stashed? Unfortunately, it is also the place where, for many couples, conflicts are played out. Such a context is hardly conducive to the "reigning" of rapturous romance, erotic ecstasy, and pleasurable passion! So set the stage, prepare the props, and enjoy the play!

> **To excel in lovemaking, we need more than tricks, toys, and techniques.**

To excel in lovemaking, we need more than tricks, toys, and techniques. We need to prioritize, plan, and purpose to become great lovers and to create a sensational sexual relationship. For many people, that involves giving ourselves permission to be adventurous and willing to let go of old inhibitions and hang ups. Again Dillow and Pintus impart godly wisdom a la Titus 2:4 by asking:

> How can American women change their mindset from boring to sizzling? By continuing to seek God's perspective on sex, a perspective that does not change or vary from culture to culture. God urges 'eat, friends; drink and imbibe deeply, O lovers' (Song of Songs 5:1) (1999, p. 180).

Speaking of that Holy Spirit-inspired poetic prose of pleasurable, passionate playfulness, Song of Songs (or Song of Solomon) is a book filled with exquisite erotic ecstasy. According to Driscoll and Driscoll (2012, p. 119), it depicts among other things: kissing (1:2), fellatio—her initiative (2:3), manual stimulation—her invitation (2:6), erotic massage—his initiative (4:5), cunnilingus—his initiative (4:12-5:1), striptease (6:13-7:9), and experimentation with new places and positions, including outdoors—her initiative (7:11-13). Somehow I get the feeling that many couples are going to do a lengthy Bible study tonight!

315

One practical suggestion Dillow and Pintus make to help women be more intentional about prioritizing their sexual relationship is to write the letters "T.S." (which is code for "think sex") on a sticky note and put it in a conspicuous place such as their mirror, refrigerator, computer monitor, or dashboard. This way they can remind themselves several times a day to think about their husband in a sexual manner. (Most husbands are already automatically hard-wired to do this!) Here are ten specific, proactive ideas that Dr. Doug Rosenau suggests can help wives keep lovemaking on the front burner:

1. Budget and spend a certain amount of money each month on your sex life.

2. Every now and then wear a sexy piece of lingerie underneath your clothing all day and allow its unusual feel to remind you of sex constantly.

3. Don't wear any underwear to a social gathering, and tell your husband on the way out the door. You will drive him crazy while you stay aroused.

4. Plan a sexual surprise at least once a month in which you try to blindside your husband in an arousing sexual way.

5. Keep a mental note, and regardless of fatigue or low interest, initiate sex at least once a week.

6. Have fun with your husband's visual arousal, and flaunt your nude body at unusual times just to enjoy his reactions.

7. Take a bubble bath and indulge in other sensual delights at the end of a tiring day—it is a great aphrodisiac and tunes you in to your body. In the midst of all your demands, you must learn to be self-nurturing. It will keep you sexier.

8. Create romantic sexual fantasies while driving in the car and share them with your mate at the end of your day. You will have to consciously think about sex more.

9. Use a special perfume that you have associated in your mind with making love, and wear it on the evening or the day you anticipate sexual activity.

10. Practice Kegel exercises (2004, p. 167).

Contrary to popular opinion, research on satisfied, successful marriages consistently shows that for healthy couples, sexual activity does not necessarily decline over the years. High sexual activity in the early years is typically followed by a decline when children are young and especially during their adolescent years. But if the couple negotiates empty nest issues effectively and nurtures their romantic relationship, there is generally a strong resurgence of sexual activity into the retirement years.

> Contrary to popular opinion, research on satisfied, successful marriages consistently shows that for healthy couples, sexual activity does not necessarily decline over the years.

Yield

The word "submit" has gotten a bad name over the years; it has been crammed down many wives' throats and beaten over their heads in a patently sexist and terribly unloving way. When most (generally male) pastors start to preach from the 'marriage passage' in Ephesians chapter 5, they typically begin with verse 22: "Wives, submit to your husbands as to the Lord." This may seem controversial, but I believe there are three basic (and serious) problems with the way I've heard this passage (mis)interpreted most of the time.

> Our horizontal relationships with others are to be contextualized within and flowing from our vertical

relationship with our Father.

To begin with, the Apostle Paul's thought originates in the previous sentence: "Submit to one another out of reverence for Christ" (vs. 21). In the Body of Christ, submission is clearly to be an interdependent, mutual dynamic—based upon, motivated by, and grounded within our reverential respect for God. As always, our horizontal relationships with others are to be contextualized within and flowing from our vertical relationship with our Father.

Secondly, the Greek word used here (*hupatasso*) and in Colossians 3:18 and 1 Peter 3:1-6 is better rendered "yield." It conveys the essence of voluntarily giving over as opposed to mandatorily giving up. The term "submission" in our culture has acquired a negative or pejorative connotation—something akin to being a doormat, or even worse, a helpless victim. But to yield is to freely and graciously allow someone else to enter the freeway ahead of us. When we yield, we are always fully in control and never feel controlled. It is a voluntary, free act of the will which is not coerced or manipulated in any way. It is about giving over, not giving up. Yielding is both honoring and honorable.

Yielding is both honoring and honorable.

And the final problem with the way this passage is typically (not) unpacked, is that the next ten verses emphasize how husbands are to self-sacrificially love their wives as Christ loved the Church! If husbands did that regularly and systematically, no wife would ever have an issue with yielding to them as the head of the home!

So what does all this have to do with sensational sex? Everything! No two people will ever have the same sexual drive, the same sexual needs, the same sexual preferences, the same sexual feelings, the same sexual desires, the same sexual energies, the same (okay, okay, I've made the point) at the exact same levels over the 78-year course of their marriage! We have to communicate, adjust, negotiate, compromise, and yield to the other's changing and ongoing differences. The point is that, "…happy and fulfilling sexual relations in marriage depend on each partner aiming to give satisfaction to the other. If it is the joy of each to make the other partner happy, a hundred problems will be solved before they happen" (Piper, 1999, p. 134).

Many couples have power struggles over sex, but, "…sex is not to be used as a bargaining chip. It is not something God allows us to withhold without consequence…the heart of marriage is one of giving ourselves to each other to meet the other's needs" (Kendrick & Kendrick, 2008, p. 157). Paul's teaching sums it up this way:

> It's good for a man to have a wife, and for a woman to have a husband. Sexual drives are strong but marriage is strong enough to contain them and provide for a balanced and fulfilling sexual life in a world of sexual disorder. The marriage bed must be a place of mutuality—the husband seeking to please his wife, the wife seeking to please her husband. Marriage is not a place to "stand up for your rights." Marriage is a decision to serve the other, whether in bed or out. Abstaining from sex for a period of time is permissible if you both agree to it, and if it's for the purposes of prayer and fasting—but only for such times. Then come back together again. Satan has an ingenious way of tempting us when we least expect it (1 Corinthians 7:2-5, The Message).

Among the myriad issues involved in the power struggles some couples have, many involve debates and controversies about what is "permissible" sexual behavior. As with other differences, we need to be able to communicate about these with safety, grace, and love. Drs. Judith and Jack Balswick advise,

319

"...if either spouse is uncomfortable with some aspect of their sexual relationship, it is imperative that they can speak their differences without being judged or feeling ashamed" (1999, p. 152). This attitude of loving consideration is essential for a healthy marriage.

What do the scriptures say? In the previously cited passage, the Greek word for "agree" is *symphonia*, from which our term "symphony" is derived. A symphony is a melodious arrangement of different instruments playing in concert and in harmony with one another. Our differences are not to make us be discordant or out of tune with each other.

> **When, not if, we experience conflicts over differing tastes, preferences, desires, and amounts of sexual appetites, we must communicate and compromise.**

When, not if, we experience conflicts over differing tastes, preferences, desires, and amounts of sexual appetites, we must communicate and compromise. If one person wants Italian and the other person wants Mexican, you could decide to alternate one meal of each on consecutive nights, compromise and have half of one and half of the other, or just go for Chinese!

Okay, but what about various sexual practices or behaviors not specifically mentioned in the Bible? In the context of discussing sexual immorality, Paul declares, "'Everything is permissible for me'—but not everything is beneficial. 'Everything is permissible for me'—but I will not be mastered by anything" (1 Corinthians 6:12). When one person has strong feelings about a certain practice, activity, or behavior, take time to listen for deeper undertones, fears, hurts, and dynamics. Don't judge and presume motives of control or rejection. Apply the relationship principles found in Romans 14:1-15:2, pertaining to how the exercise of our freedom can become a stumbling block to trip up a fellow believer who has different values, standards, or convictions. The stronger and more mature person is to be considerate and self-sacrificing in those areas of incompatibility, even when they believe they are right. If we're truly Christ-like, it's really not about us!

To summarize, "Marriage at its exquisite peak of pleasure speaks powerfully the truth of covenant-keeping love between Christ and His church. And that love is the most powerful force in the world. It is not surprising then that Satan's defeat, Christ's glory, and our pleasure should come together in this undefiled marriage bed" (Piper, 2009, p. 135). The marriage bed is perfectly pure (Hebrews 13:4) and is to be kept that way.

Dr. Kevin Leman concludes, "Sexual intimacy between a man and woman should be the culmination and expression of intimacy they share in all areas of their life together" (1999, p. 11). Sex symbolizes and summarizes a couple's entire relationship. Dr. Juli Slattery wisely concludes, "Sexuality isn't a separate compartment of your life but an expression of your heart" (2009, p. 200). Consequently, copulation is clearly the climax of a couple's conjugal closeness, consolidated commitment, and convergent communication.

A perpetually wonderful sex life doesn't just happen automatically. Passionate playmates purposely pursue one another and place a premium on pleasing their partner! My hope and prayer for you and your spouse is that your sexual relationship becomes, and remains, simply *sensational!*

Scriptural Search

1. Genesis 2:25
2. Song of Songs
3. 1 Corinthians 6:19-20
4. 1 Corinthians 7:1-15
5. Hebrews 13:4

Ponderable Points

1. What were you taught about human sexuality while growing up and by whom? When did you first learn about sex and how?

2. What is the most romantic experience you have ever initiated in your marriage relationship? What is the most romantic experience ever initiated by your mate in your marriage relationship?

3. In what ways do you and your spouse experience one-flesh intimacy? In what ways would you like to experience greater closeness?

4. In what areas in your marriage, besides sex, do you feel a lack of intimacy or closeness? What are some clear, specific things you want to change in these areas? What are you personally willing to commit to do differently?

5. What emotional and/or relational "baggage" did you and did your mate bring into the marriage bed? In what ways has this affected you, and in what ways has this affected your spouse? Consider using the communication exercises outlined in Chapter 6 to tenderly and sensitively discuss these issues.

Activation Activities

1. Consider conducting a session of "sensate focusing" where both you and your spouse take turns giving and receiving sensual but non-demand pleasure (i.e. where the desired goal or outcome of pleasuring one another does not necessarily

culminate in intercourse). Write down what you would like both your spouse and you to experience as a "take-away" from this exercise.

2. Set aside time to talk deeply about your relationship; exchange fears, feelings, and fantasies. What would you most like to be able to tell your husband or wife about what your marriage is like for you?

3. Think about how often your pursuit of sexual intimacy has been more focused on achieving an orgiastic orgasm instead of an overarching oneness. In light of God's desire that we experience and exude oneness, what changes do you need to make in your own thinking? Share with your mate some specific things you are willing to do to achieve spiritual oneness with them beyond simply achieving simultaneous orgasm.

Recommended Resources

A Celebration of Sex, Doug Rosenau (2002).
No More Headaches, Juli Slattery (2009).
Sheet Music: Uncovering the Secrets of Sexual Intimacy in Marriage, Kevin Leman (2003).
Sexy Christians, Ted and Diane Roberts (2010).
Sacred Sex, Tim Gardner (2002).

Epilogue

It is my sincere hope and prayer that this book has been a blessing to you, your spouse, and your marriage. To reiterate, there is no such thing as a state of perfect matrimony—despite all the fantasies and fairy tales you may have believed before you said, "I do." But I firmly believe that through dedicated mutual effort and the empowerment of God's Holy Spirit, all marriages can mend, meld, and morph into the marvelous and magnificent mystery (Ephesians 5:32) which God intends.

Much like a lush, verdant, fruitful garden or a gleaming new, well-tuned automobile, a magnificent marriage is a thing of beauty, which can be greatly enjoyed. But, as with luxurious landscapes and classic cars, magnificent marriages require a huge investment of time, money, and energy to get that way and to stay that way.

Therefore, I want to encourage you and your spouse to make and maintain your marriage magnificently. If you have not already done so, I would like to suggest that you go through the exercises in the companion workbook, *Marriage Maintenance Manual*, together with your spouse. The questions and growth opportunities suggested there are specifically designed to help you customize and apply the material from this book to your own marriage in a practical, personal, and powerful way. When you as a couple discuss and write down your responses to the material, it will become much more real, relevant, and relational.

Additionally, when you both take the corresponding free online *Relationship Health Score 1.0* assessment at RelationshipHealthScore.com, you will be given clear and accurate research-based feedback concerning the operational state of your marriage system. The unique, insightful, and personalized data derived from the *RHS 1.0* is both valid and valuable, and it can be used to understand and strengthen your marriage in a profoundly powerful way.

In order to receive maximum benefit from these complementary, interactive marriage-making tools, I would suggest that as a couple, you first take the *RHS 1.0,* then read this book and complete the exercises in the *Marriage Maintenance Manual,* and finally retake the *RHS 1.0* assessment. This way, you will be given solid empirical results measuring the healing, growth, and progress you have achieved toward making your marriage magnificent as a result of working through the book and workbook. And if you decide you need further, specialized assistance, we have developed a nationwide network of qualified, licensed professional marital therapists to whom you can be referred through the website.

Additionally, it is a good idea to retake the *RHS 1.0* assessment after times of concentrated work on your marriage—such as couples counseling, marriage retreats, and/or small group growth experiences—in order to track the ongoing development of your relationship. Another way to use these materials is to periodically review them at specific time intervals, such as every year on your wedding anniversary. Retaking the assessment at that time measures and monitors the growth and health of your marital relationship. Also, sometimes couples choose to commemorate significant periods of growth and/or healing in their relationship by formally renewing their wedding vows. This can be an incredible and intimate investment into your marriage that is deeply meaningful and wonderfully loving.

In conclusion, I want to encourage you to take to heart the words from a frequently quoted wedding ceremony benediction entitled the Apache Wedding Prayer* as my personal blessing and counsel for you and your spouse:

Now you will feel no rain,
for each of you will be shelter for the other.
Now you will feel no cold,
for each of you will be warmth to the other.
Now there will be no loneliness,
for each of you will be companion to the other.
Now you are two persons,
but there is only one life before you.
May beauty surround you both in the journey ahead
and through all the years.
May happiness be your companion,
and your days together be good and long upon the earth.
Treat yourselves and each other with respect,
and remind yourselves often of what brought you together.
Give the highest priority to the tenderness,
gentleness, and kindness that your connection deserves.
When frustration, difficulty, and fear assail your relationship
—as they threaten all relationships at one time or another—
remember to focus on what is right between you,
not only the part which seems wrong.
In this way, you can ride out the storms
when clouds hide the face of the sun in your lives,
remembering that even if you lose sight of it for a moment,
the sun is still there.
And if each of you takes responsibility
for the quality of your life together,
it will be marked by abundance and delight.
Go now to your dwelling place,
to enter into the days of your togetherness.
And may your days be good and long upon the earth.

*(According to most historians, this prayer did not actually originate with
the Native American Apache tribe. The first four lines are from Elliot Arnold's

1947 novel, *Blood Brother*, which was adapted into a screenplay for the 1950 film, *Broken Arrow*, starring Jimmy Stewart. The rest has been adapted down through the years by unknown authors.)

Bibliography

Alexandre, J. A. (2013), *Marital Happiness Is a Choice.*

Allender, Dan (2008), *The Wounded Heart: Hope for Adult Victims of Childhood Sexual Abuse.*

Allender, Dan and Tremper Longman (1992), *Bold Love.*

Allender, Dan and Tremper Longman (1999), *Intimate Allies: Rediscovering God's Design for Marriage and Becoming Soul Mates for Life.*

Anderson, Neil (1996), *The Christ-Centered Marriage.*

Arp, David and Claudia (1993), *Fifty-Two Fantastic Dates for You and Your Mate.*

Arp, David and Claudia (1997), *The Second Half of Marriage.*

Arp, David and Claudia (2005), *Ten Great Dates to Energize Your Marriage.*

Balswick, Jack and Judith (1999), *Authentic Human Sexuality.*

Blue, Ron (2000), *Taming the Money Monster: Five Steps to Conquering Debt.*

Bonhoeffer, Dietrich (1997), *Life Together.*

Burkett, Larry (2001), *Money Matters.*

Burns, Jim (2006), *Creating an Intimate Marriage.*

Buscaglia, Leo (1988), *Loving Each Other.*

Carder, Dave (2008), *Torn Asunder: Recovering from an Extramarital Affair.*

Chapman, Gary (2003), *Covenant Marriage.*

Chapman, Gary (2009), *The Five Love Languages.*

Clinebell, Howard and Charlotte (1970), *The Intimate Marriage.*

Clinton, Tim and Julie (2000), *The Marriage You've Always Wanted: How to Grow a Stronger, More Intimate Relationship.*

Cloud, Henry and John Townsend (2002), *Boundaries in Marriage.*

Cloud, Henry and John Townsend (2009), *Rescue Your Love Life.*

Conway, Jim and Sally (2001), *Traits of a Lasting Marriage.*

Daly, Jim (2012), *The Best Advice I Ever Got on Marriage.*

Dayton, Howard (2009), *Money and Marriage God's Way.*

Dillow, Linda and Lorriane Pintus (2009), *Intimate Issues.*

DiMarco, Hayley (2006), *Sexy Girls: How Hot Is Too Hot?*

Dobson, James (1989) *What Wives Wish Their Husbands Knew About Women.*

Dobson, James (2004), *Love for a Lifetime.*

Dobson, James (2007), *Love Must Be Tough.*

Dobson, James and Shirley (2008), *Nightlight: A Devotional for Couples.*

Driscoll, Mark and Grace (2012), *Real Marriage: The Truth About Sex, Friendship and Life Together.*

Eggerichs, Emerson (2004), *Love and Respect.*

Eggerichs, Emerson (2008), *Cracking the Communication Code.*

Egli, Glenn and Jennifer Carrell (1994), *Making Love Last.*

Eldridge, John and Stasi (2009), *Love and War: Find Your Way to Something Beautiful in Your Marriage.*

Endrei, Paul and Patti (2006), *Glue: Sticking Power for Lifelong Mariages.*

Exley, Richard (2008), *Intimate Moments.*

Exley, Richard and Brenda (1997), *Forever in Love.*

Farrell, Bill and Pam (2001), *Men Are Like Waffles, Women Are Like Spaghetti.*

Farrell, Bill and Pam (2006), *Red-Hot Monogamy: Making Your Marriage Sizzle.*

Feldhahn, Shaunti (2013), *For Women Only.*

Ferguson, David and Teresa (2000), *More Than Marriage! Ten Keys to Intimacy for a Lasting Marriage.*

Foster, Richard (1985), *The Challenge of the Disciplined Life: Reflections on Money, Sex, and Power.*

Frank, Jan and Don (1990), *When Victims Marry.*

Gardner, Tim (2002), *Sacred Sex.*

Godzich, Leo (2006), *Men Are from Dirt, Women Are from Men.*

Gottman, John (1999), *The Seven Principles for Making Marriage Work.*

Gottman, John and Julie Schwartz Gottman (2006), *Ten Lessons to Transform Your Marriage.*

Gray, John (1993), *Men, Women and Relationships.*

Gray, John (2000), *Mars and Venus in Touch.*

Hansel, Tim (1979), *When I Relax I Feel Guilty.*

Harley, Willard (2006), *I Promise You: Preparing for a Marriage That Will Last a Lifetime.*

Harley, Willard (2008), *Love Busters.*

Harley, Willard (2011), *His Needs, Her Needs.*

Hart, Archibald and Sharon Hart Morris (2003), *Safe Haven Marriage.*

Hart, Archibald, Catherine Hart Weber, and Debra Taylor (2004), *Secrets Of Eve: Understanding the Mystery of Female Sexuality.*

Hawkins, David (2005), *Nine Critical Mistakes Most Couples Make.*

Hocking, David and Carole (1986), *Romantic Lovers.*

Hunt, Mary (2003), *Debt-Proof Your Marriage.*

Ingram, Chip (2003), *Love, Sex and Lasting Relationships.*

Janssen, Al (2001), *The Marriage Masterpiece.*

Jantz, Gregory (2010), *Hope, Help, and Healing for Eating Disorders.*

Kendrick, Stephen and Alex (2008), *The Love Dare.*

Klein, Foster and Hermie (2005), *Marriage Love and Logic.*

Laaser, Mark (2004), *Healing the Wounds of Sexual Addiction.*

Leman, Kevin (2011), *How to Have a New Husband by Friday.*

Leman, Kevin (1999), *Sex Begins in the Kitchen.*

Leman, Kevin (2003), *Sheet Music: Uncovering the Secrets of Sexual Intimacy in Marriage.*

Leman, Kevin (2009), *Turn Up the Heat: A Couple's Guide to Sexual Intimacy.*

Lewis, C.S. (1971), *The Four Loves.*

Louden, Jennifer (1994), *The Couple's Comfort Book: A Creative Guide for Renewing Passion, Pleasure and Commitment.*

Markman, Howard, Scott Stanley, and Susan Blumberg (2001), *Fighting for Your Marriage.*

Mason, Mike (2005), *The Mystery of Marriage: As Iron Sharpens Iron.*

McCluskey, Kevin and Rachel (2004), *When Two Become One: Enhancing Sexual Intimacy in Marriage.*

McDonald, Cleveland and Philip (2008), *Creating a Successful Christian Marriage.*

Murrow, David (2011), *Why Men Hate Going to Church.*

Parrott, Les and Leslie (1995), *Becoming Soul Mates.*

Parrott, Les and Leslie (1998), *Relationships.*

Parrott, Les and Leslie (2004), *Love Talk.*

Parrott, Les and Leslie (2013), *The Good Fight: How Conflict Can Bring You Closer.*

Paul, Robert (2007), *Finding Ever After: A Romantic Adventure for Her, An Adventurous Romance for Him.*

Peck, M. Scott (1978), *The Road Less Travelled: A New Psychology of Love, Traditional Values and Spiritual Growth.*

Pellicane, Arlene (2012), *Thirty-One Days to a Happy Husband: What a Man Needs Most from His Wife.*

Penner, Clifford and Joyce (2003), *The Gift of Sex: A Guide to Sexual Fulfillment.*

Penner, Clifford and Joyce (1986), *A Gift for All Ages.*

Piper, John (2009), *This Momentary Marriage.*

Rainey, Dennis and Barbara (1986), *Building Your Mate's Self-Esteem.*

Rainey, Dennis and Barbara (2000), *Starting Your Marriage Right.*

Rainey, Dennis and Barbara (2004), *Rekindling The Romance.*

Ramsey, Dave (2007), *The Total Money Makeover.*

Roberts, Ted and Diane (2010), *Sexy Christians: The Purpose, Power, and Passion of Biblical Intimacy.*

Rosberg, Gary and Barbara (2000), *The Five Love Needs of Men and Women.*

Rosen, Margary (2002), *Seven Secrets of a Happy Marriage.*

Rosenau, Douglas (1991), *Slaying the Marriage Dragons.*

Rosenau, Douglas (2002), *A Celebration of Sex.*

Schaumburg, Harry (1997), *False Intimacy: Understanding the Struggle of Sexual Addiction.*

Slattery, Juli (2009), *No More Headaches.*

Smalley, Gary (1996), *Making Love Last Forever.*

Smalley, Gary (2004), *The DNA of Relationships.*

Smalley, Gary (2006), *I Promise: How Five Essential Commitments Determine the Destiny of Your Marriage.*

Smalley, Gary and Norma (2011), *Four Days to a Forever Marriage.*

Smalley, Gary and Trent, John (1993), *The Gift of the Blessing.*

Smalley, Greg (2013), *Fight Your Way to a Better Marriage: How Healthy Conflict Can Take You to Deeper Levels of Intimacy.*

Smalley, Greg and Erin (2013), *The Little Book of Great Dates: Fifty-Two Creative Ideas to Make Your Marriage Fun.*

Smedes, Lewis (1976), *Sex for Christians.*

Smith, Debi (2012), *Dance with Me.*

Snyder, Chuck and Barb (1988), *Incompatibility: Grounds for a Great Marriage.*

Stanley, Scott (1998), *The Heart of Commitment.*

Stoop, David and Jan, Eds. (2002), The Complete Marriage Book.

Talley, Jim (1991), *Reconcilable Differences: Healing for Troubled Marriages.*

Thomas, Gary (2000), *Sacred Marriage.*

Vernick, Leslie (2001), *How to Act Right When Your Spouse Acts Wrong.*

Virkler, Henry (1992), *Broken Promises: Healing and Preventing Affairs in Christian Marriages.*

Wheat, Ed and Gayle (1977), *Intended for Pleasure.*

Wilson, Barbara (2009), *Kiss Me Again: Restoring Lost Intimacy in Marriage.*

Wilson, Rodney and Selma (2006), Extraordinary Marriage.

Wright, H. Norman (1999), *After You Say "I Do": Making The Most of Your Marriage.*

Wright, H. Norman (2000), *Communication: Key to Your Marriage.*

Wright, H. Norman and Gary Oliver (1994), *How to Change Your Spouse Without Ruining Your Marriage.*